THE GUIDE TO
RALEIGH
NORTH CAROLINA AREA
REAL ESTATE

THE GUIDE TO
RALEIGH
NORTH CAROLINA AREA
REAL ESTATE

Raleigh, Cary, Apex, Wake Forest,
Holly Springs, Fuquay-Varina
and The Triangle Area Including
Chapel Hill and Durham

MICHAEL D. REGAN
with contributions from
John Streit, Bill Cobey, and Christine Nguyen

WEXFORD HOUSE BOOKS

THE GUIDE TO
RALEIGH
NORTH CAROLINA AREA
REAL ESTATE

Raleigh, Cary, Apex, Wake Forest,
Holly Springs, Fuquay-Varina
and The Triangle Area Including
Chapel Hill and Durham

MICHAEL D. REGAN
with contributions from
John Streit, Bill Cobey, and Christine Nguyen

Published by:
Wexford House Books

All rights reserved. No part of this book may be reproduced or transmitted in any form or by any means, electronic or mechanical, including photocopying, recording, or by an information storage and retrieval system - except by a reviewer who may quote brief passages in a review to be printed in a magazine or newspaper - without permission in writing from the publisher.

Copyright © 2010 by Michael D. Regan
Printed in the United States of America

ISBN
978-0-615-31852-3

ABOUT THE AUTHOR

Mike Regan is the owner of *Regan & Company Real Estate Brokers and Advisors*, a residential real estate brokerage firm with a staff of 14 agents located in Raleigh, NC. The content of this book is drawn from his experience helping hundreds of clients buy and sell homes in the Raleigh area.

John Streit, Bill Cobey, and Christine Nguyen, longtime residents of the Raleigh area and senior real estate brokers with Regan & Company, contributed significant insight to this book from their years of working with local buyers and sellers.

ACKNOWLEDGMENTS

Thank you to Marti Maguire, Clarissa del Pilar, Megan Southwick, Tracy Carr, Jennifer Ferris, Jason Korreck, Gerald Huntley, DJ Keen, Susan and Kaitlyn Darby, and Jamie Dunston, each of whom helped us with part of the research, interviewing, and writing of this book. Thank you to George Foster for the cover design, Cynthia Mallard and Ashley Mewborn for interior graphic design, Kimberly Martin for formatting, and Stacey Anfindsen for the data in the real estate graphs. Thank you to Bill and Sandy Kerwin, Jan Carmody, Crystal Wilson, Val Hurley, and Renee Rundenza for proofing and editorial assistance.

Thank you to the interviewees who boldly told us the truth as they saw it in the interviews section (names changed to protect their privacy).

Thank you to Jan Carmody, Jamie Harrison, Mandy Thomas, Sarah Leinhaas, Stacey Regan, Tabitha Cooper, Elizabeth Rivers, Sharyn Davis, Jeremy Carter, and Renee Rundenza, for their great work for our clients as real estate brokers at Regan & Company.

A BIG thank you to Brian Buffini, the best real estate mentor on the planet, and coach Billy Van Raaphorst (see *www.buffiniandcompany.com*). Thank you to Dave Ramsey, who has helped us be more wise with our personal and business finances, and Heath Hertzog for his support specific to the real estate industry (see *www.daveramsey.com*).

Finally, thank you to my Mom and Dad, my two great kids, my fabulous wife Stacey, and my Father in Heaven for all His blessings.

CONTENTS

INTRODUCTION 1
   1   Why Move to the Raleigh Area? 3

PART I
BUYING & SELLING REAL ESTATE IN THE RALEIGH AREA 21
   2   Top Tips for Raleigh Area Buyers 23
   3   Top Tips for Raleigh Area Sellers 33
   4   55+ Communities: Inside Information for Mature Adults 46

PART II
RALEIGH AREA CITIES AND TOWNS 63
   5   Wake County 65
   6   Raleigh 68
   7   Wake Forest 74
   8   Rolesville 78
   9   Cary 81
  10   Apex 85
  11   Morrisville 88
  12   Holly Springs 91
  13   Fuquay-Varina 95
  14   Garner 99
  15   Knightdale 103
  16   Wendell 107
  17   Zebulon 111

PART III
DURHAM & CHAPEL HILL/ CARRBORO 114
  18   Durham 115
  19   Chapel Hill / Carrboro 126

PART IV
INTERVIEWS 139

20	Brandon & Alicia Donley...	141
	To **Downtown Raleigh** from Aliso Viejo, California	
21	Heidi McCord	147
	To **Downtown Raleigh** from Savannah, Georgia	
22	Lane Newgard	152
	To **North Raleigh** from Los Angeles, California	
23	Mandy & Jason Hollowell...	155
	To **Raleigh** from Dayton, Ohio then to Melbourne Florida and back to **North Raleigh**	
24	John & Patricia Southwell...	159
	To **Raleigh** from Rochester, New York	
25	Danny & Elisabeth Agostini...	162
	To **Raleigh** from Atlanta, Georgia	
26	Franco & Karla Luciano..	166
	To **Raleigh** from Italy	
27	Travis & Olivia Drury..	170
	To **Raleigh** from Rochester, New York	
28	Larry & Claire Schuyler	177
	To **East Raleigh** then **Rolesville**, from central Pennsylvania	
29	Tina Franklin	181
	To **Research Triangle Park** then **East Raleigh**, from Sacramento, California	
30	James & Kristen Tugood..	187
	To **Wake Forest** from Wilmington, North Carolina	
31	Ron & Danielle Casey...	190
	To **Durham**, then **Wake Forest**, from New York	
32	Jane Mitchell	197
	To **Cary** from Howard County, Maryland	

33	Davis & Simone Canton 202
	*To **Cary** from Memphis, Tennessee*
34	Dave Creager 205
	*To **Apex** From St Paul, Minnesota*
35	Ken & Shelly Camp 209
	*To **Holly Springs** from Duxford, Massachusetts*
36	Brian & Samantha Jarman 213
	*To **Fuquay-Varina** from Washington D.C.*
37	Bobby Upshaw 219
	*To **Garner** from Wilmington, North Carolina*
38	Derek Tyborowski 223
	*To **Zebulon** from New York City*

PART V
THE NEWCOMER'S GUIDE TO THE RALEIGH AREA 227

39	Getting Settled 229
40	The Job Market 249
41	Childcare and Education 267
42	Health Care 287
43	Places of Worship 295
44	Shopping Guide 322
45	Cultural Life 340
46	Climate and Environment 368
47	Transportation in the Triangle 383
48	Sports & Recreation 399
49	Outdoor Fun (Green Space) 418

INTRODUCTION

Stacey and I moved to Raleigh from Rochester, New York in 1995, and we did our homework. We researched cities across the United States from Seattle to Austin and Boston to Savannah. Our top priorities were lots of sunshine (sorry, Seattle), economic opportunity, and a great place to settle down and start a family.

We narrowed it down to Atlanta, Charlotte, Greensboro (NC), and the Raleigh area. After more research, we decided Atlanta was too busy and developed. Then a friend told us the Charlotte business community was less open to "outsiders", compared to other areas of North Carolina.

That left Greensboro and Raleigh. We flew south to see North Carolina for the first time and visit our two remaining choices. It turned out Greensboro was not economically diversified and developed enough for us. At last, we visited Raleigh, saw all the trees and nice neighborhoods, took a walk around one of the several lakes, and felt at home. After several more job-hunting trips we made the move, and we hope to stay forever.

Since then our family has grown by two children and a dog, and both of our parents moved to the area.

If you are thinking about moving to the Raleigh area, I hope this book helps you make a good decision.

CHAPTER 1

WHY MOVE TO THE RALEIGH AREA?

People say there's power in numbers, and judging by the number of accolades the Raleigh area has received in recent years, the area is packing a lot of power.

From traditional designations such as "Best City to Live" and "Best Place for Business and Careers" to more eclectic ones including "Quirkiest New Year's Eve Drop" and "Least Miserable Airport," Raleigh has been named a top city for everything from jobs, population growth, education, and family life, and the media buzz around the city keeps on coming.

Below is a collection of some of the awards and accolades Wake County has received during the past three years. Raleigh is widely known as one of the top destinations for relocating families and professionals; as such, there are many not-so-surprising designations included in the long lists that follow (e.g. #1 Fastest-Growing Metropolitan Area in the Country). But among the expected praise, there will likely be a number of surprises.

THE GUIDE TO RALEIGH NORTH CAROLINA AREA REAL ESTATE

"BEST CITY" DESIGNATIONS

Raleigh has consistently appeared on "Best City" rankings during the past several years, thanks in large part to its diverse economy, highly educated workforce, strong housing market, and reasonable cost of living.

In September 2008, Raleigh-Cary ranked No. 2 on the Milken Institute's list of **Best Performing Cities**. Each year the Milken Institute, an independent economic think tank, ranks major metropolitan areas based on factors of economic growth, including long-term and short-term measurements of employment and salary growth and indicators of high-tech output. In 2008, Raleigh jumped eight spots in the institutes' ranking, moving to the No. 2 spot from No. 10 in 2007.

Raleigh has also been named the **Best Place to Live in the U.S.** and the **Best City of 2009**.

The Best City...

- #1 Best Place to Live in the U.S. (Raleigh, NC) - *msnbc.com*, June 2008
- #2 Best City to Live, Work and Play (Raleigh, NC) - *Kiplinger's*, July 2008
- #2 Best Performing City (Raleigh-Cary, NC) - The Milken Institute, September 2008
- #10 Best City of 2009 (Raleigh-Cary)- *Kiplinger's Personal Finance*, May 2009
- #20 Best Place to Live and Launch (Raleigh, NC) - *CNNMoney.com*, March 2008
- # 22 Best Place to Live (Holly Springs, NC) - *Money*, July 2007

ECONOMY

Most people would argue there is no such thing as a recession-proof city, but Forbes.com would disagree.

INTRODUCTION

In April 2008, Forbes.com published a list of the top ten metropolitan areas it found to be "well positioned to weather the expected downturn." According to the finance magazine, "stable home prices and growth across the different sectors of its economy have kept Raleigh strong," making Raleigh the No. 5 **Recession-Proof City** in the U.S.

One year later, as the economic situation continued to spiral downward, the foreign direct investment publication *fDi Magazine* gave Raleigh the top spot among small U.S. cities with the best economic potential.

An Economic Stronghold...

- #1 City with Best Economic Potential (Raleigh)- fDi Magazine, April 2009
- #5 Recession-Proof City (Raleigh, NC) - Forbes.com, April 2008

GROWTH AND EXPANSION

Raleigh is growing and is growing quickly. In the early 2000s, Americans were moving to the Southwest in droves, but as we get closer to the end of the 2000s, more and more Americans are turning their attention to the Southeast. Raleigh topped the U.S. Census Bureau's rankings of the **Fastest-Growing Metropolitan Area in the Country** in March 2009, and it doesn't look like growth in Raleigh is going to slow down anytime soon.

In May 2009, Forbes.com pointed to Raleigh-Cary as the No. 1 **City Where Americans Are Relocating**, and even organizations like the National Policy Research Council are highlighting the growth potential of Raleigh and the greater Triangle area. In September 2007, the National Policy Research Council named Wake County and the Triangle as top 10 **Economic Development Hot Spots**.

THE GUIDE TO RALEIGH NORTH CAROLINA AREA REAL ESTATE

A Growing City...

- #1 City Where Americans Are Relocating (Raleigh-Cary) - Forbes.com, April 2009 and May 2009
- #1 Fastest-Growing Metropolitan Area in the Country (Raleigh-Cary) - U.S. Census Bureau, March 2009
- #10 U.S. City with the Largest Numerical Increase (Raleigh, NC) - U.S. Census Bureau, July 2008
- #63 Fastest Growing Suburb in America (Apex, NC) - Forbes.com, August 2007
- #8 Fastest Growing Large City (Cary, NC) - Fast Company, July 2007
- #15 Fastest Growing Large City (Raleigh, NC) - U.S. Census Bureau, 2006 (Data released 2007)
- #8 Fastest Growing Metro in the Nation (Raleigh-Cary, NC) - U.S. Census Bureau, April 2007
- #6 Medium-Sized Metro (Raleigh-Cary, NC) - Site Selection, March 2008

Development Potential ...

- #2 Metro Entering Slow Period With Most Positive Momentum (Raleigh, NC) - bizjournals, November 2008
- #3 Economic Development Hot Spot (Wake County, NC) - National Policy Research Council, September 2007
- #10 Economic Development Hot Spot (Raleigh-Durham-Chapel Hill, NC) - National Policy Research Council, September 2007

REAL ESTATE

With the housing market in shambles, it's been difficult to find any goods news when it comes to real estate. Yet, if there is a silver lining in

INTRODUCTION

the housing crisis of 2008 and 2009, Raleigh would without a doubt be part of it.

While home values have plummeted 20% in some parts of the country, property values in the Wake County are relatively stable, and that's caught the eye of media outlets and real estate organizations alike. In December 2007, *Money* magazine recognized Raleigh as one of the **Top Appreciating Metro Areas**. More recently, Raleigh-Cary ranked 18th in the Federal Housing Finance Agency's list of **MSAs with Highest Rate of House Price Appreciation**.

The continued appreciation of home values is just one indicator of how well Raleigh's housing market is weathering the storm. Raleigh came in at No. 6 in Builderonline.com's ranking of the U.S.'s **Healthiest Housing Markets**. Builderonline.com attributes the real estate market's health to the city's continued job growth, population growth, and steady employment.

Housing Health...

- #6 Healthiest Housing Market (Raleigh) - Builderonline.com, February 2009
- Top Five Strongest Real Estate Market (Raleigh-Cary, NC) - Veros.com, January 2008
- #16 Top Real Estate Market (Raleigh, NC) - Expansion Management, October 2007

Appreciation ...

- #18 MSA with Highest Rate of House Price Appreciation (Raleigh-Cary) - Federal Housing Finance Agency, February 2009
- #7 Top Appreciating Metro Area (Raleigh, NC) - Money, December 2007

- #1 Seller's Market-Residential (Raleigh, NC) - Forbes.com, June 2007

Affordability...

- #2 Best City for Bargain House-Hunters (Raleigh, NC) - Forbes.com, February 2008
- #12 Most Affordable Real Estate Market in the Nation (Raleigh-Cary, NC) - Forbes.com, August 2007

EMPLOYMENT

For the last several years, real estate and employment troubles have gone hand in hand. However, like Raleigh's real estate market, the city's job market has remained steady as unemployment skyrocketed across the country.

In each of the last three years, Raleigh has received at least one "Best City for Jobs" recognition from a major media outlet. In 2007, *Business 2.0* named Raleigh to its **America's Best Jobs in the Hottest Cities** list, and in 2008 and 2009, Forbes.com gave Raleigh the No. 1 spot in its **Best Places for Business and Careers** rankings.

Like many others, Forbes.com attributes Raleigh's job-market stability to the presence of three major higher-education institutions, its low manufacturing base, and the big-name, big-business employers in Research Triangle Park. In fact, the corporations in RTP employ such a large number of professionals in the Triangle that Raleigh has already been recognized as a city with one of the **Largest Concentrations of Drug and Pharmaceutical Jobs** (pharmaceutical giant GlaxoSmithKline has facilities in RTP) and one of the **Highest Concentrations of Tech Workers**

INTRODUCTION

The Job Market...

- #1 Best Place for Business and Careers (Raleigh-Cary) - Forbes.com, March 2009
- #1 Best U.S. City for Jobs (Raleigh-Cary, NC) - Forbes.com, February 2007
- #1 Best Place for Business and Careers (Raleigh, NC) - Forbes.com, March 2008
- #9 Best City for Jobs (Raleigh, NC) - Forbes.com, January 2008
- #3 America's Best Jobs in the Hottest Cities (Raleigh-Durham, NC) - Business 2.0, May 2007
- One of Top10 Great Cities for Salary Growth (Raleigh-Cary) - Yahoo! Hotjobs, January 2009

The Workforce ...

- #15 Most Educated Workforce (Raleigh, NC) - Business Facilities, July 2007
- #3 Metro for College Educated Workers (Raleigh-Cary, NC) - Expansion Management, April 2007

For Recent Grads ...

- #8 Best City for Recent College Grads (Raleigh-Durham, NC) - Forbes.com, June 2008
- #4 Hottest Job Market for Young Adults (Raleigh, NC) - Bizjournals, April 2007

By profession ...

- #5 Top City for Designers and Artists (Raleigh-Cary)- ArtBistro.com, May 2009

- #6 Largest Concentration of Drug and Pharmaceutical Jobs (Raleigh-Durham, NC) - Technology, Talent and Capital: State Bioscience Initiatives 2008, June 2008
- #12 Best Market for Female Execs and Women Business Owners (Raleigh, NC) - *Bizjournals*, August 2007
- #4 MSA With Highest Concentration of Employment – Drugs and Pharmaceuticals (Raleigh-Cary, NC) - Business Facilities, July 2008
- #12 Highest Concentration of Tech Workers (Raleigh, NC) - AeA's Cybercities 2008, June 2008

BUSINESS

Businesses, both big and small, are welcomed with open arms in Raleigh, and you don't have to take a businessman's word for it. Numerous media outlets – from Forbes.com to *Chief Executive Magazine* to *Kiplinger's* – have pinpointed Raleigh (and greater North Carolina) as one of the best places in which to do business.

Since 2006, North Carolina has remained among the top four states for business, as ranked by *Chief Executive Magazine*. *Chief Executive Magazine* says it evaluates states by: taxation and regulation, workforce quality, and living environment. When it comes to small business, experts say Raleigh is just as welcoming; *Bizjournals* and Portfolio.com named Raleigh the **Top City for Small Business**.

In addition, the entrepreneurial spirit is also alive and well in Raleigh. Named a "Fast City" by *Fast Company* in 2007, Raleigh's "Fast City" designation highlighted not only the city's wide range of opportunities but also the city's propensity for innovation. In an article about the 2007 Fast Cities list, *Fast Company* writer Andrew Park commented: "Fast Cities are places where entrepreneurs and employees alike can maximize their potential … Fast Cities invest in physical, cultural, and intellectual infrastructure that will sustain growth."

INTRODUCTION

Business Friendly...

- 2nd Best State to Do Business In (North Carolina) - Chief Executive Magazine, March 2009
- #1 Top City for Small Business (Raleigh, NC) - *Bizjournals* and Portfolio.com, February 2009
- Best Large City for Business (Raleigh-Cary) - NewGeography.com, December 2008
- #2 Best City to Live, Work and Play (Raleigh, NC) - Kiplinger's, July 2008
- #2 State with the Best Business Climate (North Carolina) - Development Counselors International, July 2008
- #4 Best State for Business (North Carolina) - Forbes.com, July 2008
- #1 Pro-Business State (North Carolina) - Pollina.com, June 2008
- #1 Best Place for Business and Careers (Raleigh, NC) - Forbes.com, March 2008
- #4 Major Market in the South (Raleigh-Cary, NC) - Southern Business & Development, Winter 2008
- #23 Best Place in the South to Locate Your Company (Raleigh, NC) - Southern Business & Development, Spring 2008
- #1 Top Business Climate (North Carolina) - Site Selection, November 2007
- #1 Best Place for Business and Careers (Raleigh, NC) - Forbes, April 2007
- #10 Large Metro for Business Recruitment & Attraction (Raleigh-Durham-Chapel Hill, NC) - Expansion Management, May/June 2007

Industries and Professions ...

- #9 Market in the South for Advance Manufacturing (Raleigh-Cary, NC) - Southern Business & Development, Winter 2008
- #12 Best Market for Female Execs and Women Business Owners (Raleigh, NC) - *Bizjournals*, August 2007
- Expansion ...
- Top 50 Hottest Cities for Expanding and Relocating Companies (Raleigh-Cary, NC) - Expansion Management, February 2007
- #3 5-Star Business Opportunity Metro (Raleigh-Cary, NC) - Expansion Management, August 2007

Entrepreneurial Spirit ...

- "Fast City" for Research and Development (Raleigh-Durham, NC) - *Fast Company*, July 2007
- Top 10 Places in the South for the Creative Class (Raleigh-Durham, NC) - *Southern Business and Development*, Winter 2007
- Top Ten Great Innovation Market in the South (Raleigh-Cary-Durham, NC) - *Southern Business & Development*, Winter 2008

Technology ...

- Top Research Science Park (North Carolina State University – Centennial Campus) - The Association of University Research Parks, November 2007
- #3 Techiest City in America (Raleigh-Cary, NC) - U.S. Census Bureau, 2006 (Data released September 2007)
- #3 Most Wired City (Raleigh, NC) - Forbes.com, January 2008

INTRODUCTION

SAFETY

Safety can be a concern in quickly growing cities, but Raleigh has managed to keep its crime rate down even as its population continues to increase.

Each year, CQ Press publishes its City Crime Rating report. In the latest edition of the report, Raleigh-Cary had the lowest crime rate among metro areas in North Carolina. Moreover, Cary came in as the city with the 15th **Lowest City Crime Ranking in United States**.

Safety First...

- #1 Lowest Metro Crime Ranking in North Carolina (Raleigh-Cary) - CQ Press, November 2008
- #15 Lowest City Crime Ranking in United States (Cary) - CQ Press, November 2008

EDUCATION

Raleigh is often referred to as one of the most highly educated cities in the nation. In fact, *Business Facilities* magazine identified Raleigh as having one of the **Most Educated Workforces** in the country. So, it's no surprise that media outlets have recognized the city and surrounding municipalities for its high quality public education system and its education-friendly job market.

When it comes to public education for K-12 students, the Wake County Public School System is among the best public school systems in the country. *Expansion Management* magazine gave the Wake County Public School System a **Gold Rating** and gave Raleigh-Cary a **5-Star Public Education Metro** rating.

For higher education, college students will be able to get a great bang for their buck at nearby universities. *USA Today* named North Carolina State University, located in the heart of Raleigh, as one of the **Best Value Public Colleges for 2009**. Nearby University of North Carolina Chapel

Hill also consistently receives accolades for providing top-notch education at a great price, especially for North Carolina residents.

The Value of Education...

- #15 Most Educated Workforce (Raleigh, NC) - *Business Facilities*, July 2007

Primary and Secondary Education ...

- 5-Star Public Education Metro (Raleigh-Cary, NC) - *Expansion Management*, December 2007
- Gold Rating (Wake County Schools) - *Expansion Management's* Education Quotient, January 2007
- #1 School District in the Nation for Certified Teachers (Wake County) - National Board of Certified Teachers, January 2007

Higher Education ...

- #6 Best Value Public College for 2009 (North Carolina State University, Raleigh) - *USA Today*, January 2009

LIFESTYLE

With more and more people moving to Raleigh, it's becoming increasingly rare to meet a Raleigh native. And though some see that as an unfortunate consequence of the influx of new Raleigh residents, others see it as a great opportunity to increase the diversity of the area and to increase Raleigh's appeal to a wider range of lifestyles.

Even though Raleigh isn't the best fit for every person and every lifestyle, newcomers with certain interests will more than likely feel at home in the city. Those with a passion for politics will find themselves in good company in Raleigh, which was named the **Most Political City** in the U.S. by *Men's Health*. If technology is more up your alley, Raleigh also

INTRODUCTION

hales as the third **Most Wired City** and the third **Techiest City in America**.

And when it comes to dating and relationships, Raleigh is at the top of the list as well, according to a number of well-known media outlets. Most recently, the Triangle was named one of **America's Best Cities for Dating**. The Triangles has also been called one of the **Most Romantic City for Baby Boomers**. And if you're ready to settle down, *Men's Health* says Raleigh is the No. 5 **Best Place to Find a Mate**.

Everyday Life...

- #1 Most Political City (Raleigh, NC) - *Men's Health*, October 2008
- #15 Most Educated Workforce (Raleigh, NC) - *Business Facilities*, July 2007
- #3 Best City for African Americans (Raleigh, NC) - *Black Enterprise*, May 2007
- #1 Healthiest City for Men (Raleigh, NC) - *Men's Health*, January 2008
- #3 Most Wired City (Raleigh, NC) - Forbes.com, January 2008
- #3 Techiest City in America (Raleigh-Cary, NC) - U.S. Census Bureau, 2006 (Data released September 2007)

Dating and Relationships ...

- #4 among America's Best Cities for Dating (Raleigh-Durham-Chapel Hill) – Sperling's BestPlaces, January 2009
- Top 5 Cities for Young Singles (Raleigh, NC) - *Kiplinger*'s Best Cities for Every Stage of Your Life List, June 2007
- #5 Best Place to Find a Mate (Raleigh, NC) - *Men's Health*, March 2007

- The Best American City for Singles (Raleigh, NC) - *Every Day with Rachael Ray*, January 2008
- #7 Hottest, Hippest Destination for Educated Workers in Their 20's
- #3 Most Romantic City for Baby Boomers (Raleigh-Durham-Chapel Hill, NC) - Sperling's BestPlaces, March 2008

FOR FAMILIES

According to Worldwide ERC, a workforce mobility association, Raleigh is one of the easiest cities to relocate to for families. In its 2007 report, Worldwide ERC ranked Raleigh No. 3 among **Best Cities for Relocating Families (Medium Markets)**. The rankings take into account a number of factors including the economy, quality of life, recreation and leisure, and the health of cities' real estate markets.

In light of Raleigh's kid-friendly museums, nature parks, great schools, and numerous options for kid-centric recreational activities, it's no wonder Raleigh also ranked high among the **Best Medium-Sized Cities for Families with Children**.

Family Ties...

- #3 Best City for Relocating Families - Medium Markets (Raleigh-Cary, NC) - Worldwide ERC and Primacy Relocation, 2007 Report
- #5 Best Medium-Sized City for Families with Children (Raleigh, NC) - Who's Your City?, May 2008

RETIREES

What makes a city a top city for soon-to-be retirees? According to Robert Skladany, vice president of research and services at RetirementJobs.com, the cities that are best for soon-to-be retirees share two key

INTRODUCTION

characteristics: employment growth and availability of jobs in professions that welcome older workers. Other important characteristics include lower cost of living, lower housing costs, and high-quality healthcare services. Taking these factors into account, Raleigh-Durham ranks among the **Top 25 Places for Retirement Jobs**.

Retirement in Raleigh...

- Top 15 Place for Cultured Retirement (Raleigh, NC) - Smithsonian.com, April 2008
- Top 25 Places for Retirement Jobs (Raleigh-Durham, NC) - MarketWatch, November 2007

TRAVEL AND RECREATION

The avid traveler knows traveling through a good airport should never be underappreciated, particularly when you're stranded because of delays. RDU International Airport, the Triangle's primary airport, officially unveiled its new Terminal 2 addition on October 26, 2008. As a result, *U.S. News & World Report* named RDU to its list of the **Least Miserable Airports** (a designation that cannot be underestimated) and MSN Travel included RDU as one of the **Top 9 Amazing New Airports**.

Once visitors arrive in Raleigh, there's plenty to keep them busy. According to publishing consulting firm Carolina Publishing Associates, The North Carolina Museum of History and the North Carolina Museum of Art are the 10th and 25th **Most Visited Attractions in North Carolina**, respectively. And for Raleigh newcomers (and visitors lucky enough to be in town around the second week of October), the North Carolina State Fair is a can't-miss event.

Praise for RDU ...

- Top 9 Amazing New Airports (Terminal 2, RDU International Airport, Morrisville) - MSN Travel, September 2008
- #10 Least Miserable Airport (Raleigh-Durham Intl.) - *U.S. News & World Report*, February 2008

For Newcomers and Visitors ...

- Mobil Five-Star Award (The Umstead Hotel and Spa, Cary) - *Mobil Travel Guide*, January 2009
- #10 Most Visited Attraction in North Carolina (N.C. Museum of History, Raleigh) - Carolina Publishing Associates, January 2009
- #22 Most Visited Attraction in North Carolina (N.C. Museum of Art, Raleigh) - Carolina Publishing Associates, January 2009
- #24 Top Arts Destination among Mid-Size Cities (Raleigh) - *AmericanStyle Magazine*, April 2009
- #2 Best Festival or Fair in Readers' Choice Awards (North Carolina State Fair, Raleigh) - *Southern Living*, January 2009

FOOD

When foodies talk about the top destinations for good eats and fine dining, it's not likely Raleigh will be the first place they mention. While New York, Chicago, and San Francisco usually top the list, foodies shouldn't underestimate the restaurant gems to be found in the Triangle.

If you're craving authentic North Carolina barbeque, **The Pit**, 328 West Davie Street, Raleigh, 919-890-4500, *www.thepit-raleigh.com*, will not disappoint. It was named one of the 50 Best New U.S. Restaurants by *Travel + Leisure* magazine. You might even recognize The Pit's owner, Ed Mitchell; he won a head-to-head cook off with his Carolina Ribs on

INTRODUCTION

Food Network's reality competition show Throwdown! With Bobby Flay.

If you're in the mood to indulge, the **Angus Barn** 9401 Glenwood Avenue, Raleigh, 919-781-2444, *www.angusbarn.com*, may be more up your alley. Don't let its name fool you; the Angus Barn offers quite the dining experience. In January 2009, *Southern Living* magazine named the restaurant **No. 2 Splurge Worthy Restaurant** in its Readers' Choice Awards.

Top Foodie Picks...

- 50 Best New U.S. Restaurants (The Pit, Raleigh) - *Travel + Leisure*, April 2009
- #2 Splurge Worthy Restaurant in Readers' Choice Awards (Angus Barn, Raleigh) - *Southern Living*, January 2009
- 50 Best Burgers (Raleigh Times Bar, Raleigh) - Food Network, May 2009
- Midtown Diamond Award for Best Martini (The Red Room Tapas Lounge, Raleigh) - *Midtown Magazine*, January 2009

ODDS AND ENDS

It's usually the quirky things that give a city its character, so if Raleigh's strong job market, steady real estate market, and top-notch public education system weren't quite the characteristics you were looking for to separate Raleigh from the crowd, maybe two of the city's most unique designations will do the trick.

In the spring of 2009, four of Wake County's major municipalities – Cary, Raleigh, Wendell, Zebulon – received the **Tree City USA recognition**. The designation is awarded by the Arbor Day Foundation to cities that have established: (1) a tree board or department, (2) a tree care ordinance, (3) community forestry program with an annual budget of at least $2 per capita, and (4) an Arbor Day observance and proclamation.

Better yet, Raleigh has one of the **Quirkiest New Year's Eve Drop** as ranked by the travel Website TripAdvisor. New York may have its New Year's Eve ball drop in Times Square, but Raleigh is the only city that can lay claim to a New Year's celebration involving a 1,250-pound copper acorn.

Out-of-the-Ordinary Designations...

- Tree City USA recognition (Cary, Raleigh, Wendell and Zebulon) - Arbor Day Foundation, March 2009
- #10 Quirkiest New Year's Eve Drop (Raleigh's acorn) - TripAdvisor, December 2008

PART I

BUYING & SELLING REAL ESTATE IN THE RALEIGH AREA

CHAPTER 2

TOP TIPS FOR RALEIGH AREA BUYERS

GET YOUR FINANCING FIGURED OUT

Before you know what homes to consider, you need to know how much you can afford, and that comes down to the monthly payment amount. Between loan products and new lending rules, variable interest rates and credit score surprises, most buyers are looking in the wrong price range (too high or too low). Ask your real estate broker for a referral to a mortgage lending specialist with at least five years experience. Based on your preferred monthly payment, income, and credit scores, he will review all your loan and down-payment options and write you a "pre qualification letter" stating what purchase price you can afford. The seller's agent will need this letter in order to consider your offer. A "pre-approval letter" (as opposed to a pre-*qualification* letter) requires more labor on your part to provide additional paperwork and verification, yet it will not help you at all when making an offer on a home, so skip it.

You will get the best advice and rates from a mortgage broker who specializes in residential loans, and has access to a large variety of loan products. Loan officers who work for one of the big lenders, such as

Wells Fargo and Countrywide, tend to focus exclusively on their own products. Retail banks are busy with a wide variety of services such as checking, savings, business and auto loans, and normally offer limited lending options, so they are rarely competitive. One exception is the State Employees Credit Union. If you are a member, you should talk to them about your purchase.

Shop for the best rate for your family, but think twice about switching away from a lender who invested her time to give you advice and help, just to save an eighth of a point. Anyone can quote you a lower rate, but that lender may drop the ball later and cost you money or delay your closing. Do not use internet lenders, out-of-state lenders, or any lender who was not referred to you, unless you like surprise rate hikes the day before your closing, when it is too late to react.

A great mortgage broker can sometimes even lower your rate *after* you lock it in, by moving you to a different lender if the rates go down before closing. The best brokers will call and offer it without you having to ask. Find that broker.

Finally, when your mortgage broker asks for additional paperwork, get it to her immediately. She cannot control what the underwriter will ask for or when, and if you are late, your closing might be also.

USE A REAL ESTATE AGENT

All commissions are paid by the seller in the Raleigh area, so for a buyer, the help of a real estate agent is free. A good real estate agent will help you find the right home in the right area, guide you away from big mistakes, and negotiate a better deal for you. Some buyers think they will save money by not having an agent. Think again. The seller has agreed to pay a certain commission rate to the listing agent, regardless of whether the buyer is represented or not. If you don't have an agent, the listing agent will keep the entire amount, and you will miss out on the benefit of professional advice.

PART I: BUYING & SELLING REAL ESTATE IN THE RALEIGH AREA

Beware of agents who offer you part of their commission as a "buyer rebate". This may be a sign they are struggling to survive as real estate broker, and as a result may not be competent to represent you.

START EARLY

Most buyers purchase a home that does not match their original criteria 100%. If you start looking too late, you might buy the wrong home. It makes sense to start looking and exploring long before you are ready to buy to give yourself time to learn and think about what you see. Your criteria for your next home will evolve and change as you look at homes. Meet with a good real estate agent and tell him your criteria. Then spread out a map and ask him what areas are appreciating, and what areas to avoid.

Your broker will start sending you properties by email. Sort through them and pick the ones you like the most. When you have time, drive by these homes and see what you think about the neighborhood, the shopping, the commute to work. You will find neighborhoods you never knew existed. At this stage you are trying to figure out in which geographic area you want to live. If, while driving around, you see a "for sale" sign in front of a property you like, ask your broker for more information.

Continue to look for homes on Realtor.com and the search page on your broker's web site. You will find homes you like that do not meet your original criteria. No problem. Tell your broker about these, change your criteria if you want to, and he will send you more homes to consider.

If you see a home you absolutely love, call your broker and tell him you want to see it ASAP. No harm in looking, and if it is the perfect home, maybe it makes sense to move a little earlier than you planned.

THE GUIDE TO RALEIGH NORTH CAROLINA AREA REAL ESTATE

MOVE UP IN THE DOWN MARKET

This is the most profitable time in the history of the Raleigh area to sell your current home and purchase a more expensive home. Here is a simplified example: Let's assume the average price of a home in the Raleigh area has dropped 10% over the past 18 months. So if you own a home that would have been worth $200,000 in a normal market, you may only get $180,000 for it now, or $20,000 less than you hoped. However, you should be able to purchase your next home at a 10% discount also, so you get a $400,000 home for $360,000, which is a $40,000 savings. In total, you took a $20,000 loss and earned a $40,000 gain, and ended up with a $20,000 profit. It gets better, though. In reality, the lower-priced homes depreciated less than the higher-priced homes. So if your $200,000 home only depreciated 5%, but the $400,000 home depreciated 15%, then you would lose $10,000 on your current home and gain $60,000 on your next home, for a $50,000 profit! Compare this to moving up in a strong market, when any appreciation on your lower-priced home is wiped out by the price increase of your next home. You are actually taking a loss on the transaction. Keep in mind that getting a bargain on the higher-priced home does not necessarily mean negotiating a big reduction off the list (or "asking") price, because the list price may have already been adjusted downward to the right price.

KNOW YOUR CRITERIA

Here is a list of criteria for you to think about:
- ☐ Price range
- ☐ Detached/Townhome/Condo
- ☐ Number of bedrooms
- ☐ Living area square footage
- ☐ Master down (Y/N)
- ☐ Number of bathrooms
- ☐ Geographic area
- ☐ School district(s)
- ☐ Acreage
- ☐ Age of home
- ☐ One story (Y/N)
- ☐ Lot type (corner/cul-de-sac)
- ☐ Flat lot (Y/N)
- ☐ Basement (Y/N)

PART I: BUYING & SELLING REAL ESTATE IN THE RALEIGH AREA

- ☐ Number of garage bays
- ☐ Commute time to work
- ☐ Screened porch (Y/N)
- ☐ Fireplace (wood/gas)
- ☐ Fenced yard (Y/N)
- ☐ Exterior (brick/vinyl/etc)
- ☐ Community pool (Y/N)
- ☐ Golf course community (Y/N)
- ☐ Direction house faces
- ☐ Short-sale/foreclosure (Y/N)
- ☐ "Fixer-upper" (Y/N)
- ☐ Deck (Y/N)
- ☐ Pool (Y/N)
- ☐ Storage shed (Y/N)
- ☐ Private lot (Y/N)
- ☐ Storage space
- ☐ Water supply
- ☐ Waste services
- ☐ Extra parking (Y/N)
- ☐ County/City
- ☐ HOA Dues

Tell your real estate broker everything you want in your next home. If your search results in too many homes to choose from, you can add to your criteria. If not enough homes match your criteria, you can make your criteria less specific.

UNDERSTAND DOM AND $/SF

DOM is "Days On Market". This number is important because the longer the home has been on the market, the more likely the seller is to accept a lower offer. Reports printed by your broker from the Triangle Multiple Listing Service (MLS) have two kinds of DOM. The first, LADOM, means "Listing Agreement Days On Market". Listing agreements can be terminated and new agreements signed, agents can be fired and hired, and this number will reset to zero each time, so this number is meaningless. CDOM, "Cumulative Days On Market" is more helpful, because it is the total number of days this property has been on the market. However, even this number will be reset to zero if the property is taken off the market for 30 days. In this case, you can ask your agent to run a report on the property address and you will see the complete MLS history, including all price reductions.

When you find a home you like, how do you know it is priced correctly? Look up the homes that have sold recently in the same subdivision and find those that are of comparable quality to the home you like, considering overall condition, upgrades, lot size, etc. Look at the $/SF, or "Sales Price per Square Foot" for each of these. The home you like should sell for a similar $/SF.

Ask your broker to print out, and help you analyze a "Quick CMA" report for the properties in which you are interested. This report will automatically calculate DOM and $/SF for you. Pay no attention to SP/LP% (percentage of list price that a property sold for) on this report. This calculation is not helpful because list price depends upon random seller preference, and is based upon the latest list price, not the original list price of each property.

KNOW WHERE TO FIND THE BEST DEALS IN THE RALEIGH AREA

The best deals in the Raleigh area are homes listed at over $400,000 in the western part of Cary, the northern part of Raleigh, and any part of Wake Forest. These are the areas where builders added too much to the supply of housing in our market. This oversupply has decreased prices dramatically for both resale and finished new construction homes. The higher price ranges have decreased by larger percentages, so while a home that was $500,000 might now sell for $425,000, a home that was at $1,500,000 may now sell for $900,000.

You can also get excellent deals on high-quality townhomes off Glenwood Avenue between routes 440 and 540. This area has been a magnet for younger people, and is convenient to shopping, the airport, Research Triangle Park, and major highways. A half-dozen developers built too many townhomes in this area, and prices have dropped an average of 15% in the past year. The price ranges are currently $160,000 to $220,000 in this area.

PART I: BUYING & SELLING REAL ESTATE IN THE RALEIGH AREA

If you like appreciation (and projects), the best deal is to find a home that has all the "right things" wrong with it (out-of-date or worn out carpet, countertops, wallpaper, fixtures, etc) and fix them yourself. You will want to look for properties listed for low $/SF in a subdivision where there are many homes selling for higher $/SF, which theoretically means the property in question could sell for that higher $/SF if you bring it up to snuff. Most of these are "as-is" properties, which means you still get a chance to inspect it thoroughly after putting it under contract, and can terminate if you do not like what you see. Enlist your broker (and her inspector and contractor friends) to help make sure you do not get stuck with a lemon.

For all the properties mentioned in this section, be prepared to stay in the home for several years until the market turns around. It always does.

UNDERSTAND SHORT SALES AND FORECLOSURES

A "short sale" is a situation in which the seller owes more on the home than it is worth, and does not have the funds to come up with the difference at closing. In North Carolina, the seller must disclose that it is a short sale, and when an offer is made, both buyer and seller must sign a "Short Sale Addendum". Once an offer is accepted by the seller, the listing agent submits it to the seller's lender for approval. In rare circumstances this approval can happen quickly, but most often it takes several months, and even then the answer might be "no". So it is possible to get a good deal on a short sale, but the lower the offer, the less chance that the lender will approve it, because the bank wants to recover as much of their money as possible. If you want certainty about when (or if) you will be able to actually occupy the property, setting your heart on a short sale can be extremely frustrating. The listing agent will try to keep you waiting by giving you hopeful updates, but oftentimes the process drags on indefinitely. My advice is to make your offer on the short sale property, knowing the addendum allows you to withdraw it at any time before it is accepted, and keep looking for another property. If your original offer gets accepted, you can celebrate. If you find a better property in the meantime, cancel your offer on the short sale property and buy the new one instead.

If a homeowner stops making mortgage payments, the bank will eventually foreclose on the property, taking ownership and listing it for sale with a real estate agent. At the beginning, the bank will price the property high, hoping to recover the amount owed. Then the bank will drop the price substantially every few months until it sells. The strategy is to understand the value of the property (see below) and make offers at or below that value regardless of the current list price. The bank will either accept the offer or say "no" (they rarely counter). If they say "no", make another offer. Recently we submitted a $760,000 offer on a home listed at $850,000. The bank said "no". We made another offer at $761,000, and the bank accepted it. You just need to get lucky by making the offer at the right time, when the bank has just reduced the list price or is about to. Since you do not know when that will be, just keep making offers.

UNDERSTAND HOW TO DETERMINE THE TRUE VALUE OF A PROPERTY

A home is worth whatever a buyer is willing to pay and a seller is willing to accept. The best source to estimate the true market value of a property is an experienced, busy real estate broker, because they are working with buyers and sellers in the current real estate market, and they have access to the best data (from the MLS). They will also correctly adjust for quality and feature differences.

The second best valuation source is an experienced, busy appraiser. They have access to the same data, but they work for banks, not buyers and sellers. In addition, they are constrained by inflexible appraisal rules which do not allow them to consider some relevant information and comparable properties.

PART I: BUYING & SELLING REAL ESTATE IN THE RALEIGH AREA

Inexperienced real estate brokers and appraisers can be wildly inaccurate. Web sites like Zillow.com calculate market values without the input from human experience or judgment and they use incomplete data from county tax records. The "value" found in the county tax records is not useful, because it is calculated for the purposes of property tax assessment. Further, in the Raleigh area, this number is updated only once every eight years, the last time being January 2008. Up until that time most properties sold for far above tax value. Since then I have seen properties sell for $100,000 above and below tax value.

ASK TWO KEY QUESTIONS IN A COMPETITIVE SITUATION

Even in a challenging market, you could find yourself competing against another buyer for a low-priced property (see "Understanding Short Sales and Foreclosures" above). The listing agent is prohibited from disclosing details of any offers received, so she will ask both buyers to return with their "best and highest offer". She will then choose one buyer with whom to negotiate a final agreement acceptable to the seller. When considering your offer price, ask yourself, "If we lose this property at this price, will I regret not offering more?" If so, you might want to increase your offer. Conversely, ask yourself "If we get this property at this price, will we regret paying that much?" If so, consider decreasing your offer. Rarely will the other buyer offer more than list price, so if you feel the property is a bargain, consider offering just a little over list price. Even $100 over can create goodwill with the seller and get the property for you. Finally, offering to close in less than 30 days may be very attractive to some sellers, especially if it is a bank-owned property.

WALK THE NEIGHBORHOOD BEFORE MAKING AN OFFER

Before committing to purchase a home, take a few slow walks through the neighborhood at different times of day. Listen for barking dogs. Look for children playing if that is important to you (the law prohibits your broker from discussing "familial status"). Introduce yourself to a few neighbors, tell them which home you are thinking about, and ask them what they know. Neighbors love to talk and you might be glad you listened.

CHAPTER 3

TOP TIPS FOR RALEIGH AREA SELLERS

MAKE BUYERS FALL IN LOVE WITH YOUR HOME

Buyers keep looking until they fall in love. They are not looking for "a" home, they are looking for "the" home, their "dream" home. They are tired of seeing homes (9 out of 10) that are not ready for sale. They want a clean, fresh, move-in-ready home. Most do not want to do even minor projects.

As a seller, you must understand the mind of the buyer. Buyers do not buy homes; they buy the feeling they get when they are looking at a home. They are not using their brains to decide, they are using their hearts. And in good markets or tough markets, when a buyer finds the right home, they will fall in love, and that home will sell for the highest possible price.

We have witnessed a buyer considering two identical homes on the same street, in the same neighborhood, with identical lots, and pay $15,000 more for the one that spent $750 preparing the home for sale. We have seen homes sit on the market for a year, then sell in 30 days (at a higher list price) after a few small adjustments to improve the buyer perception of the home.

If you want to sell your home for the highest price in the shortest amount of time, emphasize or add elements with which buyers will fall in love, and fix or remove issues that will cause them to hesitate.

There are a few investor types out there who truly decide with their brain, and whose first priority is a good deal. But we do not want anyone getting a good deal on your home, right? So we can ignore them. What we want is a buyer to come to your home, fall in love, and impulsively write an offer at (or near) your asking price. So we will concentrate on those buyers instead.

MAKE A PROFIT WHEN YOU SELL WITH SMART INVESTMENTS

By making the right investments in your home, you will not only cause buyers to fall in love, but you will also make a profit. Depending on your neighborhood, your price point, and the size of your home, the following improvements will generally produce at least $2 or more in increased sales price for every $1 you invest. And anything that increases your price will also reduce your "days-on-market."

- ☐ **Granite countertops in the kitchen**. They are almost a necessity in the Raleigh area if you expect your home to sell for over $250,000. You should be able to get them for $45 per square foot, installed. Go with a standard, lower-priced choice. For higher-end homes, consider granite in the master bath as well. For homes under $250,000, consider granite-looking laminate countertops, or if there is an island in the kitchen, you can consider putting granite there only.
- ☐ **Stainless steel appliances**. You should be able to get a refrigerator, oven, microwave, and dishwasher for under $2500. If your current appliances are white or cream color, this is especially important. Black appliances may be okay if they are fairly new.

- ☐ **Replace old carpets**. If they are over five years old, they will not look new when cleaned, unless they are very good quality. New carpet also helps a home smell new.
- ☐ **Remove wallpaper**. Buyers today strongly dislike wallpaper, except for a very subtle pattern in the powder room.
- ☐ **Refinish dull and scratched hardwood floors**. Shining floors make a stunning impact on buyers.
- ☐ **Paint**. Go with a medium beige in the inside, darker than what was, in the past, considered "builder beige". It makes the home look more expensive and makes white trim "pop". Paint your front door and shutters black.

This advice is subject to modification based on the specifics of your home, and over time as buyer tastes evolve. In a few years buyers will probably love wallpaper again. I recommend getting the advice of a staging consultant who works with real estate agents. Most interior decorators do not specialize in preparing homes for buyers.

Fixing problems is always better than offering an allowance, because to make up for the problem you will have to reduce your price more than it would have cost you to fix it.

DO THESE EASY THINGS

Here are a list of low-cost, easy improvements which will pay for themselves many times over:

- ☐ **Clean every inch of your home.** Get help if you need it.
- ☐ **Spread new mulch.** Use dark brown "triple-shredded stained bark." The stain keeps it looking better much longer. Pine straw is cheaper but it also looks cheaper.
- ☐ **Plant many, many flowers.** More than you think you need. Flowers may be the single best investment you can make to sell your home.

- ☐ **Remove clutter.** Remove personal pictures. Remove everything from horizontal surfaces except a few decorations.
- ☐ **Remove window treatments.** Leave blinds.
- ☐ **Remove basketball goals, play sets, and tree houses**. These will turn some people off, and no one will ever say "I would have bought that home if only it had a basketball goal." If you have a flat driveway they can install one themselves. Especially remove trampolines. They make many mothers nervous.

USE TEMPORARY STORAGE CONTAINERS

Our sellers have had very good experiences using temporary storage containers (such as PODS or PackRat) to store clutter while preparing their home for sale. Some sellers end up using them for the entire move, often in combination with hired labor. As of this writing, a 16-foot container (holds approximately 4 rooms) was $69 for drop off and pick up, plus $155/month for secure, climate-controlled storage, plus a second $69 at final drop off and pick up. The other alternative is hauling material to and from a storage location, which is less expensive, but more work for you.

GET YOUR IMPROVEMENTS PERMITTED AND INSPECTED

If you have made any structural changes to your property that were not permitted and inspected, you will have to tell the buyer on the required Residential Property Disclosure Statement. That will make most buyers nervous, and even if they are not concerned, they will use it as a negotiating lever. As a result, it is almost always better to get the space inspected and make any necessary repairs. If you did it right in the first place, it is usually not a big deal. The inspections are inexpensive and fairly quick. If you have questions, call the city or town (or the county if you are not in an incorporated area) and ask them anonymously.

PART I: BUYING & SELLING REAL ESTATE IN THE RALEIGH AREA

PRICE YOUR HOME REALISTICALLY

The price you want, or need, to get for your home does not matter to buyers. Yes, making smart investments and otherwise preparing your home for sale will definitely increase the value, but if your asking price is too much above that value, it will not sell. In fact, because the market is much more price-sensitive than most sellers realize, you may not even get any showings.

Do not make the mistake of thinking, "I'll price it high, because the buyer will make a low offer, and we'll meet in the middle." That is not how it works. Buyers very rarely make low offers, at least in the first 30-60 days a home is on the market. Buyers do not like conflict, they do not want to make sellers upset. Neither do their agents, because they hope to work with the listing agent many times again in the future. The buyers have the data, they know what the comparable properties sold for, and if your home is overpriced they assume you will only accept offers close to your list price. Rather than argue about it, they will just ignore your home.

I am not suggesting that you under-price your home to motivate buyers to come see it. Your well-prepared home is motivation enough, and you deserve every penny you can get from the sale, right? An *accurately-priced* home will sell just as quickly as an under-priced home (in fact, under-priced homes look suspicious to buyers). But price cannot be an obstacle either. If your home is prepared correctly, the fair-market value for your property will be near the top of the range of the comparable homes that have sold recently. List your home at about two percent above fair-market value, and that is enough "negotiating room" for most buyers to feel like they "won."

UNDERSTAND HOW BUYERS FIND THE HOME THEY PURCHASE

You have prepared your home for the market and priced it realistically. Now you need to market it effectively. In order to do that, you need to know how buyers in the Raleigh area find the home they purchase. Almost every buyer searches for homes on the internet, but except for a small percentage, that is not how they find the home they actually purchase.

- The vast majority of Raleigh-area buyers (approximately 80%) become aware of the home they actually **purchase through a real estate broker**. That is because most buyers purchase a home different from the criteria they originally defined, and good brokers find homes buyers miss when searching on their own. So as a seller you should be marketing more to real estate brokers than to buyers. Easier said than done, because brokers get so bombarded with emails and flyers that they just end up deleting or throwing them away. The key here is to realize that 10% of the brokers sell 80% of the property. You need to find out who these brokers are and somehow get them to pay attention to your home. The only way I know to do that is to have your agent bring buyers to see their listings, and ask the other agent to return the favor.

- About nine percent of Raleigh-area buyers become aware of the home they purchase **through a friend who lives in the same neighborhood as the home being sold**. The best way to make this fact work for you is to call your neighbors and invite them to come to see your home, then ask them if they know any friends or relatives that might want to live in the neighborhood. They will be especially curious to see your home if you have made significant improvements to prepare it for sale.

- Six percent of Raleigh-area buyers find the home they buy because they saw the **"for sale" sign** while they were exploring the neighborhood. To maximize this traffic, have a high-quality sign, preferably one hanging from a post. A better sign is more noticeable, and it adds to the perception of quality of your home. Also, skip the brochures in front of your home. Most of them get

- picked by neighbors anyway, and real buyers use them more to eliminate your home than to schedule a showing. Most buyers will call the number on the sign if they are interested, and you or your broker can sell your home more effectively than a brochure.
- Five percent of buyers do actually find the home they purchase **through the internet**. This is not a big percentage, but do not ignore it. Ask your broker to list it on Realtor.com, and see if she can arrange to get it listed on the websites of the other real estate firms in town. Re-list your home on Craigslist every three days so it does not get too far down on the page. Definitely list it on Zillow.com and Trulia.com (two of the most popular real estate web sites), and if you search you will find at least 30 other real-estate related sites on which to place it.
- **Do not invest in print advertising**, either in the newspaper or the real-estate-related magazine you see in the grocery store. They are very expensive, and statistically they generate almost zero results.
- Finally, **I advise against open houses**. The Raleigh-area is not an open-house oriented market. The chance of selling your home this way (less than 1%) is not worth the safety concern of having unrepresented strangers exploring your home.

These statistics come from our experience with hundreds of buyers and sellers in the Raleigh area. You might find statistics different from those above regarding how buyers find homes. For example, the statistics available from the National Association of Realtors are different, because they are national statistics. Every local market is different, and you have to market to the buyers in your market, not a market in a different part of the country.

SELL YOUR HOME QUICKLY

Brokers set up searches in the Multiple Listing Service for their clients, so that when a home comes on the market that meets their buyer's criteria, it gets sent to the buyer automatically. So when your home is activated in the MLS, it will be emailed to hundreds of potential buyers all at the same time. Some of these buyers just started looking, so even if they see and love your home, they are not ready to make a decision. They need to see more homes first, and might not have their financing figured out. The majority of the buyers, though, have been looking for a while and are ready to buy immediately, when they find the right home. These buyers are the key to success, and you have one chance at them. They will see the listing and look at the pictures and the price, and decide whether or not to schedule a showing to see your home. If they decide "no", they will never see your home again. If they decide to come see your home, they will decide to either buy it, or not. If they decide "no", they will never see your home again. If you do not sell your home to one of these ready-to-buy buyers, you may be in for a long wait, because every buyer who sees your home from then on will be a "new buyer" who is not ready to buy yet.

If your home is prepared right, priced right, and marketed right, you should be able to sell it quickly, in any market, to one of these "ready-to-buy" buyers. In less than 30 days. And the faster you sell your home the better price you will get. Here is why: if a buyer walks into your home and falls in love, and the home has been on the market only a few days, they will think, "If we love it, someone else will love it too. We can't let someone else get it first. So let's make an offer today, and let's make it close to asking price. We are not going to let a few thousand dollars get between us and our new home."

After your home has been on the market 30 days, this sense of urgency among buyers is gone. Buyers start saying "Hmm, if this home is so great, why hasn't anyone else bought it yet? I wonder what's wrong with it?" Or, "We like it, but it's been here this long already. It'll be here for a while longer. Let's keep looking in case we find something better." Not good for you.

If you over-price your home you will get less in the end, because buyers will ignore it until you fix the price, and by then you will have missed all the "ready-to-buy" buyers. Do not have the attitude of "I'll wait for my price". The longer your home sits, the lower it will go. After 90 days buyers will think you are desperate, and they will start to "low-ball" you.

Selling a home is a pain. But, you have the choice of: (1) experiencing that pain, at the beginning, for the short amount of time required to get your home ready the right way, or (2) trying to avoid pain at the beginning, and experiencing pain for six months (or more) of price reductions and showings. Constantly having your home ready for showings is stressful. Especially if you have kids or pets.

You have one chance to get the best price in the shortest amount of time. Do the work, be realistic, and get it over with.

HIDE THE PETS

I know you love your pets. I love mine too. But buyers do not like pets. In our experience, 70% of buyers will not consider buying your home if they see you have a cat. Too many people are allergic, or have friends or relatives who are. Thirty percent of buyers will not consider your home if they see you have a dog. To a lesser extent, it is the same for hamsters, ferrets, rabbits, turtles, etc. So, as much as possible, take the pets out of the home during showings, and hide the evidence left behind (pet food, bowls, litter boxes, and beds). For the average home, this effort will increase your sales price by over $5,000, and reduce the days-on-market by 50%. It's worth the trouble.

MAKE PRICE ADJUSTMENTS QUICKLY BASED ON SHOWING TRAFFIC

Insufficient showings means your home is overpriced. In our market, if you get three or fewer showings in the first 30 days, the market is telling you your home is overpriced by at least 10%. If you get between 4 and 12 showings, you home is 4% to 7% overpriced. If you get 12 or more showings in the first 30 days, but no offer, your home is about 3% overpriced. For higher-priced or very unique properties, you should expect slightly fewer showings, but the conclusions remain the same. Adjust your price immediately. The longer your home is on the market, the lower the eventual price will be.

BE SMART ABOUT WHAT OFFER YOU ACCEPT

It is very difficult for a seller to back out of a North Carolina real estate contract, so think carefully before signing on the dotted line.

I advise not considering a contract that is contingent upon the sale of a home that does not already have a contract on it. Your buyer may not have properly prepared their home for sale, and/or may be unrealistic about asking price. Sometimes a seller will accept such an offer, while retaining the right to continue marketing their property, while giving the buyer a 48-hour notice when another offer is received to either terminate their offer or drop the contingency. This will not help much because the Triangle Multiple Listing Service will require you to list your property as "Active-Contingent", which will reduce your showings by 75%. In the case where the buyer's home is already under contract, it depends upon how good the contract is. Have your broker contact the listing agent for the buyer's home. If everything looks solid, you should feel good about moving forward.

Make sure the buyer's financing is in good shape. Certainly ask for a pre-qualification letter, but I also recommend having your broker ask permission to contact the buyer's lender to see how much research the lender has really done.

For homes below $250,000 it is very common for buyers to ask for "seller paid closing costs". Think of these as "buyer-financed closing costs", and when considering an offer, mentally subtract this amount (found in section 10 of the North Carolina Offer to Purchase and Contract) from purchase price on the first page of the offer, because that is the price the buyer is really offering you, and negotiate accordingly. The buyer often needs this money to purchase your home because they do not have enough cash to cover both the down payment and closing costs such as inspection, appraisal, loan origination, etc. The risk to the seller is that the home must appraise for the total amount, including the closing costs. If it does not, the buyer will ask you to reduce your price to the appraised value (still including closing costs), and if you refuse they might be unable to close.

IF BUYING ALSO, GO FOR A SIMULTANEOUS CLOSE

If you are both selling and buying a home, the timing is important. If you sell your home before you find the next one, you will end up moving twice, once into a temporary location, then later into your new home. If you buy your new home before you sell your current home, you will end up paying two mortgages for a while (which also requires the approval of your lender). However, with a smart strategy, you might be able to sell and buy on the same day.

The key is to work on finding your next home while preparing your current home for sale. With the right advice from a good real estate broker, and a realistic price, you should be able to get a contract on your Raleigh-area home within 60 days. If you have done your homework on the buying side, you will already have a few top choices for your next home. If so, go ahead and get your top choice under contract, contingent on the closing of the existing contract on your home. If not, negotiate a longer closing date on your current home to give you more time, and get to work finding the right home. In either case, you should be able to arrange the same closing date for both homes.

If you do not need the cash from your current home in order to purchase the next home, and your lender approves you for a loan on your next home while you still own your first home, it can be very convenient to close on your new home a week or so early to make the move easy.

However, most sellers will need to schedule the closing of their current home in the morning on the closing date, then get that attorney to wire the proceeds to the next attorney in order to close later that day on the home they are buying. In North Carolina a real estate closing is more of an accounting function than a legal representation, so I recommend using the same attorney for both closings in this case, even if that means using your buyer's attorney for your purchase. That way you can skip the wire transfer and close back-to-back in the same office.

No matter how much you prepare, keep this important fact in mind: although 95% of real estate closings happen on time, they can be delayed for a dozen different reasons, many of which (such as the buyer's lender) are out of your control. The standard North Carolina contract allows a buyer ten days delay without penalty, but in most cases delayed closings will take place by the end of the next business day. Try to stay calm, and prepare in advance. When choosing a moving company ask them how much it will cost you if they have to hold onto your belonging for an extra day or more (see the "Storage Container" section above for a different strategy).

GET AN EXPERIENCED, FULL-SERVICE BROKER AND LISTEN TO HER

Not all brokers perform equally. Ten percent of brokers are responsible for over 80% of all sales in the Raleigh area. As of this writing, the

PART I: BUYING & SELLING REAL ESTATE IN THE RALEIGH AREA

average "days-on-market" for sold listings in the Raleigh area is 110 days, but some of the best agents are averaging less than 40 days for 2009.

A tough real estate market is a "professional's market". You need a full-service agent to help you do everything right so your home will be the one buyers choose. "Limited service" brokers do not have time to help you get everything right, and trying to sell your home by yourself will leave you helpless. In the Raleigh area, 80% of buyers find their home through a broker, and brokers do not like "For Sale by Owner" properties because they are difficult to deal with.

A busy, experienced agent is by far the best qualified person to calculate an accurate fair-market-value for your home. He works with buyers and sellers all the time, and has his finger on the pulse of the market. Good agents have ongoing, productive relationships with other good agents, and can get them to bring buyers to your home.

Find a good agent and listen to her. She might upset you in the beginning when she tells you the truth about your home and the market, but she knows that is better than upsetting you every day for six months while your home sits unsold.

A good agent knows how to negotiate the best price for you. He will prove it to you by sticking to his commission rate when you meet him. If he does not believe in himself enough to charge his full commission, then you should not believe in him either. Just tell him to get to work and earn it. Real estate brokerage is like any other business. You get what you pay for, and paying less will cost you more in the end.

CHAPTER 4

55+ COMMUNITIES: INSIDE INFORMATION FOR MATURE ADULTS

WHY MOVE TO THE RALEIGH AREA?

The rise in Wake County's popularity as a retirement destination coincides with declining interest in more traditional retirement locations like Florida. "Halfback," a term usually associated with football, has been used to describe a growing group of older Americans who initially relocated from Northern states to the deep South, but later moved *half way back* – ending up in places like North Carolina and Tennessee.

Wake County's municipalities are consistently ranked among the best places in the country to live, work, buy a home and *retire*. Raleigh, for example, ranked fourth in CNNMoney.com's 2006 list of the Best Big Cities for Retirement.

COMMUNITIES FOR OLDER ADULTS

There are many communities in the Raleigh area that cater to older adults. These communities can be divided into four categories: Active

PART I: BUYING & SELLING REAL ESTATE IN THE RALEIGH AREA

Adult Communities, Continuing Care Retirement Communities, Retirement Rental Communities, and Age-Targeted Communities.

The first three categories are often referred to as age-restricted communities, and, as such, must adhere to certain requirements set forth by the Fair Housing Act of 1968 and the Housing for Older Persons Act of 1995. In addition to these federal laws, individual developments may institute their own rules regarding age-restrictions.

ACTIVE ADULT COMMUNITIES (55 AND OVER)

Americans are living longer, healthier lives. As the baby-boomer generation reaches retirement age, Active Adult communities continue to gain in popularity. As the title suggests, these developments emphasize activities and amenities such as fitness centers, cooking classes, golf outings and pools. Some developments are designed to be self-contained communities and include everything from grocery stores to doctors' offices, restaurants to walking trails.

Most Active Adult communities offer homes for purchase, though some developments offer rental options as well. Another common feature of Active Adult communities is low-maintenance housing – lawn care and exterior building maintenance are often included in homeowners' association (HOA) fees.

Home styles range from large multi-level houses to ranch-style villas, townhouses to apartments. An Active Adult development might include a variety of home styles, or just one.

In order to be identified as a fifty-five and over community, 80% of occupied units must be inhabited by at least one person who is fifty-five or over. Individual communities and HOAs will define additional age requirements and guidelines. For example, most Active Adult communities do not allow anyone under the age of nineteen to be a full-time resident.

ACTIVE ADULT COMMUNITIES IN WAKE COUNTY

Carolina Preserve at Amberly (55+)
Municipality: Cary
Description: Carolina Preserve, a Del Webb community, offers a wide range of clubs and classes from fitness to cooking. There are seventeen different home models to choose from.
Types of Homes: Single Family, Townhouse
# of Homes/Sites/Units: 1300
Price Range: $100,000 - $400,000
HOA Fees: $200+/month
Developer: Pulte Homes
Construction Dates: 2006-11
Nearby: RDU Airport, Golf, Hospitals, Interstate 40
Activities and Amenities: Activity Center, Teaching Kitchen, Ballroom, Fitness Center, Pools, Tennis, Chipping and Putting Greens, Trails
Address: 107 Arvind Oaks Circle**,** Cary, NC 27519
Phone: (919) 460-7170
Web site: *www.pulte.com/delwebb*

Heritage Pines(55+)
Municipality: Cary
Description: Multi-unit villas and single-family residences are available at Heritage Pines. Residents can play tennis and shuffleboard in the recreational complex.
Types of Homes: Apartment, Single Family
# of Homes/Sites/Units: 298
Price Range: $200,000 - $300,000
HOA Fees: $174/month
Developer: K. Hovnanian Homes
Construction Dates: 2000-06
Nearby: RDU Airport, Golf, Hospitals, Interstate 40

PART I: BUYING & SELLING REAL ESTATE IN THE RALEIGH AREA

Activities and Amenities: Clubhouse, Fitness Center, Pool, Library, Trails, Tennis, Shuffleboard, Foreign Language Clubs
Address: 2000 Heritage Pines Drive, Cary, NC 27519
Phone: (919) 466-0016
Web site: *www.heritagepinesnc.com*

SummerWind Plantation (55+)

Municipality: Clayton
Description: When complete, SummerWind Plantation will feature a stocked fishing pond, a professional/medical office complex and a fitness center. The development currently offers nine different home models as well as custom options.
Types of Homes: Single Family, Townhouse
# of Homes/Sites: 530
Price Range: $150,000 - $300,000
HOA Fees: $220+/month
Developer: Parker Development Ltd.
Construction Dates: Under Development
Nearby: Golf, Hospitals, Interstate 40
Activities and Amenities: Fitness Center, Indoor & Outdoor Pools, Wellness Center, Fishing Pond, Gated Community, Tennis
Address: Glen Road, Clayton, NC
Phone: (919) 369-7344
Web site: *www.parker-dev.com*

Ivy Hall (55+)

Municipality: East Raleigh
Description: Ivy Hall offers one-story, maintenance-free homes in East Raleigh between the 440 and 540 interstates.
Types of Homes: Single Family
# of Homes/Sites: 116
Price Range: $200,000 - $250,000

HOA Fees: $170/month
Developer: WKB Properties, Inc.
Construction Dates: 2006-10
Nearby: Downtown Raleigh, Golf, Interstate 440, Interstate 540
Activities and Amenities: Clubhouse, Pool, Lawn Maintenance, Two Car Garages, Fireplaces
Address: 4710 Ivy Crest Court, Raleigh, NC 27604
Phone: (919) 235-0508
Web site: *www.trianglenewhomes.com*

The Village at Aversboro (55+)

Municipality: Garner
Description: Six different ranch-style home models are available at The Village at Aversboro, all feature brick exteriors and two car garages. Lake Benson offers recreation opportunities within walking distance.
Types of Homes: Single Family
# of Homes/Sites: 147
Price Range: $200,000 - $400,000
HOA Fees: $100/month
Developer: S. Wake Properties, Inc.
Construction Dates: 2008-09
Nearby: Downtown Raleigh, Golf, Interstate 440
Activities and Amenities: Clubhouse, Community Potluck Dinners and Brunches, Lawn Maintenance
Address: 401 Aversboro Road, Suite 100, Garner, NC 27529
Phone: (919) 662-5507
Web site: *www.thevillageataversboro.com*

PART I: BUYING & SELLING REAL ESTATE IN THE RALEIGH AREA

CONTINUING CARE RETIREMENT COMMUNITIES (62 AND OVER)

Continuing Care Retirement Communities (CCRC) are developments that provide a continuum of care to residents from independent living to skilled nursing. CCRCs offer the opportunity for an individual to remain in one location for the rest of his or her life. While exceptions are made, sixty-two is the minimum age for residency at all of Wake County's CCRCs. In the case of couples, only one person must meet the age-requirement.

Upon first entering a CCRC, most residents move into an independent living situation (a single-family home, townhouse or apartment). Like Active Adult communities, CCRCs offer activities and amenities such as restaurants, fitness centers, book clubs and on-site health care. What makes CCRCs unique is that they also offer assisted living and skilled nursing care to their residents, should the need arise.

Contracts are another distinguishing feature of CCRCs. Residents must enter into a contract with a CCRC prior to moving in. Most contracts include both entrance fees (some of which may be refundable) and monthly fees. Some CCRCs also offer the ability to purchase a home. There are four basic kinds of contracts:

- **Extensive** – Extensive contracts are all-inclusive. Housing, community services and access to all levels of care are included in the price.
- **Modified** – Modified contracts provide housing, community services and a specified amount of long-term care, after which the resident must make additional payments.
- **Fee-for-Service** – Fee-for-Service contracts provide housing, community services and guaranteed access to health care at the going rate.
- **Equity** – Some CCRCs offer the opportunity to purchase property.

Because of the many different options involved with Continuing Care Retirement Communities, prices vary greatly, both between communities and within communities.

The North Carolina Department of Insurances oversees all Continuing Care Retirement Communities in the state. Please visit their Web site for more information: *www.ncdoi.com/FED/SE/fed_se_ccrc_guide.asp*

CONTINUING CARE RETIREMENT COMMUNITIES IN WAKE COUNTY

Glenaire (62+)
Municipality: Cary
Description: Glenaire is located on a 30-acre wooded site within the suburban community of Cary. In 2007, the community center was expanded to include an aquatic center and a larger library.
Types of Homes: Apartment, Single Family
# of Homes/Sites/Units: 332
Entrance Fees: $56,000 - $276,000
Monthly Fees: $1850-$3000
Contract Type: Modified
Construct. Dates: 1993-2007
Nearby: RDU Airport, Downtown Cary
Activities and Amenities:Fitness Center, Pool, Library, Community Center, Pond, Trails
Address: 4000 Glenaire Circle, Cary, NC 27511
Phone: (919) 480-8095
Web site: *www.gleanaire.org*

PART I: BUYING & SELLING REAL ESTATE IN THE RALEIGH AREA

Searstone (62+)

Municipality: Cary
Description: Located in Cary, Searstone will offer over 20 different floor plans in 3 different home styles. Specialty Village, located within Searstone, will feature shopping, dining, medical offices and professional services.
Types of Homes: Apartment, Townhouse, Single Family
# of Homes/Sites/Units: 200
Entrance Fees: $310,000-$900,000
Monthly Fees: $1200-$4500
Developer: John R. McAdams Company, Inc.
Construction Dates: Under Construction
Nearby: RDU Airport, Downtown Cary
Activities and Amenities: Fitness Center, Pool, Arts Studio, Dining, Housekeeping Service, Health Care Center
Address: 106 Walker Stone Drive, Cary, NC 27513
Phone: (919) 466-9366
Web site: *www.searstone.com*

The Cypress of Raleigh (62+)

Municipality: North Raleigh
Description: The Cypress of Raleigh is located on a 48-acre campus situated within the suburban surroundings of North Raleigh. The campus features two lakes circled by walking trails, and the Rosewood Health Center, an onsite clinic specializing in long-term care and rehabilitation.
Entrance Fees: Varied
# of Homes/Sites: 203
Contract Types: Equity
Monthly Fees: Variable
Developer: The Cypress Company
Construction Dates: 2007-08

THE GUIDE TO RALEIGH NORTH CAROLINA AREA REAL ESTATE

Nearby: RDU Airport, Golf, Downtown Raleigh, Interstate 540
Activities and Amenities: Fitness Center, Pool, Arts Studio, Dining, Housekeeping Service, Health Care Center
Address: 8801 Cypress Lakes Drive, Raleigh, NC 27615
Phone: (919) 870-9007
Web site: *www.thecypressofraleigh.com*

The Cardinal at North Hills (62+)

Municipality: Raleigh
Description: When construction is complete, The Cardinal at North Hills will open its doors within the mixed-use development of North Hills in Midtown Raleigh. The Cardinal will offer dining, shopping, fitness facilities and a partnership with the Duke University Health System.
Types of Homes: Apartment
# of Homes/Sites/Units: 202
Entrance Fees: $300,000-$1,000,000
Monthly Fees: $1800-$3200
Developer: Kane Realty, Banyan Senior Living
Construction Dates: 2008-11
Nearby: North Hills Mall, Downtown Raleigh, Interstate 440
Activities and Amenities: Clubhouse, Restaurants, Shopping, Fitness, Housekeeping, Concierge Service, Arts Studio, Billiards Room
Address: 4421 Six Forks Road, Suite 123, Raleigh, NC 27609
Phone: (888) 781-2021
Web site: *www.thecardinalatnorthhills.com*

Springmoor (62+)

Municipality: North Raleigh
Description: Springmoor offers nine different types of accommodations from apartments to single-family homes. Amenities include a pool, chapel, and library. Nearby Wildwood Green provides golfing privileges.

PART I: BUYING & SELLING REAL ESTATE IN THE RALEIGH AREA

Types of Homes: Apartment, Single Family
# of Homes/Sites/Units: 591
Entrance Fees: $86,900 - $196,100
Monthly Fees: $1839-$3200
Contract Options: Modified
Construction Dates: 1984
Nearby: Golf, Crabtree Valley Mall, Interstate 440
Activities and Amenities: Lakes, Health Center, Pool, Chapel, Bank, Pharmacy, Library, Garden Plots, Billiards Room
Address: 1500 Sawmill Road, Raleigh, NC 27615
Phone: (919) 848-7000
Web site: *www.springmoor.org*

Windsor Point (62+ - Spouses must be 55+)

Municipality: Fuquay-Varina
Description: Windsor Point admits residents into independent or assisted living levels of care. The family owned operation features a country store and auditorium.
Types of Homes: Apartment, Single Family
# of Homes/Sites/Units: 281
Price Range: entrance fees $53,000 - $233,000
Monthly Fees: $2306-$2506
Contract Types: Modified or Rental (No Entrance Fee)
Construct. Dates: 1998-2004
Nearby: Downtown Fuquay-Varina, Golf
Activities and Amenities: Dining, Country Store, Computer Room, Billiards Room, Auditorium, Fitness Center
Address: 1221 Broad Street, Fuquay Varina, NC 27526
Phone: (919) 552-4580
Web site: *www.windsorpoint.com*

Whitaker Glen (62+)

Municipality: Raleigh
Description: Whitaker Glen is located on a 14-acre campus inside the I-440 beltline in Raleigh. The development offers one- and two-bedroom apartments with full kitchens.
Types of Homes: Apartment
# of Homes/Sites/Units: 235
Entrance Fees: $79,000 - $98,000
Monthly Fees: $1696-$2326
Contract Options: Fee for Service
Construction Dates: 1984
Nearby: Interstate 440, Downtown Raleigh
Activities and Amenities: Transportation, Fitness Center, Greenhouse, Barber and Beauty Salon, Dining
Address: 501 East Whitaker Mill Road, Raleigh, NC 27608
Phone: (919) 839-5604
Web site: *www.whitakerglen.com*

RENTAL RETIREMENT COMMUNITIES

Developments in this category offer independent living situations, assisted living services, skilled nursing care, or some combination of the three. Home styles range from apartments to stand-alone cottages. Except where noted, contact the community for information about pricing and age-restrictions.

RENTAL RETIREMENT COMMUNITIES IN WAKE COUNTY

Abbotswood at Stonehenge

Municipality: North Raleigh

PART I: BUYING & SELLING REAL ESTATE IN THE RALEIGH AREA

Description: Abbotswood at Stonehenge offers independent living apartments with full-size kitchens and private baths. The campus features a library and recreation room.
Type of Units: Apartment
Services Offered: Independent Living
Nearby: Golf, Crabtree Valley Mall, Interstate 540
Activities and Amenities: Courtyard, Library, Recreation Room, Game Room, Wellness Programs
Address: 7900 Creedmoor Road, Raleigh, NC 27613
Phone: (919) 847-3202
Web site: www.abbotswoodtour.com

Alta Oakridge

Municipality: North Raleigh
Description: Alta Oakridge is an independent living complex that offers one- and two-bedroom apartments. A cocktail lounge is located on-site.
Type of Units: Apartment
Services Offered: Independent Living
Nearby: Golf, Crabtree Valley Mall, Interstate 540
Address: 10810 Sandy Oak Lane, Raleigh, NC 27614
Phone: (919) 848-2088
Web site: www.altaoakridge.com
Activities and Amenities: Clubhouse, Billiards Room, Dining, Library, Game Room, Cocktail Lounge

The Gardens at Wakefield Plantation

Municipality: North Raleigh
Description: Part of the larger Wakefield Plantation development, The Gardens at Wakefield Plantation complex offers independent living within close proximity to medical offices, banks, shopping and dining.
Type of Units: Apartment

Services Offered: Independent Living (62+)
Nearby: Downtown Wake Forest, Golf, Interstate 540
Activities and Amenities: Transportation, Community Trips, Recreational Program
Address: 12800 Spruce Tree Way, Raleigh, NC 27614
Phone: (919) 562-5580
Web site: *www.thegardensatwakefield.com*

The Heritage of Raleigh

Municipality: North Raleigh
Description: The Heritage of Raleigh offers one- and two-bedroom apartments with full kitchens. The community features a wellness clinic and walking trails.
Type of Units: Apartment
Services Offered: Independent Living, Assisted Living
Nearby: North Ridge Shopping Center, Golf, Interstate 440
Address: 1200 Carlos Dr, Raleigh, NC 27609
Phone: (919) 747-3213
Web site: *www.brookdaleliving.com/the-heritage-of-raleigh.aspx*
Activities and Amenities: Dining, Café, Indoor Pool, Game Room, Arts Studio, Wellness Clinic, Fitness Center

Independence Village of Olde Raleigh

Municipality: West Raleigh
Description: Independence Village of Olde Raleigh offers one- and two-bedroom apartments as well as studios. Amenities include housekeeping and linen service, day trips, a library and a billiards room.
Type of Units: Apartment
Services Offered: Independent Living
Nearby: North Ridge Shopping Center, Umstead State Park, Interstate 440

PART I: BUYING & SELLING REAL ESTATE IN THE RALEIGH AREA

Activities and Amenities: Library, Billiards Room, Day Trips, Housekeeping, Exercise Room
Address: 3113 Charles B. Root Wynd, Raleigh, NC 27612
Phone: (919) 781-8226
Web site: *www.independencevillageofolderaleigh.com*

Jordan Oaks Retirement Community
Municipality: Cary
Description: Studio suites, one-bedroom and two-bedroom apartments are available at Jordan Oaks. The dining hall features an executive chef.
Type of Units: Apartment
Services Offered: Independent Living
Nearby: Hemlock Bluffs State Natural Area, Cary Towne Center, Interstate 40
Address: 10820 Penny Rd , Cary, NC 27518
Phone: (919) 387-8250
Web site: *www.jordan-oaks.com*
Activities and Amenities: Dining with Executive Chef, Library, Housekeeping, Internet Access, Fitness Center, Billiards Room

Magnolia Glen
Municipality: Raleigh
Description: Magnolia Glen is a Kisco Senior Living Community. The complex is located on 12 wooded acres, and backs up to the Brookhaven Nature Park. Magnolia Glen offers single-family cottage style homes and apartments.
Type of Units: Apartment, Single Family
Services Offered: Independent Living, Assisted Living
Nearby: Brookhaven Nature Park, Crabtree Valley Mall, Interstate 440
Activities and Amenities: Dining, Library, Computer Center, Indoor Pool, Wellness Programs, Trails

Address: 5301 Creedmoor Road, Raleigh, NC 27612
Phone: (919) 841-4747
Web site: *www.kiscoseniorliving.com/communities_magnolia.asp*

Woodland Terrace

Municipality: Cary
Description: Woodland Terrace is a Kisco Senior Living Community. The campus features landscaped gardens and a lake. Woodland Terrace offers single-family cottage style homes and apartments.
Type of Units: Apartment, Single Family
Services Offered: Independent Living, Assisted Living, Dementia, Alzheimer's Care
Nearby: Cary Towne Center, Interstate 440, Golf
Address: 300 Kildaire Woods Drive, Cary, NC 27511
Phone: (919) 465-0356
Web site: *www.woodlandterracetour.com*
Activities and Amenities: Gardening, Library, Housekeeping, Dining, Wellness Programs, Trails

Brighton Gardens of Raleigh

Municipality: Raleigh
Description: Brighton Gardens, managed by Sunrise Senior Living, Inc. offers assisted living and Alzheimer's care.
Type of Units: Apartment
Services Offered: Assisted Living, Alzheimer's Care
Nearby: Crabtree Valley Mall, Downtown Raleigh, Interstate 440
Activities and Amenities: Faith-based Activities, Outings, Fitness and Music Classes, Cognitive Skills Activities, Nature Walks
Address: 3101 Duraleigh Road, Raleigh, NC 27612
Phone: (919) 571-1123
Web site: *www.sunriseseniorliving.com*

PART I: BUYING & SELLING REAL ESTATE IN THE RALEIGH AREA

Sunrise of Raleigh

Municipality: Raleigh
Description: Sunrise of Raleigh, managed by Sunrise Senior Living, Inc. offers assisted living and Alzheimer's care.
Type of Units: Apartment
Services Offered: Assisted Living, Alzheimer's Care
Nearby: Crabtree Valley Mall, Downtown Raleigh, Interstate 440
Activities and Amenities: Faith-based Activities, Outings, Fitness and Music Classes, Cognitive Skills Activities, Nature Walks
Address: 4801 Edwards Mill Road, Raleigh, NC 27612
Phone: (919) 787-0777
Web site: *www.sunriseseniorliving.com*

Sunrise at North Hills

Municipality: Raleigh
Description: Sunrise at North Hills, managed by Sunrise Senior Living, Inc. offers assisted living and Alzheimer's care.
Type of Units: Apartment
Services Offered: Assisted Living, Alzheimer's Care
Nearby: North Hills Mall, Downtown Raleigh, Interstate 440
Activities and Amenities: Faith-based Activities, Outings, Fitness and Music Classes, Cognitive Skills Activities, Nature Walks
Address: 615 Spring Forest Road, Raleigh, NC 27609
Phone: (919) 747-3213
Web site: *www.sunriseseniorliving.com*

AGE-TARGETED

By law, communities in the first three categories are only available to those who meet certain age requirements. Age-targeted communities are developments that choose to market themselves towards the fifty-five and over community, but have no legal age-restrictions. These developments may offer many of the same conveniences and amenities as Active Adult communities, such as low-maintenance housing or golf privileges, but they are open and occupied by people of all ages.

Communities that market to older adults in the Raleigh area include: Wakefield Plantation, Johnson's Landing, The Villas at Wake Forest and Heritage Spring.

ADDITIONAL RESOURCES

The following organizations provide services of particular interest to older adults in Wake County.

- **Resources for Seniors**, formerly the Council on Aging in Wake County, provides a wealth of information and services to seniors. *www.resourcesforseniors.com*
- **Cary Senior Center** *www.townofcary.org*
- **Raleigh Senior Center** *www.raleigh-nc.org*

PART II

RALEIGH AREA CITIES AND TOWNS

The Raleigh area consists of 12 municipalities within Wake County, including the city of Raleigh, and the towns of Wake Forest, Rolesville, Cary, Apex, Holly Springs, Fuquay-Varina, Garner, Knightdale, Wendell, and Zebulon, and those areas of the county not officially incorporated into any of those towns.

In this part of the book we will describe the history of each municipality, and share data about home prices, the number of home sales, population growth, and how many new homes are being built to accommodate the increased population. We will start with a look at Wake County as a whole.

Raleigh is one of the three corners of an area known as *The Triangle*. In the next part of this book we will cover the other two corners, Durham and Chapel Hill, as destinations. *Research Triangle Park*, another well-known area, located mostly in Durham County, is home to 130 research facilities and 39,000 employees.

CHAPTER 5

WAKE COUNTY

The earliest inhabitants of Wake County were the Tuscarora Native Americans. They were defeated in 1711 during the Tuscarora War, and moved to New York to join the Iroquois nation. The county was officially formed in 1771 and was named after Margaret Wake, the wife of then-Governor William Tryon.

No matter where you end up in Wake County, you will probably think of yourself as living in one of the 12 municipalities described in the following chapters. In some cases, your home may be outside the incorporated limits of a municipality (saving you municipal property taxes), but your mailing address will normally match up with the nearest city or town.

Among the important functions of the county government are running the school system, the sheriff's department, and human services. In addition, ownership and tax information for all property in Wake County is listed on the web site below.

WAKE COUNTY CONTACT INFORMATION

Web Site: *www.wakegov.com*
Main Office: 919-856-6160

THE GUIDE TO RALEIGH NORTH CAROLINA AREA REAL ESTATE

Wake County Map and Population

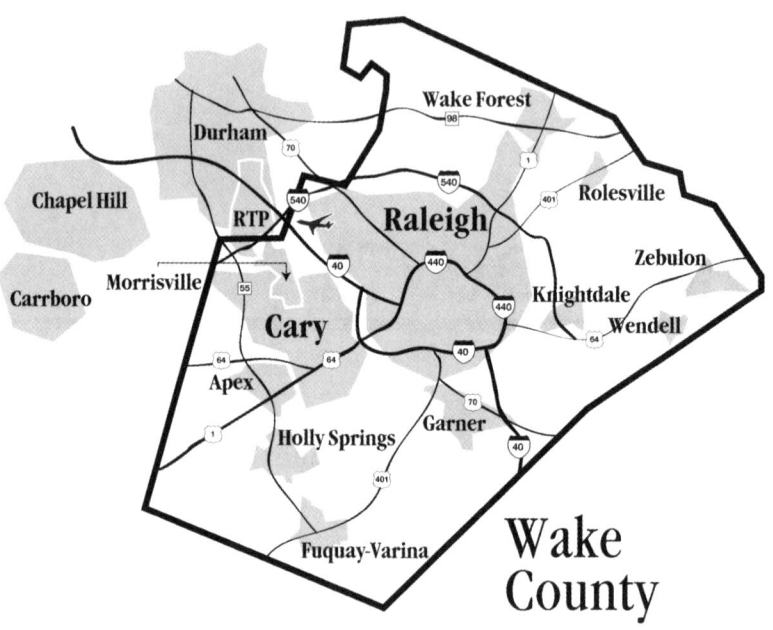

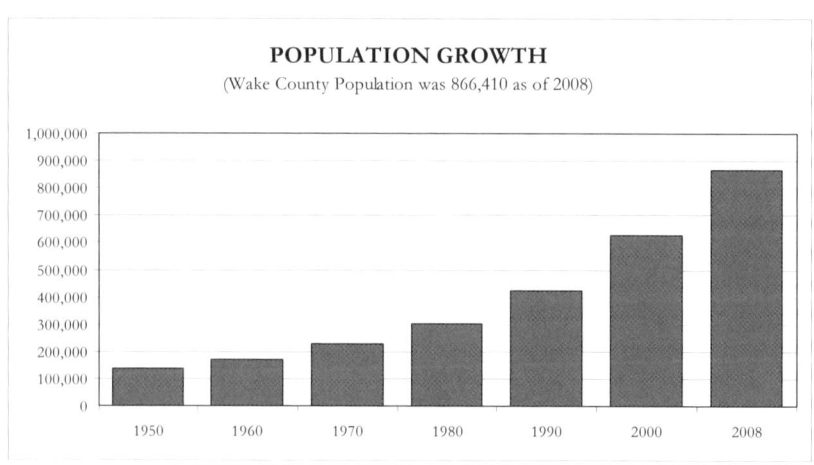

SOURCE: US Census Data (2009 data not available at time of printing)

PART II: RALEIGH AREA CITIES AND TOWNS

Wake County Real Estate Data

SOURCE: Stacey Anfindsen of Birch Appraisal (2009 data not available at time of printing)

AVERAGE SALES PRICE OF HOMES IN WAKE COUNTY
(Interpret as AFFORDABILITY: Reflects appreciation and price of new construction homes)

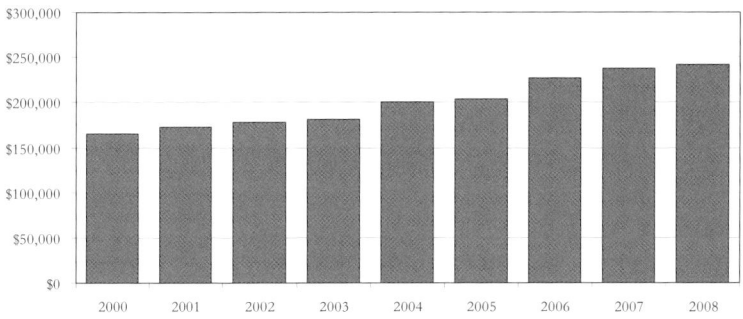

NUMBER OF HOMES SOLD
(New and Resale in all of Wake County)

NEW CONSTRUCTION ACTIVITY
(Permits Issued to Build New Homes in all of Wake County)

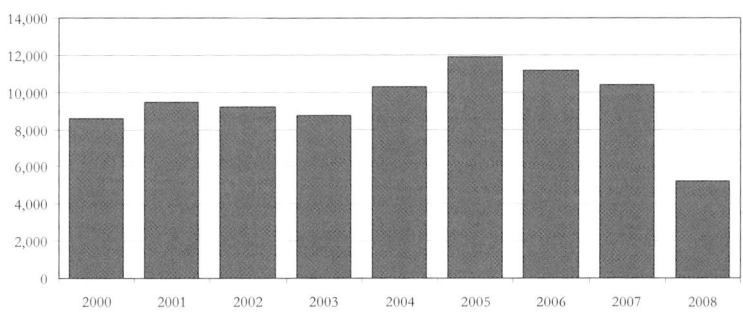

CHAPTER 6

RALEIGH

Raleigh was named after Sir Walter Raleigh, even though he had never set foot in North Carolina, let alone Wake County. He earned this honor by sponsoring the establishment of the first English colony in North Carolina two centuries earlier, at Roanoke Island.

The City of Raleigh was created by government mandate in the wake of the Revolutionary War. Representatives from the western part of the state were tired of traveling to the previous capital in New Bern, so the North Carolina General Assembly authorized the Constitutional Convention to establish a permanent state capital in a more central location. The Convention began gathering at Isaac Hunter's Tavern in March of 1792, and they were so impressed by the hospitality of the tavern that they recommended to the General Assembly that the new capital be located within ten miles of it. Commissioners selected the land in 1792 and hired a surveyor to lay out the city. In 1794, the General Assembly met in their new Statehouse in Raleigh for the first time. The Governor's residence was officially shifted to the new capital in 1798, and by 1800, Raleigh boasted a population of 669 people, making Raleigh one of a handful of cities in the United States established and built specifically to house a state capital.

PART II: RALEIGH AREA CITIES AND TOWNS

Raleigh Location and Population

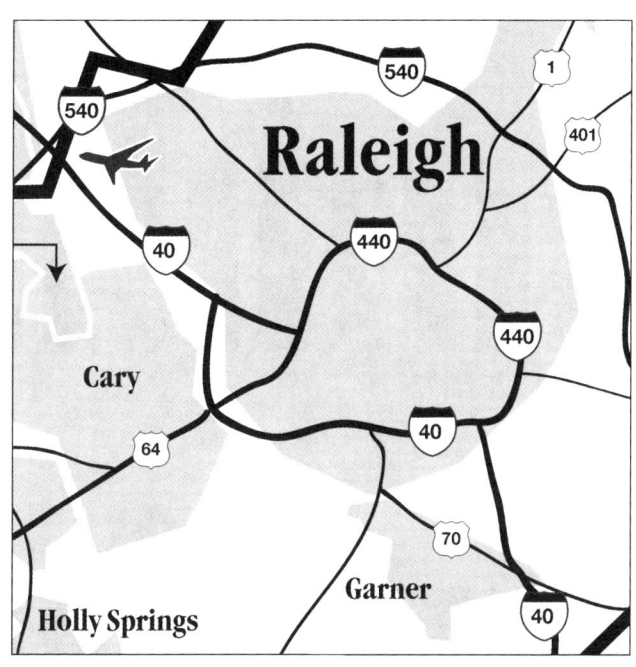

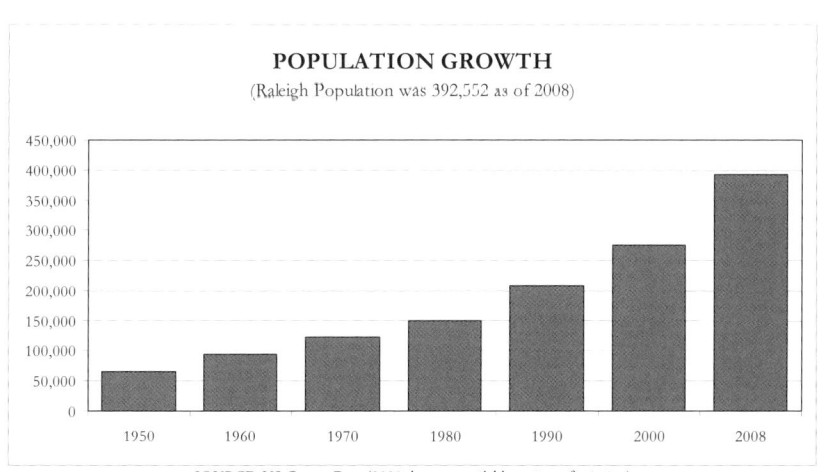

THE GUIDE TO RALEIGH NORTH CAROLINA AREA REAL ESTATE

Raleigh Real Estate Data

SOURCE: Stacey Anfindsen of Birch Appraisal (2009 data not available at time of printing)

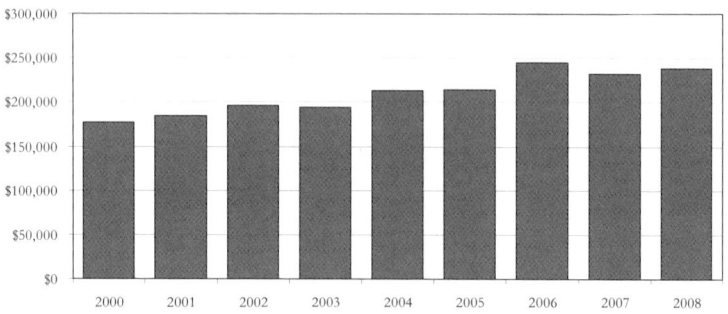

AVERAGE SALES PRICE OF HOMES IN RALEIGH
(Interpret as AFFORDABILITY: Reflects appreciation and price of new construction homes)

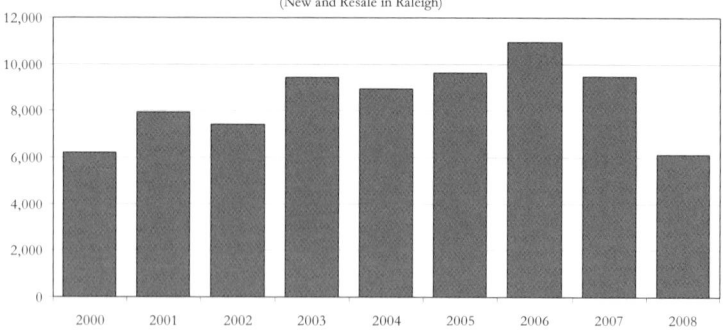

NUMBER OF HOMES SOLD
(New and Resale in Raleigh)

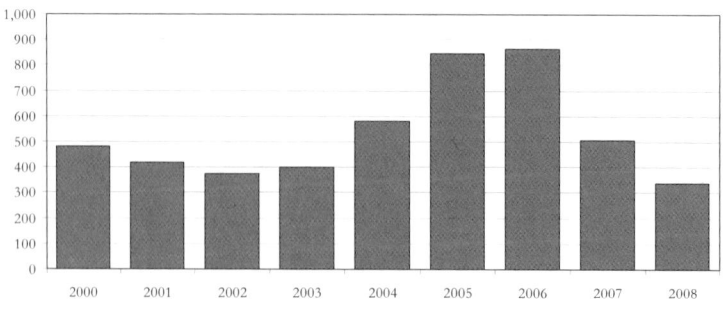

NEW CONSTRUCTION ACTIVITY
(Permits Issued to Build New Homes in Raleigh)

PART II: RALEIGH AREA CITIES AND TOWNS

DOWNTOWN RALEIGH ("INSIDE-THE-BELTLINE")

In recent years, the City of Raleigh has focused much of its attention on revitalizing the downtown area. With so many office buildings and trendy nightlife hotspots, downtown had always attracted plenty of commerce, but a lack of land for housing had caused the area inside the beltline to stagnate. However, in 2006, Raleigh undertook a comprehensive urban renewal plan to make the downtown area a place where people can – in the words of DowntownRaleigh.com – "Live. Work. Play." Luxury condos and town homes have started springing up all over downtown, aimed squarely at the young urban professional demographic that is increasingly attracted to the capital city.

In addition to the wealth of new condominiums available between Glenwood Avenue and Dawson Street, there are many beautiful historic homes. Some of these homes have been lovingly restored, and others are in need of some TLC, but even if you're not in the market for an older home, it's worth a drive through Oakwood (19th century homes near Oakwood Cemetery), Brooklyn (on Glenwood just north of Peace Street) or Boylan Heights (at South Boylan and Cabarrus). These neighborhoods showcase some of Raleigh's rich history and the beautiful architectural styles of Raleigh's oldest homes.

How you define "downtown Raleigh" depends as much on where you live in relation to it as it does on any map. Some define it as the area immediately surrounding the nightclubs and restaurants on South Glenwood between Peace Street and Hillsborough Street. The Downtown Raleigh Alliance defines five distinct but interconnected districts, including Glenwood South, the Capitol, the Warehouse District, Fayetteville Street, and Moore Square. Check out *www.godowntownraleigh.com* for more information about these districts and what you'll find there. Those who live "Outside the Beltline" tend to define downtown as anything "Inside the Beltline," I-440, which encircles the central part of Raleigh.

THE GUIDE TO RALEIGH NORTH CAROLINA AREA REAL ESTATE

WEST RALEIGH

West Raleigh includes NC State and the surrounding area and stretches roughly from Pullen Park and Cameron Village in the East to the State Fairgrounds and the Cary town limit to the West. It extends as far north as Glenwood Avenue and as far south as I-40, covering a diverse area that includes students, young singles, and families.

Much of the area immediately around NC State is devoted to student housing, which includes apartments and investment properties that are rented out to undergraduates and graduate students at NC State or Meredith College. As you move towards the Cary town limit, however, the area becomes more diverse, and the houses and lots grow larger. The Medfield area, near Trinity Road, is almost entirely occupied by families, many of whom have a connection to NC State in some capacity but are not necessarily full-time students.

West Raleigh contains the North Carolina State Fairgrounds, Carter-Finley Stadium (where the NC State Wolfpack plays), and the RBC Center, home of the Carolina Hurricanes professional hockey team. For the outdoorsman, fishing, boating, hiking, and biking are all available at Lake Johnson Park on Avent Ferry Road.

NORTH RALEIGH

Abundant employment, shopping, and recreational opportunities, combined with a variety of housing options and convenience to Research Triangle Park, downtown, and the rest of Wake County have made North Raleigh one of the most desirable areas in the Triangle. Geographically large, culturally diverse, and teeming with localized commercial and retail districts, North Raleigh truly does have something for just about everyone.

PART II: RALEIGH AREA CITIES AND TOWNS

EAST RALEIGH

East Raleigh is bisected by New Bern Avenue, which stretches from the current state capital towards North Carolina's first capital at the coast, New Bern. To the north and south lie the eastern part of Raleigh, bounded to the south by I-40 and to the north by Capital Boulevard. Eventually, the eastern border of East Raleigh will be formed by the Outer Beltline, I-540. Currently, only the northern portion of the loop is complete, but this section of highway already makes the trip to North Raleigh fast and easy. Meanwhile, East Raleigh is connected to the southern and western parts of Wake County via Highway 64, I-440, and I-40.

SOUTH RALEIGH

South Raleigh stretches from the southern border of I-440 to the Garner town limits at Tryon Road. Its eastern boundary is marked by Lake Wheeler Road, and I-40 curves sharply southward at the I440/I-40 split to separate South Raleigh from the eastern part of the city. Residents of South Raleigh enjoy all the conveniences and benefits of being inside the capital city limits with the added benefit of a quieter, more laid-back lifestyle.

CITY OF RALEIGH CONTACT INFORMATION

Web Site: *www.raleighnc.gov*
Main Office: (919) 996-3000

CHAPTER 7

WAKE FOREST

The beginnings of Wake Forest can be traced to the North Carolina Baptist Convention's purchase of a 615-acre plantation a mile north of the small community of Forestville in 1832. There, they opened the Wake Forest Institute in 1834. It was re-chartered as Wake Forest College in 1838. In 1840, the Raleigh and Gaston Railroad was completed east of campus, but the closest depot and post office were in Forestville. The outbreak of the Civil War closed the college, as the students and some of the faculty left to enlist. A depleted college reopened in 1866.

In 1874, college officials paid to have the rail depot relocated from Forestville to Wake Forest itself. This caused a boom in commercial development, and the community incorporated as the Town of Wake Forest College in 1880. In the succeeding years, the college established a School of Law followed by a School of Medicine. In 1909, the town was re-chartered as the Town of Wake Forest, removing the word "College" from the name. Which was prescient, because in 1946, as a result of large gifts from the Z. Smith Reynolds Foundation, the entire college agreed to move to Winston-Salem. The move was completed in 1956. Southeastern Baptist Theological Seminary, which began offering classes in 1951,

PART II: RALEIGH AREA CITIES AND TOWNS

is now located on the site of the original Wake Forest College and is the beautiful historic centerpiece of the current Town of Wake Forest.

Wake Forest, with approximately 26,000 residents today, combines small-town charm with a lively downtown and, just down the highway toward Raleigh, all the shopping conveniences you could desire. Planned developments such as Heritage Wake Forest include everything from townhomes to million dollar residences, offering something for every lifestyle and budget. Set amid central North Carolina's beautiful rolling hills, Wake Forest boasts excellent schools, a low crime rate, and amenities that create high quality of life.

TOWN OF WAKE FOREST CONTACT INFORMATION

Web Site: *www.wakeforestnc.gov*
Town Hall Service: (919) 554-6100

Wake Forest Location and Population

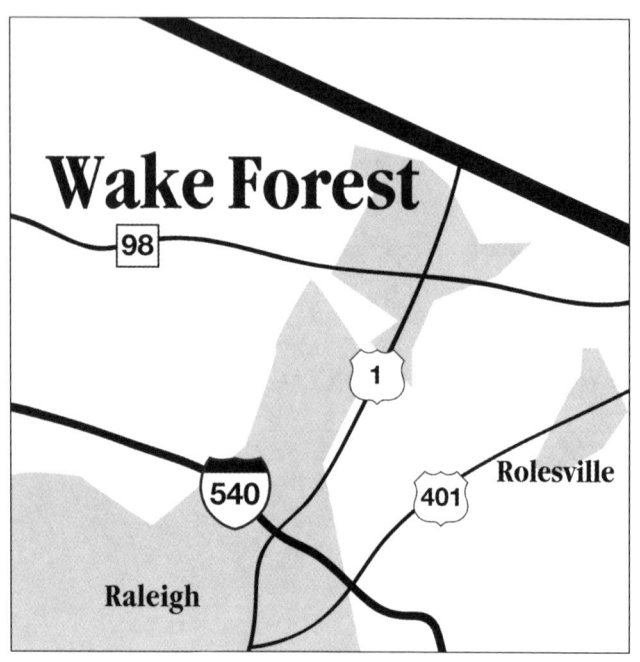

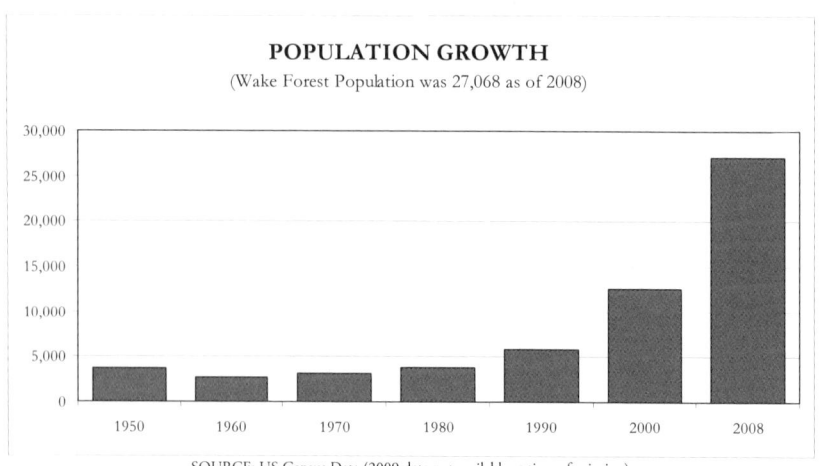

POPULATION GROWTH
(Wake Forest Population was 27,068 as of 2008)

SOURCE: US Census Data (2009 data not available at time of printing)

PART II: RALEIGH AREA CITIES AND TOWNS

Wake Forest Real Estate Data

SOURCE: Stacey Anfindsen of Birch Appraisal (2009 data not available at time of printing)

AVERAGE SALES PRICE OF HOMES IN WAKE FOREST
(Interpret as AFFORDABILITY: Reflects appreciation and price of new construction homes)

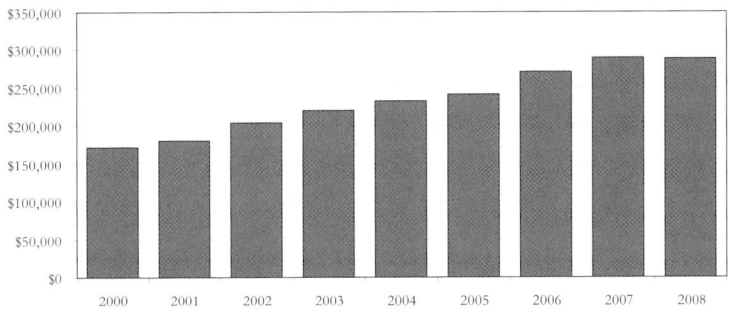

NUMBER OF HOMES SOLD
(New and Resale in Wake Forest)

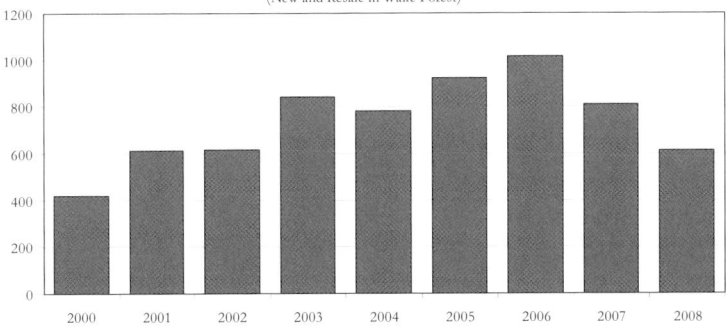

NEW CONSTRUCTION ACTIVITY
(Permits Issued to Build New Homes in Wake Forest)

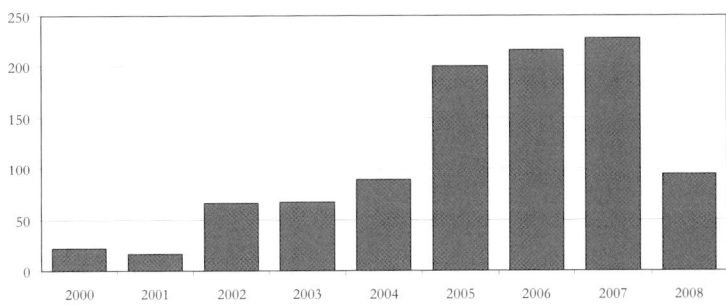

CHAPTER 8

ROLESVILLE

Rolesville is the second-oldest town in Wake County, and the least populous, at 2,844 persons in 2008. It was named for an early prominent citizen, William "Billy" Roles. He was a landowner, merchant, cotton broker, cotton gin owner, postmaster, and deacon and trustee of the Baptist Church. He also founded the first local school in 1832. The town was originally incorporated in 1837. It became a stage stop on the north-south route between Richmond and Fayetteville, and the stage traffic supported the local economy until the advent of the railroad. Rolesville was reincorporated in 1941, and its boundaries were expanded in 1945.

Rolesville is growing more than it ever has and is constantly focused on remaining a great place to live, work, play, relax, and raise a family, while maintaining its small town charm.

TOWN OF ROLESVILLE CONTACT INFORMATION

Web Site: *www.ci.rolesville.nc.us*
Town Hall Service: *(919) 556-3506*

PART II: RALEIGH AREA CITIES AND TOWNS

Rolesville Location and Population

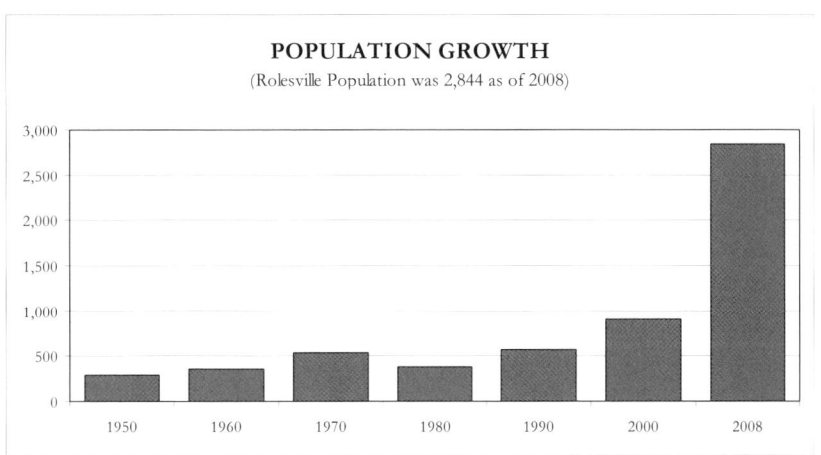

SOURCE: US Census Data (2009 data not available at time of printing)

Rolesville Real Estate Data

SOURCE: Stacey Anfindsen of Birch Appraisal (2009 data not available at time of printing)

AVERAGE SALES PRICE OF HOMES IN ROLESVILLE
(Interpret as AFFORDABILITY: Reflects appreciation and price of new construction homes)

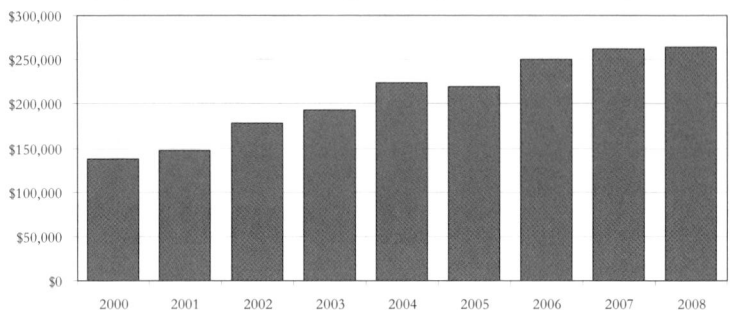

NUMBER OF HOMES SOLD
(New and Resale in Rolesville)

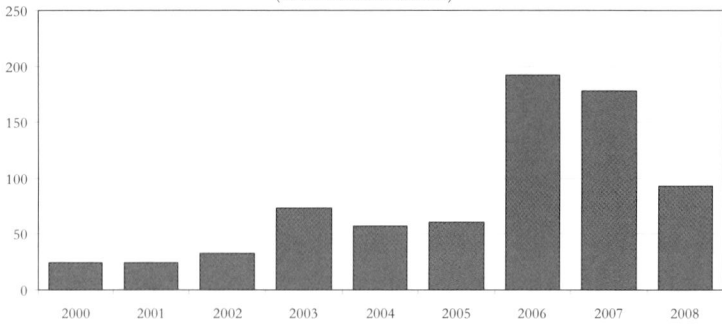

NEW CONSTRUCTION ACTIVITY
(Permits Issued to Build New Homes in Rolesville)

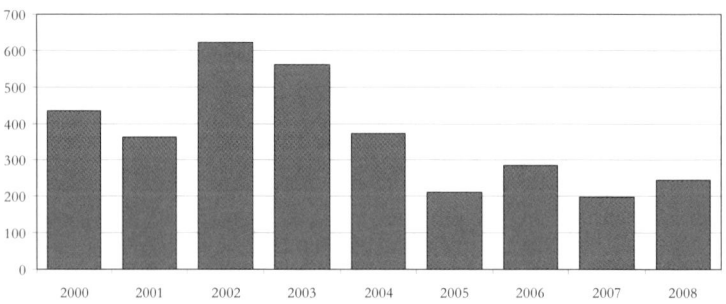

CHAPTER 9

CARY

The site that would later become the Town of Cary was home to a settlement called Bradford's Ordinary as early as 1750. Modern Cary began to grow from these pre-Revolutionary roots when Allison Francis "Frank" Page bought 300 acres in the tiny community in 1854. He laid out the first streets of what would come to be called Cary, named after Samuel Fenton Cary, a prominent prohibitionist from Ohio. Page was Cary's first developer, mayor, postmaster, and railroad agent, and also built Cary's first hotel, the Page-Walker Hotel. In the 1860s the Seaboard and North Carolina Railroads formed a junction in Cary, contributing greatly to the community's growth. The town was officially incorporated in 1871. It remained a sleepy town of a few thousand people until the 1960s, when Research Triangle Park began to bring rapid growth to the area. The population of Cary tripled in the 1970s, doubled in the 1980s, and doubled again in the 1990s.

Cary, once a small bedroom community, has blossomed into a fully functional, self-contained hub of commerce, industry, and suburban living. Cary boasts several high-end planned developments such as Preston, Lochmere, and MacGregor Downs and has many established, mature neighborhoods in central Cary as well. *Money* magazine put Cary on the map in 2006 by declaring it one of America's five best places to live, citing the town's beautiful rolling hills, excellent schools, low crime rate, and plentiful employment opportunities.

TOWN OF CARY CONTACT INFORMATION

Web Site: *www.townofcary.org*
Town Hall Service: (919) 319-4500

PART II: RALEIGH AREA CITIES AND TOWNS

Cary Location and Population

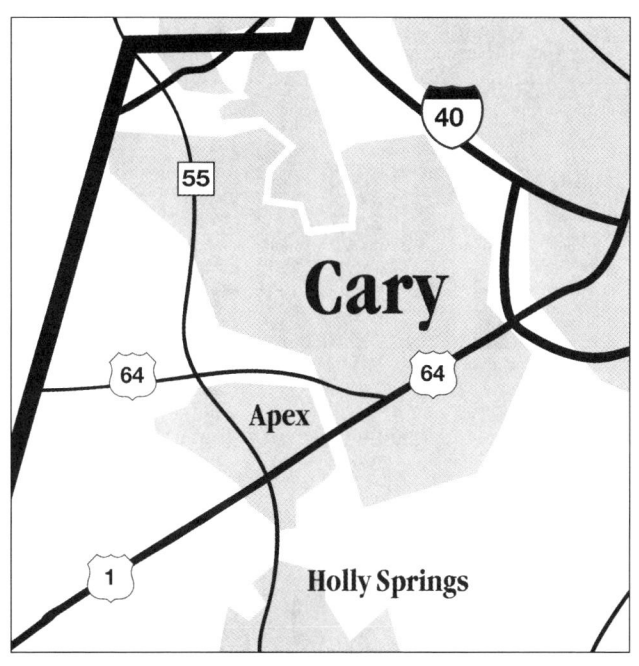

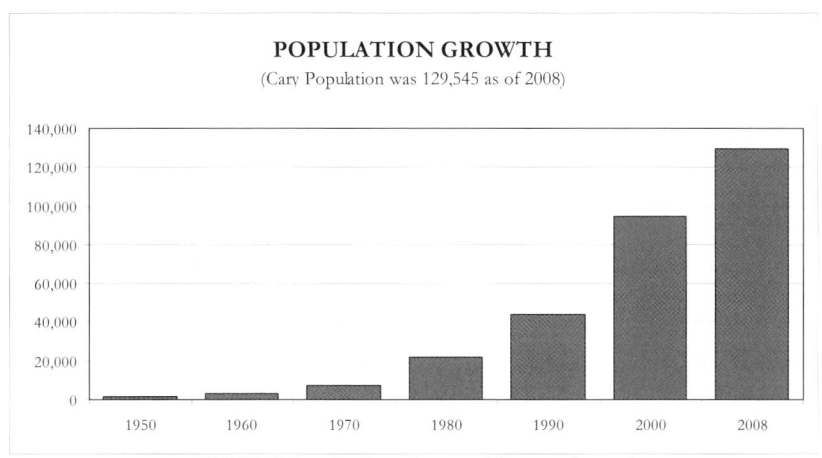

SOURCE: US Census Data (2009 data not available at time of printing)

Cary Real Estate Data

SOURCE: Stacey Anfindsen of Birch Appraisal (2009 data not available at time of printing)

AVERAGE SALES PRICE OF HOMES IN CARY
(Interpret as AFFORDABILITY: Reflects appreciation and price of new construction homes)

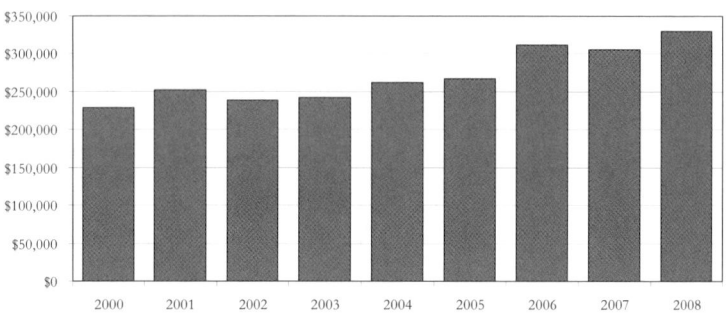

NUMBER OF HOMES SOLD
(New and Resale in Cary)

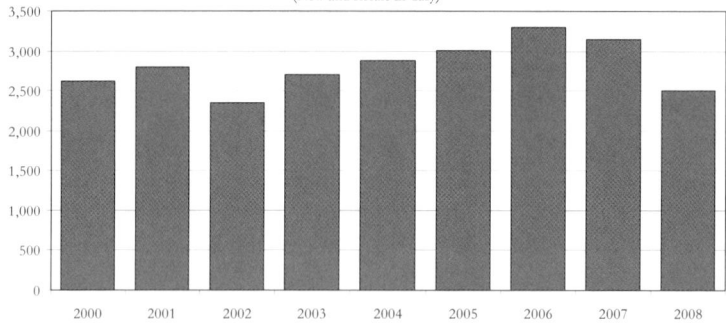

NEW CONSTRUCTION ACTIVITY
(Permits Issued to Build New Homes in Cary)

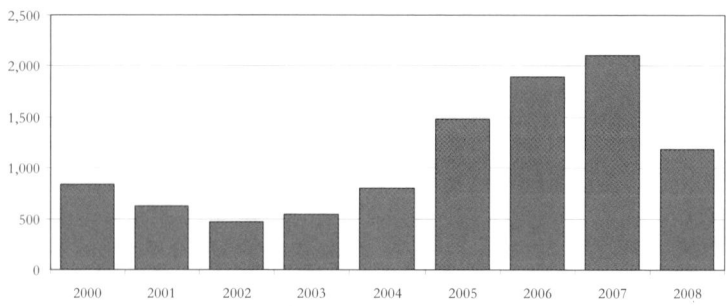

CHAPTER 10

APEX

Apex, like so many towns in central North Carolina, has the railroad to thank for its inception. The town gradually formed around a railroad station on the Chatham Railroad, which connected Raleigh with the coal fields in Chatham County to the west. Although begun in 1854, delays due to war and reconstruction resulted in the completion of the rail station around 1867. Located in the middle of a pine forest, the community became a shipping point for products such as tar, turpentine, and lumber. Apex takes its name from the fact that the community was located on the highest point on the Chatham Railroad between Richmond, Virginia and Jacksonville, Florida. A play on words and this geographical fact, the town's current motto is "The Peak of Good Living." Apex was officially incorporated in 1873.

Apex, located to the south and west of Cary, has long stood in the shadow of its rapidly expanding neighbor. However, recent retail and industrial developments in Apex have brought the conveniences of modern suburban life to the quaint, small, southern town.

TOWN OF APEX SERVICES DIRECTORY

Web Site: *www.apexnc.org*
Main Office: (919) 249-3400

THE GUIDE TO RALEIGH NORTH CAROLINA AREA REAL ESTATE

Apex Location and Population

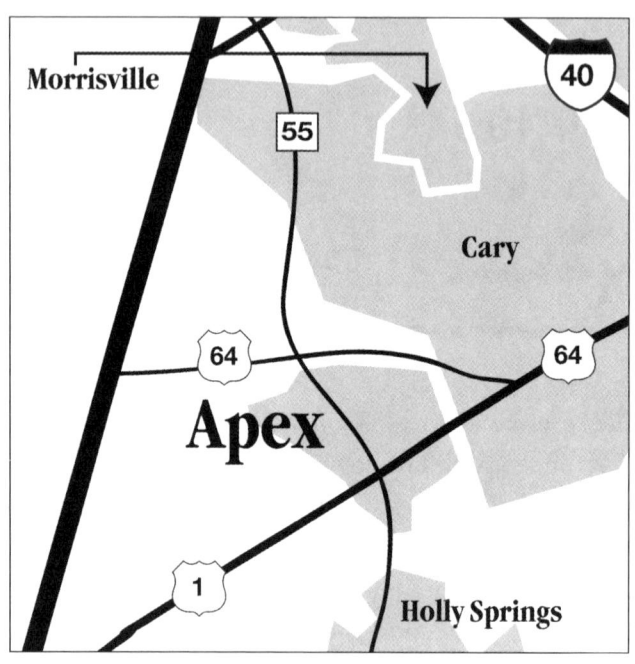

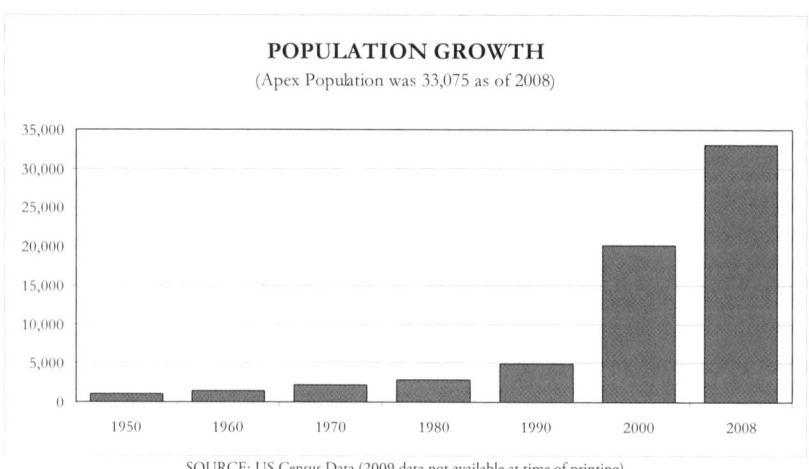

SOURCE: US Census Data (2009 data not available at time of printing)

PART II: RALEIGH AREA CITIES AND TOWNS

Apex Real Estate Data

SOURCE: Stacey Anfindsen of Birch Appraisal (2009 data not available at time of printing)

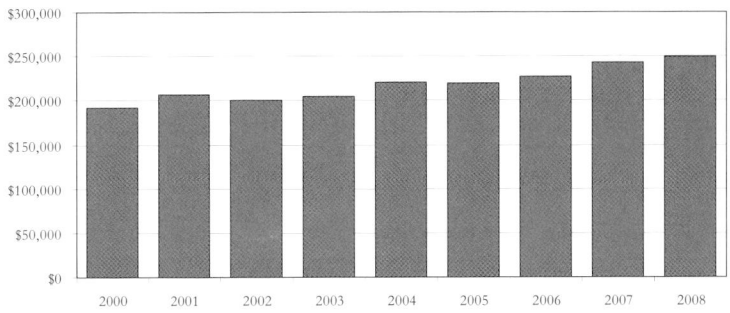

AVERAGE SALES PRICE OF HOMES IN APEX
(Interpret as AFFORDABILITY: Reflects appreciation and price of new construction homes)

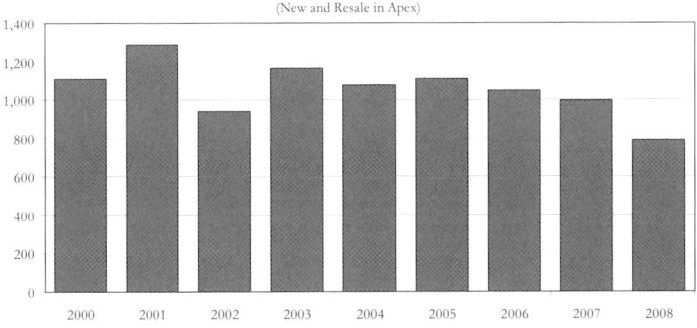

NUMBER OF HOMES SOLD
(New and Resale in Apex)

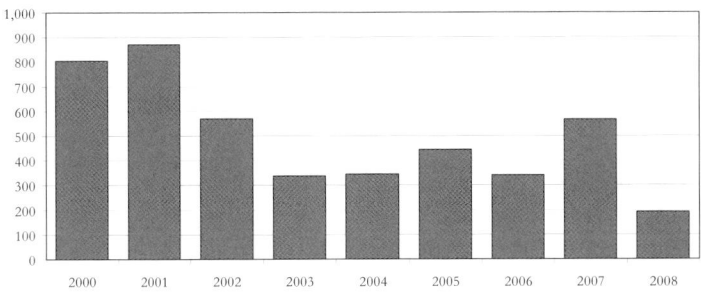

NEW CONSTRUCTION ACTIVITY
(Permits Issued to Build New Homes in Apex)

CHAPTER 11

MORRISVILLE

The Town of Morrisville is situated on the western border of Wake County. It is named for Jeremiah Morris, who donated 3 acres of land to the North Carolina Railroad in 1852 for a water station, woodshed, and other support buildings. Morris also established the first post office that year, and served as its first postmaster. The North Carolina Railroad from Goldsboro to Charlotte was completed in 1856, and Morrisville was made a polling place by the county government in 1859. One of the last battles of the Civil War was fought in Morrisville on Apr 13, 1865.

The town was chartered in 1875, but that charter was repealed by a vote of the citizenry in 1933. The town was re-chartered in 1947, acquired its first Town Hall in 1976, and had a population of a little over 1000 in 1990. Thanks to its central location, safe neighborhoods, thriving businesses, excellent schools, Morrisville has experienced growth of over 150% in the past ten years to its current population of 15,000.

TOWN OF MORRISVILLE SERVICES DIRECTORY

Web Site: *www.ci.morrisville.nc.us*
Town Hall Service: (919) 463-2600

PART II: RALEIGH AREA CITIES AND TOWNS

Morrisville Location and Population

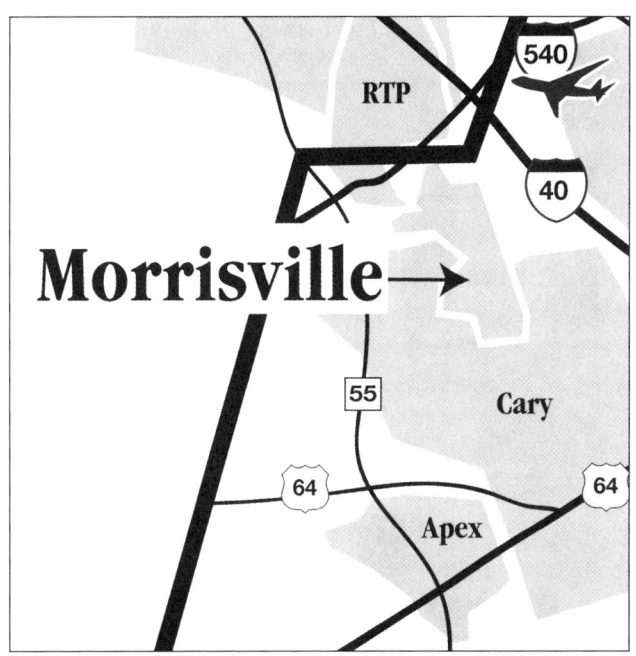

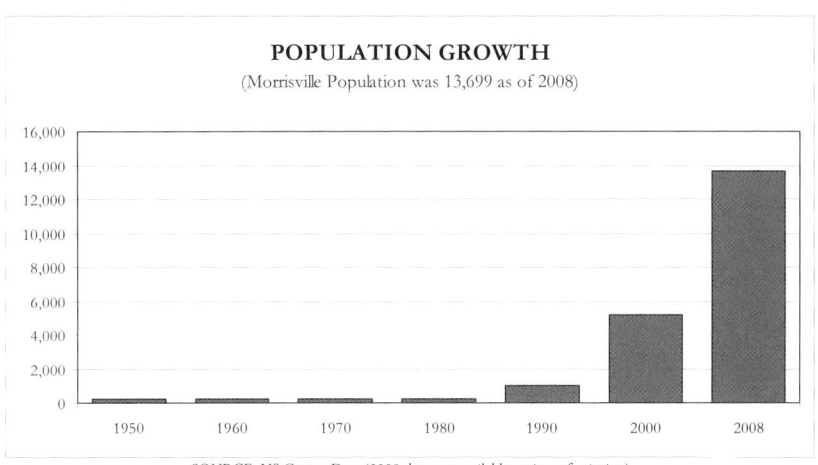

Morrisville Real Estate Data

SOURCE: Stacey Anfindsen of Birch Appraisal (2009 data not available at time of printing)

AVERAGE SALES PRICE OF HOMES IN MORRISVILLE
(Interpret as AFFORDABILITY: Reflects appreciation and price of new construction homes)

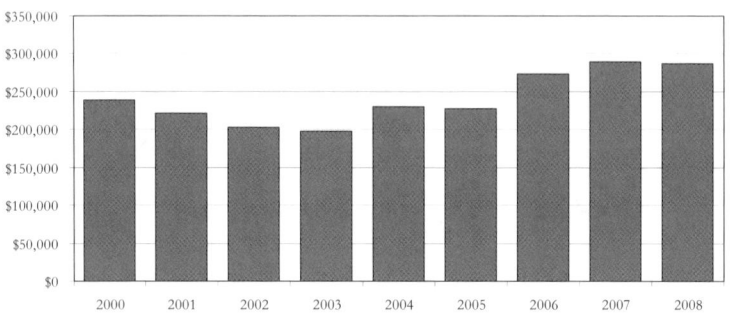

NUMBER OF HOMES SOLD
(New and Resale in Morrisville)

NEW CONSTRUCTION ACTIVITY
(Permits Issued to Build New Homes in Morrisville)

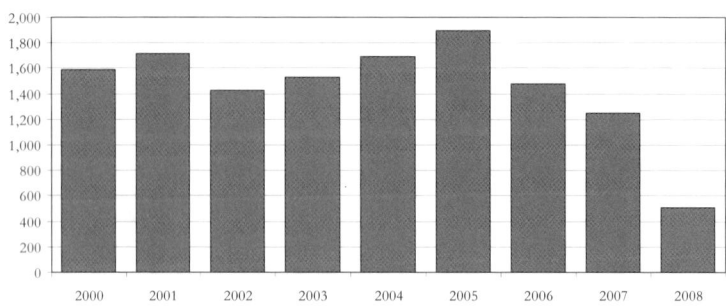

CHAPTER 12

HOLLY SPRINGS

Holly Springs has seen its ups and downs during the course of its history. Although not incorporated until 1877, the first settlements around the spring under the holly trees predate the Revolution. The community church was one of the first four to join the Raleigh Baptist Association in 1805. But the Civil War stripped the community of fighting-age men, and the town was slow to recover from the destruction in the wake of defeat, derailing the progress of what had been a thriving community. Additionally, the construction of the Chatham Railroad through neighboring Apex lured economic momentum down the road to the new community.

In 1875, however, Colonel Alford moved his businesses to Holly Springs, generating new economic life. He and other prominent citizens convinced what would become the Durham and Southern Railroad to build to Holly Springs. Colonel Alford founded a newspaper in the community, and he led the effort that resulted in the town's incorporation in 1877. The town's boundaries, a one-mile square, would remain unchanged for 110 years.

Recently, though, Holly Springs has the distinction of being the fastest-growing town in the fastest-growing county in the fast-growing state of North Carolina. In 2007, Holly Springs was listed in the #18 slot on the Forbes list of fastest-growing suburbs in America. The population has grown from 900 in 1992 to more than 17,400 in 2007, and it's still climbing. Voted #22 on Money Magazine's Best Places to Live in 2007, Holly Springs is a young town with a median age of 30 years, five years younger than the state average.

TOWN OF HOLLY SPRINGS CONTACT INFORMATION

Web Site: *www.hollyspringsnc.us*
Town Hall: (919) 552-6221

PART II: RALEIGH AREA CITIES AND TOWNS

Holly Springs Location and Population

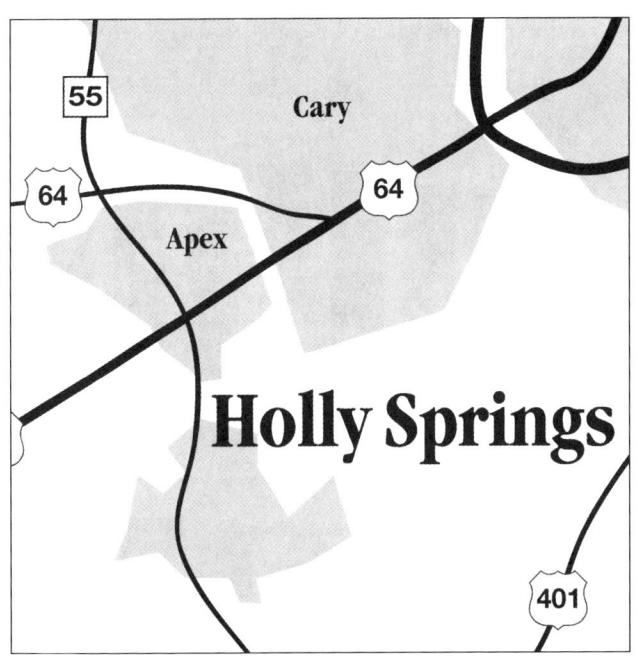

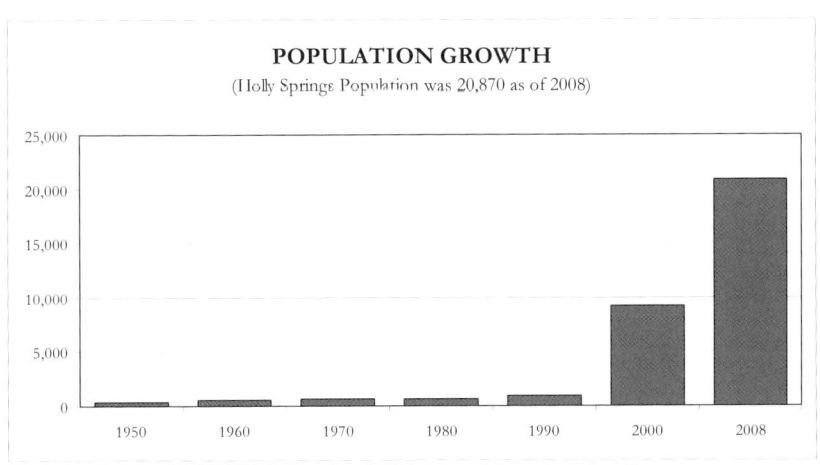

Holly Springs Real Estate Data

SOURCE: Stacey Anfindsen of Birch Appraisal (2009 data not available at time of printing)

AVERAGE SALES PRICE OF HOMES IN HOLLY SPRINGS
(Interpret as AFFORDABILITY: Reflects appreciation and price of new construction homes)

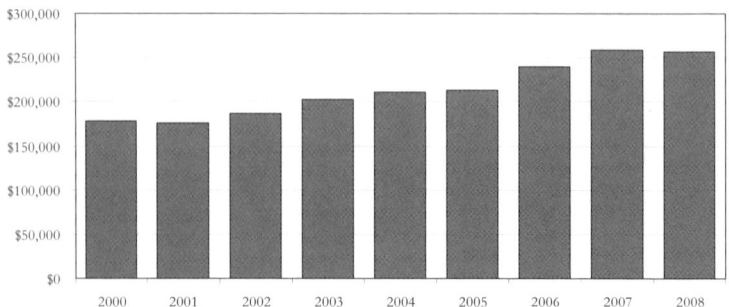

NUMBER OF HOMES SOLD
(New and Resale in Holly Springs)

NEW CONSTRUCTION ACTIVITY
(Permits Issued to Build New Homes in Holly Springs)

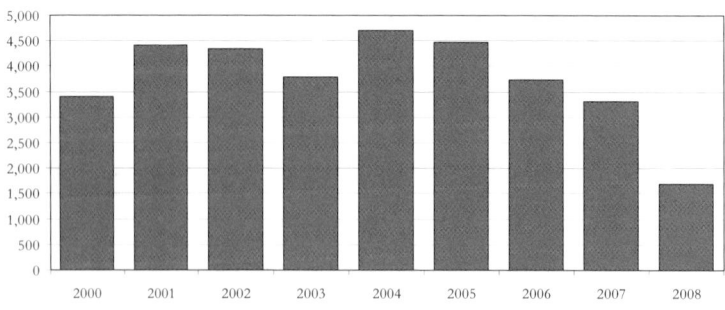

CHAPTER 13

FUQUAY-VARINA

Fuquay-Varina derives its unusual name from its history as two distinct communities. Historians believe the first European to settle in the area was a Frenchman named William Fuquay. William's grandson, David Crocket Fuquay, is supposed to have given the community its name. He and his wife lived in the small farming community then known as Sippihaw, from the name of the local Indian tribe. David's son discovered a mineral spring on his property, and it gained local fame as having healing properties. Tourists began coming to "take the waters," and hotels and businesses were established to cater to the visitors. Sippihaw was renamed Fuquay Springs in 1902 and incorporated in 1907.

Varina, although never officially incorporated, grew next to Sippihaw as an independent community. It was founded after the civil war by Confederate veteran J.D. Ballentine, who had been the first schoolmaster of Sippihaw. To promote the morale of southern troops, many young women wrote to the soldiers, and Ballentine received letters written by a young woman under the pen name Varina. She eventually gave him her real name – Virginia Avery – and after the war they met, fell in love, and were married. Ballentine called his wife Varina for the rest of his life. They settled in Sippihaw, and Ballentine founded a general store called the Varina Mercantile Company. The community of Varina developed around this store, and although parts of it were eventually included in the corporate limits of Fuquay Springs, it retained its separate identity until the two communities reincorporated together as the town of Fuquay-Varina in 1936.

Fuquay-Varina is North Carolina's second hyphenated town, after Winston-Salem. With less than 7 square miles of land and under 15,000 residents, Fuquay-Varina is the embodiment of small-town charm in Wake County. As such, it is a family-oriented town with lots of green, open space and a close-knit community.

TOWN OF FUQUAY-VARINA CONTACT INFORMATION

Web Site: *www.fuquay-varina.org*
Town Hall Main Office: (919)552-1401

PART II: RALEIGH AREA CITIES AND TOWNS

Fuquay-Varina Location and Population

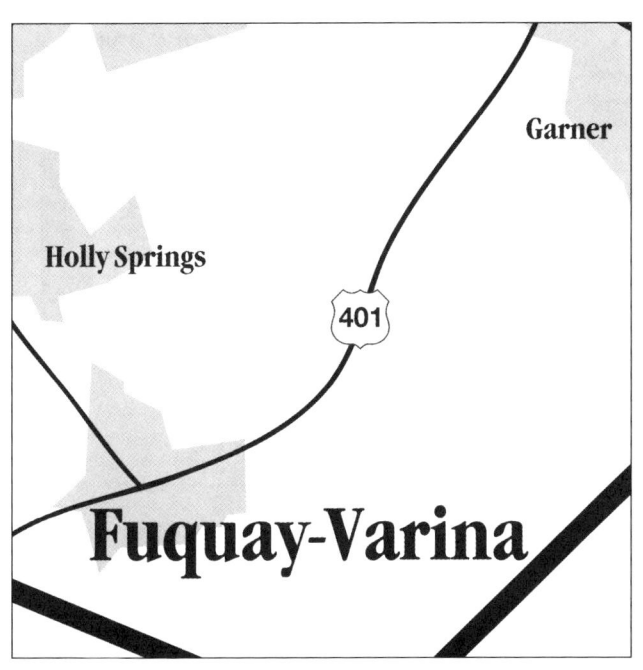

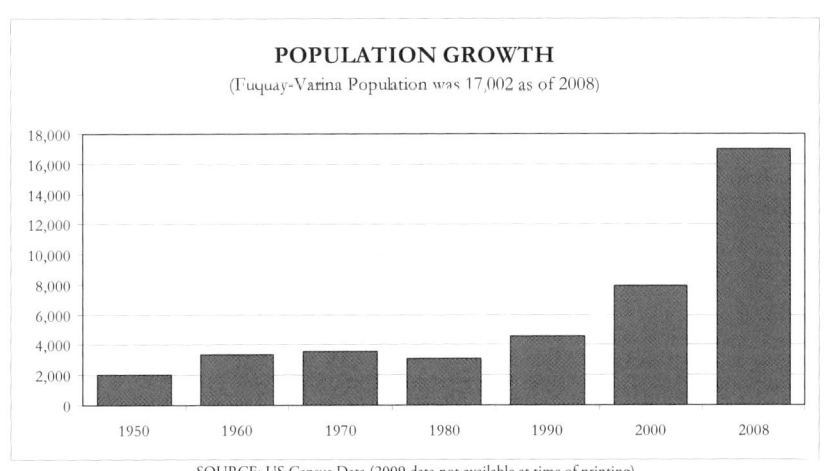

POPULATION GROWTH
(Fuquay-Varina Population was 17,002 as of 2008)

SOURCE: US Census Data (2009 data not available at time of printing)

Fuquay-Varina Real Estate Data

SOURCE: Stacey Anfindsen of Birch Appraisal (2009 data not available at time of printing)

AVERAGE SALES PRICE OF HOMES IN FUQUAY-VARINA
(Interpret as AFFORDABILITY: Reflects appreciation and price of new construction homes)

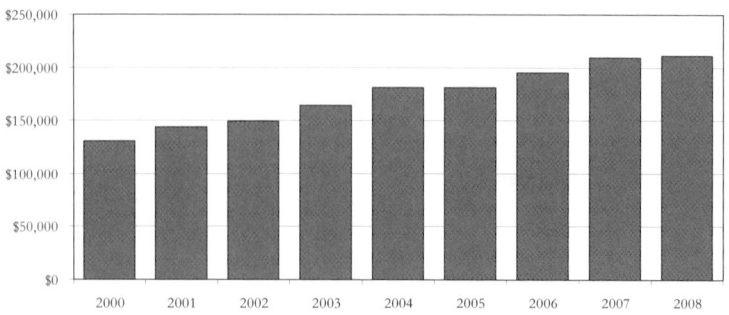

NUMBER OF HOMES SOLD
(New and Resale in Fuquay-Varina)

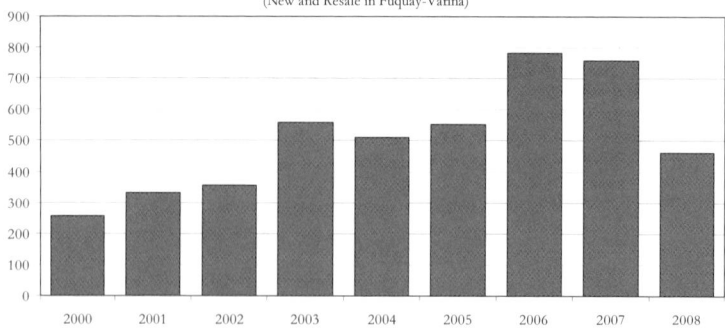

NEW CONSTRUCTION ACTIVITY
(Permits Issued to Build New Homes in Fuquay-Varina)

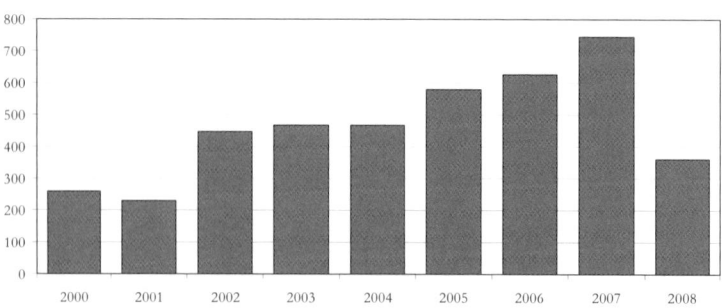

CHAPTER 14

GARNER

Although settlement in the Garner area predates the Revolutionary War, the community did not really take shape until the North Carolina Railroad connecting Goldsboro and Charlotte chose what is today Garner as the location for a new "wood and water" stop around 1870. This stop obviously proved to be a great economic driver; by 1878 the settlement had grown large enough that it required its own post office. It was incorporated as the Town of Garner Station in 1883. This charter was repealed for unknown reasons in 1891, but the community reincorporated as the Town of Garner in 1905, after a railroad depot was built in the town. The origin of the name "Garner" is uncertain – it may have been the name of a prominent citizen in the early years of the community.

Garner's convenient location at the intersection of Hwy 70 and I-40 has helped it blossom into a bustling, growing community in the central part of southern Wake County. Garner's population increased from 17,757 in 2000 to more than 26,000 in 2009, and along with this population growth came new schools, restaurants, shopping centers, and employment opportunities. Smaller and slower-paced than its western Wake County cousin, Garner has many of the same amenities as Cary but with one-fifth of Cary's population.

TOWN OF GARNER CONTACT INFORMATION

Web Site: *www.ci.garner.nc.us*
Town Hall: (919)772-4688

PART II: RALEIGH AREA CITIES AND TOWNS

Garner Location and Population

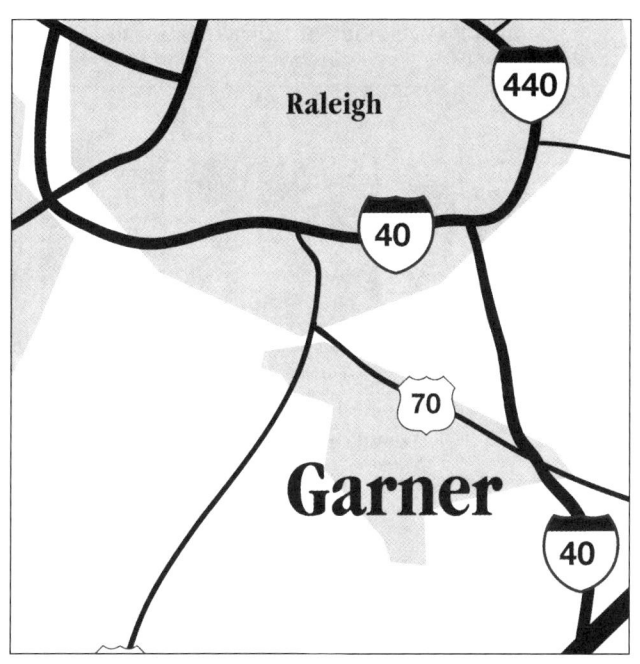

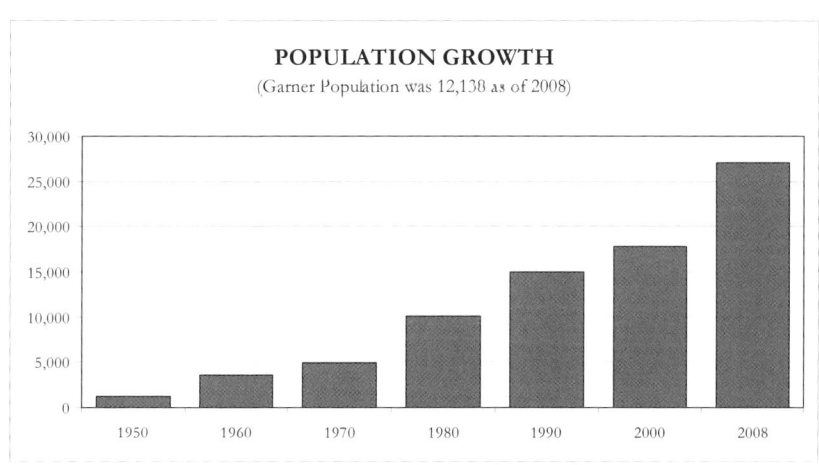

POPULATION GROWTH
(Garner Population was 12,138 as of 2008)

SOURCE: US Census Data (2009 data not available at time of printing)

THE GUIDE TO RALEIGH NORTH CAROLINA AREA REAL ESTATE

Garner Real Estate Data

SOURCE: Stacey Anfindsen of Birch Appraisal (2009 data not available at time of printing)

AVERAGE SALES PRICE OF HOMES IN GARNER
(Interpret as AFFORDABILITY: Reflects appreciation and price of new construction homes)

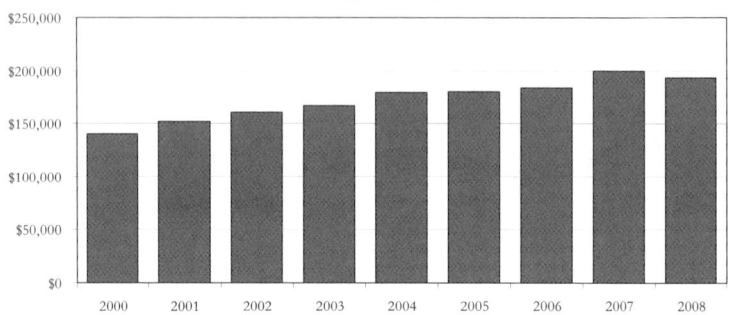

NUMBER OF HOMES SOLD
(New and Resale in Garner)

NEW CONSTRUCTION ACTIVITY
(Permits Issued to Build New Homes in Garner)

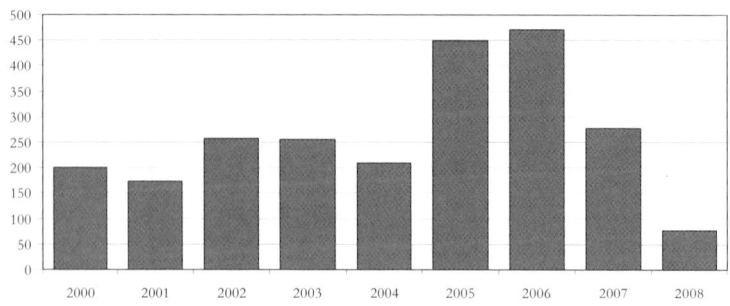

CHAPTER 15

KNIGHTDALE

The area that would come to be known as Knightdale was originally settled around 1730 by John Hinton. After the Revolution, tobacco and cotton farming became the economic mainstays of the community. The Civil War wreaked considerable devastation, and the settlement was reduced for a time to little more than a crossroads served by a post office, according to contemporary accounts.

The modern town of Knightdale takes its name from Henry Haywood Knight, a prominent resident who, in 1852, donated some of his land to the Norfolk and Southern Railroad in the hopes of attracting the economic growth that accompanied the arrival of a railroad in a community. The railroad did come in the first decade of the 20th century, and the Town of Knightdale was incorporated in 1927.

Now one of the fastest-growing towns in Wake County, Knightdale has more than tripled its population during the 1990s, growing from a tiny village of 1,700 people in 1990 to 6,000 in 2000. Knightdale's population continues to grow by leaps and bounds and was estimated at just under 9,000 in 2008.

Before the completion of the Northern Wake Expressway -- better known as I-540 -- Knightdale was a small country town whose professional citizenry faced a long commute to Raleigh or Research Triangle

Park. Now, however, I-540 and the NC-64 bypass have connected Raleigh's suburbs more efficiently than ever, and commuters can reach downtown Raleigh in 20 to 30 minutes or RTP in 30 to 45 minutes, depending on traffic.

TOWN OF KNIGHTDALE CONTACT INFORMATION

Web Site: *www.ci.knightdale.nc.us*
Main Office: (919) 217-2212

PART II: RALEIGH AREA CITIES AND TOWNS

Knightdale Location and Population

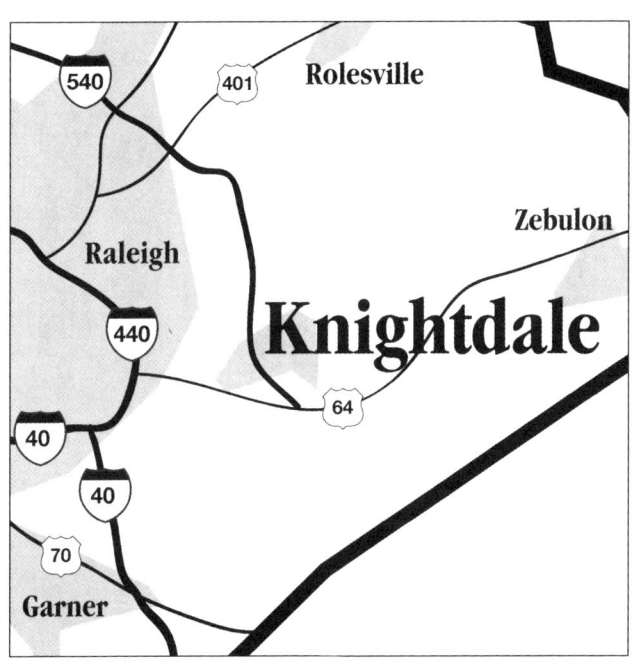

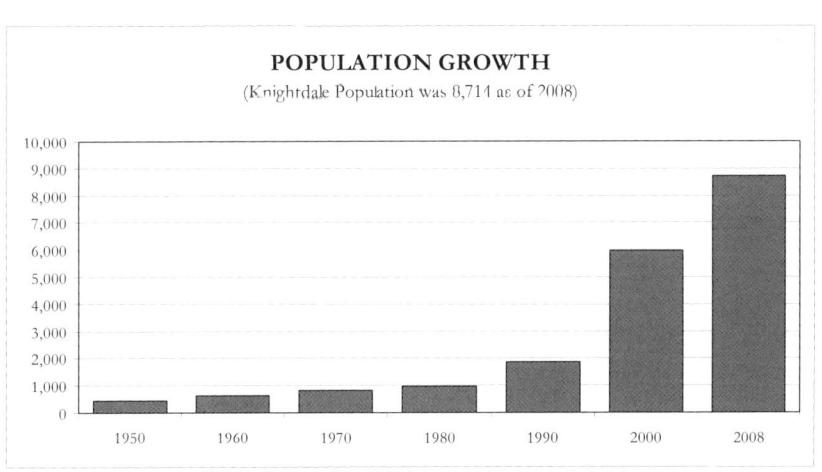

THE GUIDE TO RALEIGH NORTH CAROLINA AREA REAL ESTATE

Knightdale Real Estate Data

SOURCE: Stacey Anfindsen of Birch Appraisal (2009 data not available at time of printing)

AVERAGE SALES PRICE OF HOMES IN KNIGHTDALE
(Interpret as AFFORDABILITY: Reflects appreciation and price of new construction homes)

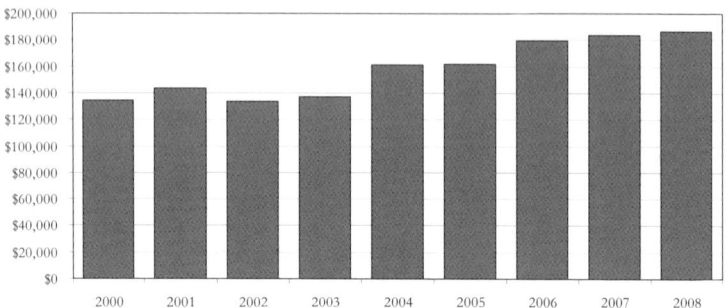

NUMBER OF HOMES SOLD
(New and Resale in Knightdale)

NEW CONSTRUCTION ACTIVITY
(Permits Issued to Build New Homes in Knightdale)

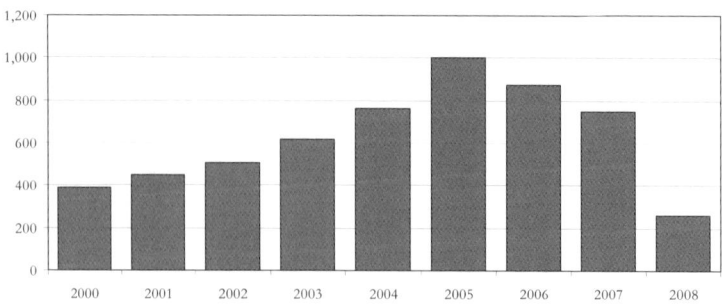

CHAPTER 16

WENDELL

What would become the Town of Wendell was originally settled by tobacco farmers from Granville County in the 1850s. They moved to Wake County in search of fertile land in the wake of the failure of the Granville County tobacco crop. As the settlement grew, residents decided they needed a name for their community. They asked the schoolmaster for a suggestion, and the schoolmaster, being a fan of the poetry of Oliver Wendell Holmes, suggested Wendell. The town's name acquired its distinctive pronunciation from the train porters, who would call out the name of the station with strong emphasis on each syllable. The locals adopted this alteration, which continues to this day. Wendell's first post office was opened in 1891, and was incorporated in 1903.

With just 2 square miles of land and 5,300 residents, Wendell is one of Wake County's smallest towns, roughly equal in population to Zebulon but with slightly less land area. But its convenient location off I-64 and the completion of the Northern Wake Expressway (I-540) must have inspired the slogan on Wendell's town web site: "Small Town Charm – Capital City Connection." Nestled between Knightdale and Zebulon, Wendell is a thirty minute drive from Downtown Raleigh and just 25 minutes from the shops and conveniences of Capital Boulevard. A new development, Wendell Falls, was approved in 2008 and is currently underway. Wendell Falls would provide enough housing to nearly double Wendell's current population and promises to bring new retail and commercial developments – and thus more jobs – to the area.

Town of Wendell Contact Information

Web Site: *www.townofwendell.org*
Town Hall: (919) 365-1521

PART II: RALEIGH AREA CITIES AND TOWNS

Wendell Location and Population

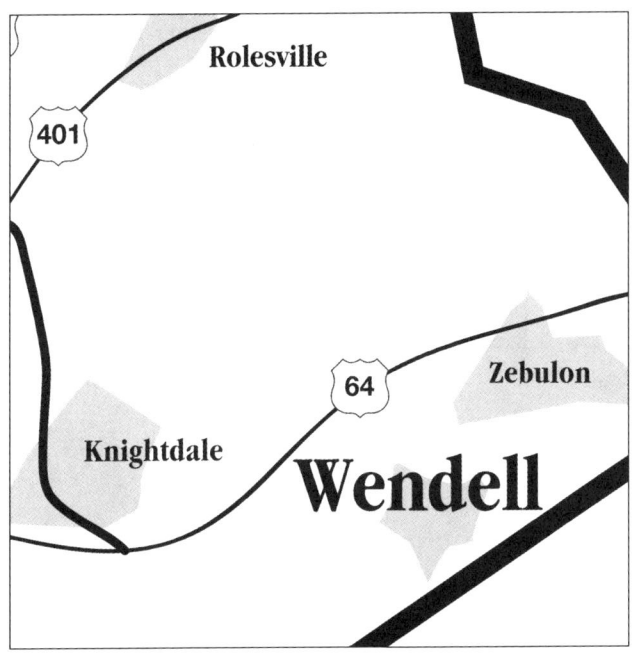

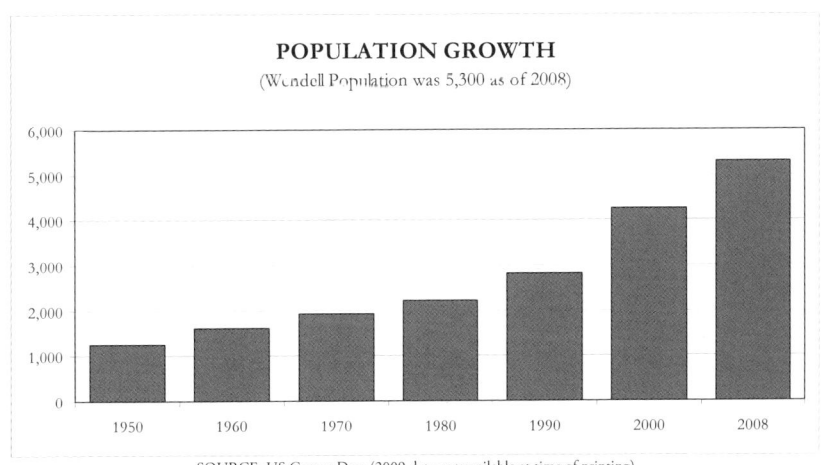

SOURCE: US Census Data (2009 data not available at time of printing)

THE GUIDE TO RALEIGH NORTH CAROLINA AREA REAL ESTATE

Wendell Real Estate Data

SOURCE: Stacey Anfindsen of Birch Appraisal (2009 data not available at time of printing)

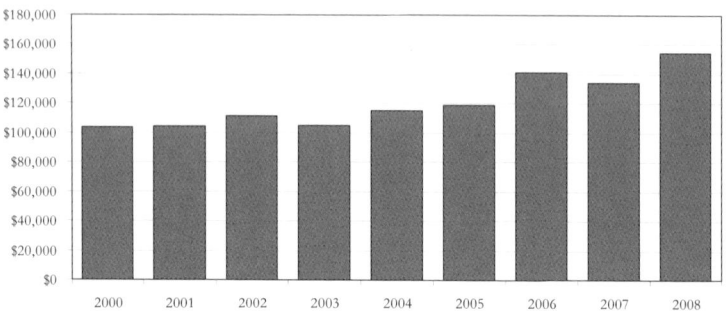

AVERAGE SALES PRICE OF HOMES IN WENDELL
(Interpret as AFFORDABILITY: Reflects appreciation and price of new construction homes)

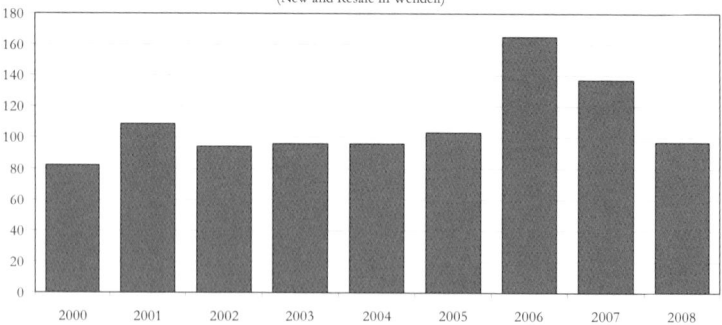

NUMBER OF HOMES SOLD
(New and Resale in Wendell)

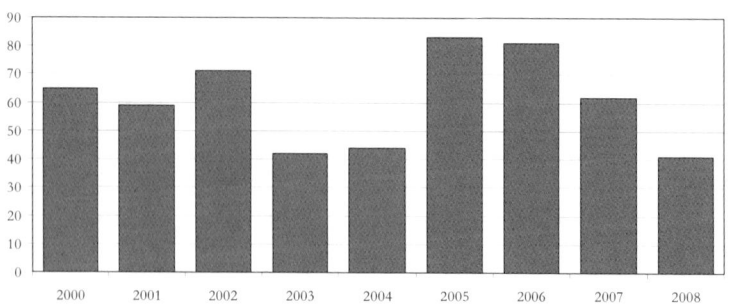

NEW CONSTRUCTION ACTIVITY
(Permits Issued to Build New Homes in Wendell)

CHAPTER 17

ZEBULON

The Town of Zebulon takes its name from Zebulon B. Vance, who was the governor of North Carolina during the Civil War. Zebulon came into existence when the Raleigh and Pamlico Sound Railroad Company decided to run a rail line through a dense stand of pines between two farms in 1906. The Zebulon Company for development organized, and divided 49 acres into lots, blocks, and streets and roadways. A year later, in February 1907, the town was officially recognized as the Town of Zebulon, and its first elections were held in May of that year.

The town of Zebulon bills itself as "A Town of Friendly People", and with just 4,732 residents, it is also Wake County's second least populous town. Zebulon is connected to the rest of Wake County via I-64 and lies just east of Wendell in the northeastern quadrant of the county.

TOWN OF ZEBULON CONTACT INFORMATION

Web Site: *www.ci.zebulon.nc.us*
Town Hall: (919) 269-7455

THE GUIDE TO RALEIGH NORTH CAROLINA AREA REAL ESTATE

Zebulon Location and Population

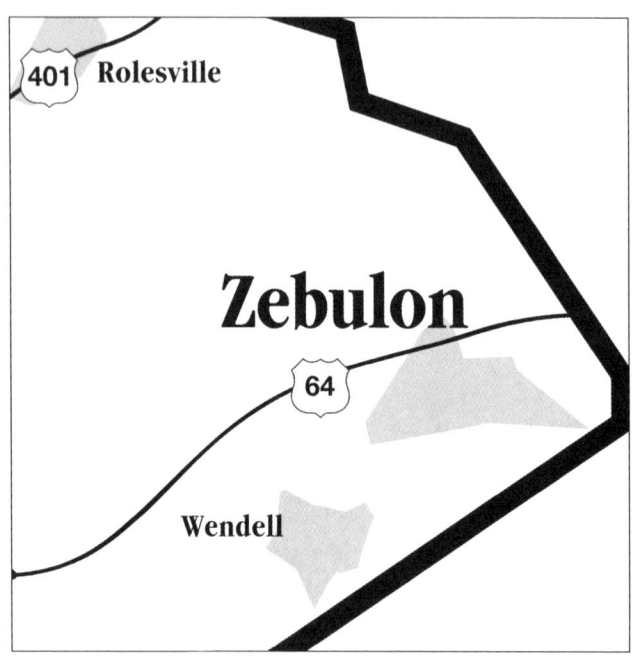

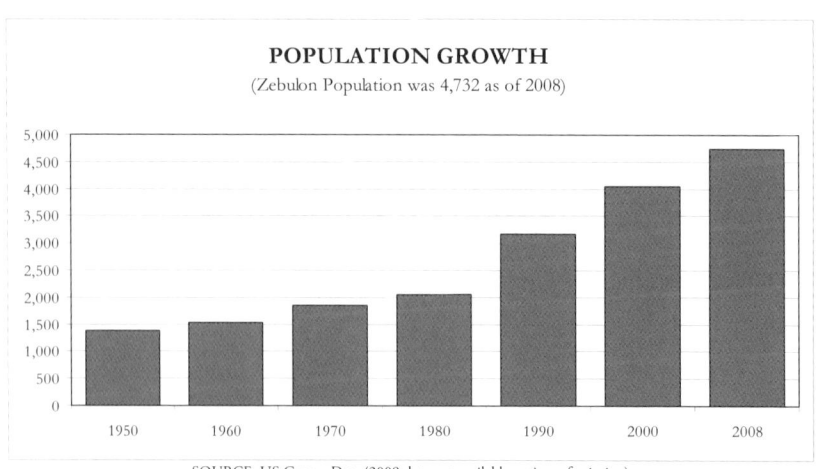

PART II: RALEIGH AREA CITIES AND TOWNS

Zebulon Real Estate Data

SOURCE: Stacey Anfindsen of Birch Appraisal (2009 data not available at time of printing)

AVERAGE SALES PRICE OF HOMES IN ZEBULON
(Interpret as AFFORDABILITY: Reflects appreciation and price of new construction homes)

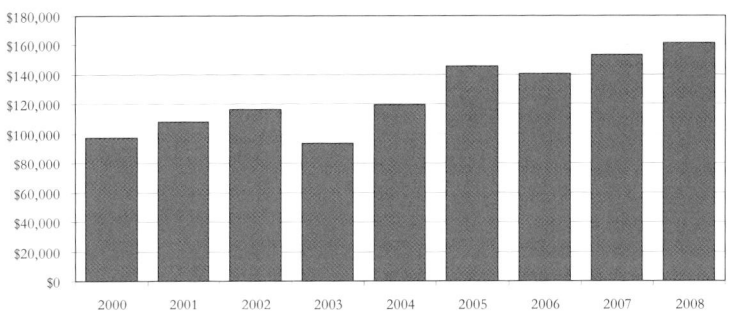

NUMBER OF HOMES SOLD
(New and Resale in Zebulon)

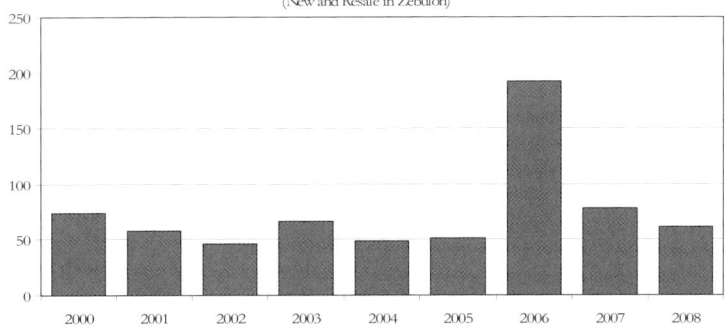

NEW CONSTRUCTION ACTIVITY
(Permits Issued to Build New Homes in Zebulon)

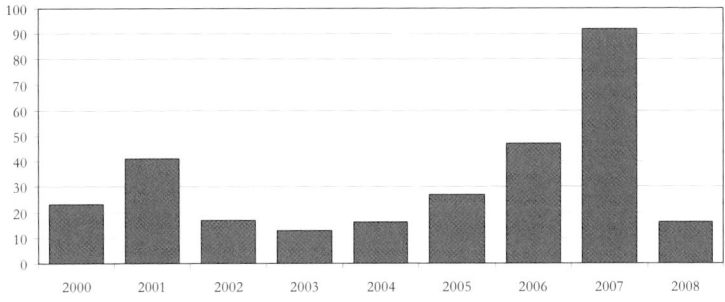

PART III

DURHAM & CHAPEL HILL/ CARRBORO

Durham and Chapel Hill/Carrboro are featured in this book as destinations for those considering a move to the Raleigh area, and wonderful destinations they are. Raleigh area residents enjoy these nearby municipalities for terrific restaurants, internationally acclaimed educational opportunities, nationally renowned collegiate and professional sports, health care, shopping, cultural activities and much more.

CHAPTER 18

DURHAM

CITY OF MEDICINE

Established in 1881, Durham, NC, is just a short trip down I-40 West from Raleigh and is quickly gaining a reputation as a true renaissance city. With a population of 257,947 in 2008, and more than 6 million visitors each year, Durham has grown into a center for learning, creativity, research and industry.

Originally believed to be the site of an ancient Native American village called Adsusheer, Durham was settled by both the Eno and Ocaneechi tribes long before the Europeans arrived. In 1701, explorer John Lawson labeled the area "the flower of the Carolinas." By the end of the Civil War Durham was well on its way to becoming a center for tobacco, particularly the Brightleaf variety, and soon gave birth to one of the largest tobacco centers in the country, which grew to include American Tobacco, Liggett & Myers and R.J. Reynolds.

Now known as the City of Medicine, USA, Durham is home to the Research Triangle Park -- which boasts more than 140 major research companies and employs 39,000 people. Healthcare is a major industry here, with more than 300 medical and health-related companies and practices.

Education is a major influence in Durham, which hosts Duke University, recently ranked in the top 10 best colleges for 2010 by *USNews & World Report*, North Carolina Central University, Durham Technical Community College, the North Carolina School of Science and Math, numerous private schools and the Durham Public School System – the 7th largest in the state with 31,000 students and 4,500 employees.

Durham is also a center for the arts, sciences and history – and is fast growing into a foodie destination. In the following pages you'll find the very best of what to see, eat and do in Durham, whether you stop by for a day or just a few hours.

FOR THE ART CONNOISSEUR

Over the years, Durham has established itself as a center for the arts, including historical art, photography, music, dance and more. Below you'll find where to go, what to see and what to do.

Visual Arts

- **Nasher Museum of Art** – In 2008 shows at the Nasher Museum were selected by Vogue magazine as some of the top cultural highlights of the year. Located at Duke University, the museum currently displays a Picasso collection and frequently hosts lectures and other events centered around the visual arts. *nasher.duke.edu*
- **NCCU Art Museum** – This museum, located within North Carolina Central University, is known for its collection of 19th and 20th century African-American art. It also houses an impressive collection of art from North Carolinian artists like Henry O., Jacob Lawrence and Minnie Evans. *web.nccu.edu/artmuseum*
- **Somerhill Gallery** – Called one of the premier galleries in the Southeast, Somerhill has spent the last 36 years filling its 9,600

square feet with abstract and representational work across all disciplines. With an open-air atrium for special exhibits and a sculpture court, this gallery located in the renovated historic Venable Center is a must-see for modern art aficionados. *somerhill.com*

Music

In addition to any number of local coffeehouses, restaurants and clubs that offer live music on a weekly basis, there are a few special events that you won't want to miss if you are a music lover.

- **Bull Durham Blues Festival** – Designed to draw attention to the rich blues history of Durham, this festival draws people from all over North Carolina. Each September, performers like the Jon Shain Trio, Delta Moon and Cool John Ferguson gather to bring the blues to the Bull City. After 22 years, you know it's the real deal. *bulldurhamblues.org*
- **Troika Music Festival** – Going strong since November of 2002, the Troika Music Festival spans 3 days and features acts from all over the Triangle area. Whether you are after indie rock, a bit of punk or just some good old country, this is one festival not to miss. *troikamusicfestival.org*

Where to Go

Here are a few places in Durham that you'll want to keep your eyes on for special events, including film festivals, dance performances and more.

- **Carolina Theatre** -- This renovated 1926 beaux-arts-style building holds both the Fletcher Hall, used for performances, and the theatre itself, known for its indie movie lineup. Be sure to check out the Full Frame Documentary Film Festival and the Nevermore Horror and Gothic Film Festival. Fletcher Hall boasts

national comedy, music and theatrical performances. *carolinatheatre.org*
- **Durham Performing Arts Center** – This state-of-the-art performance center was designed with the audience in mind. No seat is more than 135 feet from the stage and the technology used makes you feel right in the middle of the action. Located in the American Tobacco District, DPAC is perfect for a date night, with restaurants open late and plenty of sights and sounds to take in. DPAC has hosted the Suntrust Broadway series and acts such as Robin Williams, David Copperfield and Roger Daltrey – among many more. *dpacnc.com*

Can't-Miss Events

- **Festival for the Eno** – Each year since 1980, West Point on the Eno plays host to this amazing festival, full of music, art and food. Attracting artists like James Taylor, Shirley Caesar and more, the festival has a long and storied history in raising money to help protect the Eno River. It usually occurs in July, so be sure to check the website for dates.
enoriver.org/festival
- **Centerfest** – For the past 35 years, North Carolinians have looked forward to Durham's fall Centerfest, a gathering of more than 150 juried artists, craftsmen and performers from all over the country. Designed to delight everyone from the youngest child to the oldest art-lover, Centerfest is easily one of the most-loved events in Durham.
centerfest.durhamarts.org
- **American Dance Festival** – Heralded as "one of the nation's most important institutions" by the New York Times, the American Dance Festival comes to Durham each summer, pressing the boundaries of modern dance. A magnet for

PART III: DURHAM & CHAPEL HILL/CARRBORO

internationally renowned choreographers and dancers, the ADF presents world-class workshops, classes and, of course, performances each year. *americandancefestival.org*

FOR THE FOODIE

Durham boasts an ever-growing number of renowned restaurants. The following are just a few highlights to look out for on your visit to the city.

- **Wimpy's Grill** – As rundown as it appears on the outside, the burgers (and made-fresh-daily banana pudding) more than make up for it. Recently featured on The Travel Channel's *Man vs. Food*, Wimpy's hand-grinds their burger meat daily, and as for toppings? Anything you can imagine, including homemade chili and slaw. If you plan to be there between 11 and 1, be prepared to stand in line! *wimpysgrillnc.com*
- **Magnolia Grill** – A 2007 James Beard nominee for Best Restaurant in America, the Magnolia Grill is tucked away in a non-descript grey building on Ninth St. But don't let the building fool you – inside you will quickly learn why the restaurant has earned its distinctions, including twice being ranked number 11 on *Gourmet* magazine's Top 50 Restaurants in the Country. Chef-owners Karen and Ben Barker produce seasonal cooking with a traditional Southern sensibility. It's a can't-miss when you are in town. *magnoliagrill.net*
- **Café Parizade** – Owner Giorgios Bakatsias is a pillar of the Durham restaurant scene, having opened and owned restaurants here for more than 30 years. Parizade boasts contemporary food with a heavy Mediterranean influence – the duck breast is not to be missed. *ghgrestaurants.com/parizade/parizademaster.html*

- **Whiskey** – Known for its specialty cocktails and liqueurs, Whiskey is just the place to go for wine by the glass or bottle, or any one of the 16 North Carolina-brewed beers they have on tap. If you are feeling a little adventurous, give the Monkey Gland a try (made with Bombay gin, fresh orange juice, pomegranate grenadine, and Absinthe). *whiskeydurham.com*
- **Bull Durham Bar** – Located at the Washington Duke Inn, the Bull Durham Bar is the perfect place for afternoon drinks after a round of golf. Casual, but with a warm and welcoming atmosphere, the fireplace invites you to cozy up with a cocktail. Or, enjoy a drink at the bar along with their artisanal cheese plate. Either way, you'll never want to leave. *washingtondukeinn.com/dining/bull_durham_bar.asp*

Can't-Miss Events

- **Bull City Chili Challenge** – Going strong for 7 years now, the Chili Challenge is organized each year to benefit the North Carolina Special Olympics. Expect to taste chili from divisions like: vegetarian, restaurant, freestyle and Texas style – they even have a division for juniors. Get there early, because the samples go fast!
- **The Doughman** – Where else but Durham would you find a quadrathlon in which the events are: eat, bike, run, swim? Combining competitive eating with a traditional triathlon, the Doughman raises funds and awareness for the Durham Inner-City Gardeners program at SEEDS. Watch as teams of four compete in a relay race with eating and activity at each leg. *doughman.pratt.duke.edu*

PART III: DURHAM & CHAPEL HILL/CARRBORO

FOR THE HISTORY BUFF

For those interested in soaking up some of the history of the area, a visit to the following is definitely in order.

- **Bennett Place** – In April of 1865, Generals Joseph Johnston and William Sherman met at Bennett Place to sign the surrender papers for Confederate armies in the Carolinas, Georgia and Florida. Bennett Place today hosts special living history events such as re-creations of the life of Southern soldiers during the war, the road to secession and Christmas in the Carolinas during the Civil War. Make sure you are there for the special Civil War Surrender Commemoration.

    nchistoricsites.org/Bennett/Bennett.htm

- **Duke Homestead** – Tobacco is an enormous part of Durham's history, and Washington Duke was there at the very beginning. Duke Homestead gives you the opportunity to see where he first grew and processed tobacco, kicking off what would soon make North Carolina the center of a tobacco empire. Don't miss Christmas at the Homestead, which recreates an 1870s Christmas with period decorations, hot cider and caroling.

    nchistoricsites.org/duke/DUKE.htm

- **Historic Stagville** – The remnants of one of the largest plantations of the South before the Civil War, Stagville once held more than 900 slaves and sat on 30,000 acres of land. There are special events throughout the year, but they go all out at Christmas time, allowing you to try your hand as a blacksmith or experience traditional African American storytelling. *stagville.org*

- **Historic Durham Athletic Park** – If you are a film buff, you'll recognize the park from its starring role in Kevin Costner's classic movie *Bull Durham*. If you are just a baseball fan, you'll love the old ball park for its long history (it was built in 1926) as home to the Durham Bulls and its new life as the location for numerous

festivals and special events such as the Durham Blues Festival and the World Beer Festival.
- **Historic Brightleaf** – The Brightleaf area of downtown Durham is housed in former American Tobacco Company warehouses, replete with original brick and iron work. Inside the buildings, you will still find the original post-and-beam construction, created out of local brick and heart pine timber. Today, Brightleaf is home to dozens of unique shops and restaurants, and hosts a summer concert series each year. Thanks to the Bull City Carriage Company, you can now take a horse-drawn carriage ride through the district and along Duke University's East Campus to drink in the history of this beautiful place. And if the wind is blowing just right, you can still smell the tobacco leaves from Liggett and Myers, just down the road. *historicbrightleaf.com*

Can't-Miss Events

- **Native American Pow-Wow** – Each February, the North Carolina School of Science and Math hosts an authentic Native American pow-wow, replete with dancers, a feast and native music. There are often more than 150 dancers and six drums in attendance and is a traditional pow-wow in every sense of the word. Traditional arts and crafts are also on display and available for purchase. *ncssm.edu/powwow/event.html*

FOR THE SPORTS FAN

Durham has a long and storied history with sports of all kinds – from the Durham Bulls to the NCCU Eagles and, of course, Duke University athletics. If you can get to town for any of these games, consider yourself lucky.

- **Durham Bulls Baseball** – First formed in 1902, this season's Durham Bulls are the 2009 National Champions. Througout the spring and summer, you can find loyal fans down at the ballpark, drinks and dogs in hand, cheering on their team. Tickets are fairly easy to get, so don't miss your chance to see the champs in action. *dbulls.com*

- **Duke University Basketball** – A game in Cameron Indoor Stadium is a truly unique experience. While you may not be able to score tickets to a game versus UNC, tickets are often available for other games. Duke basketball is an institution in Durham, and is not to be missed! *goduke.com*

Can't-Miss Events

- **Bull City Classic Basketball Tournament** – One of the premier high school basketball invitationals in the country, the Bull City Classic each year showcases the talents of the up-and-comers on the basketball scene. McDonald's All-Americans and other award winners gather to showcase their talent. If you are a basketball fan, don't miss this opportunity to see the future stars of college – and professional – basketball. *bullcityclassic.com*

FOR THE OUTDOORSMAN

Durham is lucky to be home to the Eno River, thousands of acres of forest land and hundreds of miles of hiking and biking trails, as well as the more refined Sarah P. Duke Gardens. Below you'll find a bit more information about each, just in case you are craving a bit of outdoor activity.

- **Eno River State Park** – With its 2700 acres and 21 miles of hiking trails, the Eno River State Park is the perfect escape from its urban surroundings. Offering canoeing, kayaking, hiking and fishing, as well as educational programs, the many facets of the park are well worth a look, especially when you need a little

escape. Be sure not to miss the West Point Grist Mill at West Point on the Eno. *enoriver.org*
- **Duke Forest** – Since the early 1930s Duke Forest has been in use for research and teaching purposes, with its 7,060 acres of land. Populated by a variety of ecosystems, plant species and soil types, Duke Forest provides not only recreation but education. Hiking, biking and horseback riding are allowed, as are fishing and picnicking. *dukeforest.duke.edu*
- **Sarah P. Duke Gardens** – Spread over 55 acres, Duke Gardens is considered by many to be the crown jewel of Duke University. Known as one of the premier gardens in the country, the gardens attract more than 300,000 visitors each year. With a water lily gallery, terraces and a lush rose garden, this is one Durham attraction you can't miss.
hr.duke.edu/dukegardens/

OTHER POINTS OF INTEREST

As you can see, Durham is full of exciting places to go and interesting things to see. But there are a few more places and activities you might want to consider during your trip to the city.
- **Museum of Life and Science** – Voted 2009's "Top Place to Bring Your Children in the Triangle" by *Cary Magazine*, the 60-plus year-old Museum of Life and Science is enjoying a period of rejuvenation. With a newly renovated dinosaur trail, a butterfly house and education programs for all ages, it is perfect for a day trip. And be sure to look out for their special events, like the Butterfly Bash, the Science Spooktacular and the always popular Santa Train. *ncmls.org*
- **Duke Lemur Center** – Famous around Durham for its lemurs, bush babies and other primates, the Duke Lemur Center is the perfect place to get up close and personal with these wide-eyed

PART III: DURHAM & CHAPEL HILL/CARRBORO

animals. You'll have to make an appointment to take a tour, but it's well worth the visit.
lemur.duke.edu

- **Golden Belt** – Once a historic textile campus founded by Julian Carr, the Golden Belt is now a hub for creativity. With dining and shopping areas, this newly restored set of buildings also holds retail space and 35 artist studios – all open to the public – that spill out into a central, artist-run gallery.
goldenbeltarts.com

- **Carolina Barnstormers** – Want to tour Durham from the air? Mike Ratty will be happy to take you – in his vintage Waco biplane. Tour Duke University (the Chapel is quite a sight from the air), Falls Lake and more. *carolinabarnstormers.com*

Durham's wide variety of cultural opportunities makes it the perfect day trip for those living in the Raleigh area. For more information on what to do and where to go in the City of Medicine, check out *durham-nc.com*.

CHAPTER 19

CHAPEL HILL / CARRBORO

WHERE THE SOUTHERN PART OF HEAVEN MEETS THE PARIS OF THE PIEDMONT

A vibrant pair of sisters as smart as they are creative, the towns of Chapel Hill and Carrboro comprise the northwestern corner of the research triangle. A mere 40-minute jaunt up I-40 from the center of Raleigh lands travelers in a destination rich with opportunity: World-renowned cuisine, top-notch collegiate sports, rich cultural activities, beautiful landscapes, quaint boutiques and more can all be found in this 25-square-mile area.

Tucked in among the gently rolling hills of the eastern Piedmont, these small towns' roots were in the establishment of a university more than two centuries ago. The University of North Carolina, the country's oldest state school, began construction in 1793 and its creation was concurrent with the founding of Chapel Hill. As the university population grew, so did the town and local industry.

Seeking to increase commerce, local officials built a train depot in 1882. University laws required it to be at least a mile away from campus

PART III: DURHAM & CHAPEL HILL/CARRBORO

to avoid corrupting students with "city temptations." The depot, named West End, soon spawned a town, Venable, which would eventually be renamed Carrboro after a local mill owner who supplied the town with electricity.

In its early days, Carrboro was a mill town, yielding hosiery and cotton from the large works near the railway. Eventually the mills fell into disuse and the railroad stopped passenger service. The town began the process of reinvention with an act by the town board in 1975 to preserve the old mill as a shopping center. It was around that time it earned the nickname, "The Paris of the Piedmont," a moniker residents have fostered by opening numerous art galleries, performance spaces and trendy eating establishments.

Today Carrboro (population: 17,000) is known as a hub for arts, environmental sustainability and a prevailing politically liberal spirit. Locals, who call themselves "Carburbans," or "Carburetors," can be found riding their bicycles to work, shopping at the twice-weekly farmers' market or putting in their volunteer hours at the food co-op that serves as the center of the community.

Nearby Chapel Hill, which lies to the east of Carrboro, shares with it a love of the arts and a politically liberal philosophy, but differs in many ways. This town of 60,000 is home to a mixed group: older, affluent homeowners share the town with many of the university's body of 28,000 students.

The most popular local tourist destination is Chapel Hill's downtown area, a business district home to series of bars and restaurants along Franklin Street and adjacent to the UNC campus. However, the "Southern Part of Heaven," as the town likes to call itself, is more than just a university and a few watering holes along the main drag. Interesting stops can be found scattered throughout the burb's 20 square miles.

THE GUIDE TO RALEIGH NORTH CAROLINA AREA REAL ESTATE

FOR THE GOURMAND

Named by Bon Appétit magazine as "America's Foodiest Small Town," Chapel Hill has offerings to sate even the most particular palate. From Carolina-style barbecue to big-city fusion cuisine, these tiny towns have it all.

Restaurants

- **Crooks Corner** – Nationally recognized as the final word in true southern cooking, Crooks Corner sits humbly in a small building on the Chapel Hill-Carrboro border. You'll know it by the giant pig statue perched above its entrance but you'll remember it for the delicacies such as shrimp and grits or honeysuckle sorbet turned out by celebrity chef Bill Smith and his top-notch staff. Find out why The New York Times calls it "Sacred Ground for Southern Foodies." *crookscorner.com*
- **Fiesta Grill** – Down N.C. 54 West, about five miles west of Carrboro, is the best authentic Mexican food this side of the border. Locals know to arrive early to grab one of the 10 tables in this tiny eatery. Gourmet Magazine called Fiesta Grill's Molé sauce a can't-miss, and customers rave about everything on the menu from the carnitas to the enchiladas. Inexpensive and delicious, Fiesta Grill is worth the trip off the beaten path. *fiestagrill.us*
- **Allen & Son Pit Cooked BBQ** – If barbecue is the official food of North Carolina, then Allen & Son is the official purveyor of the slow-cooked pulled pork that could make even a vegetarian drool. With all the atmosphere of a hunting lodge and a hard-to-find location, this is not the place to go for a formal meal. But for hungry patrons looking for the true, hickory-smoked taste of the Carolinas, this is not just a restaurant, it's a destination. Allen & Son's spicy, vinegar-based barbecue sauce delights the taste buds

PART III: DURHAM & CHAPEL HILL/CARRBORO

while the Brunswick stew can fill even the hungriest belly. *919-942-7576*

- **The Lantern** – From the Wall Street Journal to Food & Wine, publications across the country can't stop raving about The Lantern's fusion fare. Chef Andrea Reusing's insistence on using only locally-grown, seasonal ingredients in her dishes earned her restaurant the number 47 spot on Gourmet's 2006 list of America's top restaurants. But The Lantern is not content to rest on its accolades. This Franklin Street staple mixes up its menu nightly, serving everything from Vietnamese-style seafood to Japanese wagyu steak with ponzu sauce. *lanternrestaurant.com*
- **Locopops** – Going to a shop that sells only popsicles sounds like boring child's play. But this local business takes the frozen confection and turns it into something irresistible. From the exotic (hibiscus-pomegranate) to the deliciously mundane (cookies-and cream), Locopops turns the Mexican traditional street food, *paletas*, into a Chapel Hill staple. Be sure to bring cash for the $2.50 pops, since they don't take plastic. With two locations, one on Franklin Street and one on Elliott road, you are never far from a sweet (and cheap!) dessert. *ilovelocopops.com*
- **Foster's Market** – Both the best place for a quick lunch and the best place to drink a bottle of wine with friends, Foster's Market makes comfort food seem classy. After working for years side-by-side with Martha Stewart, Sara Foster set out on her own, opening a catering business and café in Durham. A second location in Chapel Hill soon followed and now the homey, art-filled space draws in students and tourists alike with its specialties which range from grilled ham and brie sandwiches to French silk pie. *fostersmarket.com*

NIGHTLIFE

Many bars in Chapel Hill require membership before pouring patrons a drink. If the establishment serves food, typically the rules don't apply. But if you are asked to apply for membership it is typically a one-time fee.

- **Top of the Hill** – One of Chapel Hill's two microbreweries, Top of the Hill is *the* place to grab a pint and watch the world go by. Situated on the third floor and overlooking the heart of the Franklin Street business district, this brewery is a favorite for locals and tourists alike. Featuring a full menu of hearty main courses to pair with its spirits and a porch with a view of downtown that can't be beat, Top of the Hill is the kind of place to while away a whole evening. *topofthehillrestaurant.com*
- **Carolina Brewery** – Down at the West End of Franklin Street near the Carrboro border is another brewing company with a personality all its own. The Carolina Brewery is a more casual destination and Friday night finds customers lining up for a chance to quaff some of the distiller's popular Flagship IPA and seasonal brews. A full menu features a range of dishes from salad to steak. *carolinabrewery.com*
- **Halloween on Franklin** – Home to raucous bar-hopping co-eds on even the quietest of nights, Franklin Street truly comes alive on Halloween. From 9 p.m. until 2 a.m. the town closes off the street for a wild party that draws crowds of more than 50,000 costumed revelers. Public drinking is not allowed in Chapel Hill, so the dozens of bars along this mile-long thoroughfare do a brisk business, serving up spooky beverages to their creepy customers. *ci.chapel-hill.nc.us*

PART III: DURHAM & CHAPEL HILL/CARRBORO

FOR THE ART AFICIONADO:

Famous performers from Andy Griffith to James Taylor have called Chapel Hill home, so it's no wonder the area is rich with artistic opportunities. Whether you're into pottery or opera, Chapel Hill and Carrboro have something to offer.

Visual Arts

- **2ⁿᵈ Friday Artwalk** – A surefire way to to see the best that Chapel Hill and Carrboro galleries have to offer, the 2ndFriday Artwork happens, as indicated by its name, on the second Friday of every month. Down Main Street in Carrboro all the way to the University Mall, art lovers can take in the sights (and drink a little wine) at more than 18 locations throughout both towns. Small galleries such as Wootini at Carr Mill Mall showcase offbeat artists from around the country, while Tyndall Galleries on Estes Drive in Chapel Hill is home to contemporary art from sculpture to mixed-media. *2ndfridayartwalk.com*
- **Ackland Art Museum** – Built as a final resting place for its namesake, the Ackland Art Museum is home to some of the most diverse collections in the South. Religious artifacts from the 16th century mingle with modern avant garde works in this stately building on the edge of the UNC campus. More than 15,000 works – among them the state's premiere collection of Asian art – are on display in this well-curated collection. *ackland.org*

Music

- **Carrboro Music Festival** – Every September more than 170 bands take to the streets of Carrboro to fill the town with the sounds of every type of music imaginable. Blues? Check! Old-time Klezmer? Check! Indie Synth-pop? Of course! Local businesses host small stages and attendees wander the streets taking in all the free music they can handle. The draw for this homegrown event is the people-watching as much as the music. Put on your walking shoes and sun hat and take a stroll through the best local music in the Triangle. *carrboromusicfestival.com*

Performance

- **DSI** – The Dirty South Improv Theater, stashed away in the back of Carr Mill Mall, is home to some of the most talented, most boisterous actors the area has to offer. These diamonds-in-the-rough perform in a variety of improvisational formats in the small, 100-seat theater. Audience participation is encouraged and laughter is a given at the short shows, which are reminiscent of "Who's Line is It Anyway?"
dsicomedytheater.com

Where to Go:

- **Cat's Cradle** – For more than three decades, there hasn't been a band worth its salt that hasn't played a gig at "the Cradle." A piece of rock n' roll history whose stage has been home to artists from R.E.M. to Vanilla Ice, this smoke-free venue hosts mainly touring rock acts from around the world. Tucked in among the shops on Main Street in Carrboro, the best way to find this hip spot is to follow concert fliers and tour buses to its nondescript front door. *catscradle.com*
- **Memorial Hall** – Recently the recipient of an $18 million renovation, Memorial Hall is the premiere location to see the biggest-name performers. The Bolshoi Ballet has taken the stage here as has Chapel Hill native James Taylor. Built in 1931, this UNC campus landmark features state-of-the-art sound and lighting systems and comfortable seats. Season subscriptions are available as are single-event tickets for the public speakers,

orchestras, operas, dance troops and musicians who perform in this historic venue. *carolinaperformingarts.org*

FOR RETAIL THERAPY:

Dotting the streets of Chapel Hill and Carrboro are some of the best shopping opportunities in the Triangle. Crafty artisans mingle with purveyors of gourmet wares along the retail corridors of these towns.

- **Carr Mill Mall** – Situated in the heart of Carrboro, this mill-turned-mall is a cute place to fill your belly and shop. The most noticeable tenant, Weaver Street Market, is a crunchy food co-op which is open to the public. The lawn in front of this granola grocery is a gathering place for a colorful assortment of people, and is a great place to stop for lunch. Other stores at this mall include an outdoor outfitter, a unique toy store and several small clothing boutiques. *carrmillmall.com*
- **University Mall** – The only place to find a department store and one of few locations to host national chains such as Bed, Bath and Beyond, this small shopping center is a great stop on a shopping expedition. Home to more than 50 shops, here you can find anything from a UNC T-shirt to a piece of fine art. *universitymallnc.com*
- **A Southern Season** – This 60,000-square-foot gourmet store at the eastern end of University Mall must be seen to be believed. Prepared hot foods and a bakery share space with a selection of kitchen tools unrivaled on the Eastern Seaboard. Fresh exotic flowers, delicate stemware and the finest wines can all be found among A Southern Season's labyrinthine aisles. Upstairs is a first-rate cooking school which hosts nightly classes and tastings and downstairs is a restaurant, The Weathervane, which serves up breakfast, lunch and dinner. *southernseason.com*

- **Franklin Street** – While it is best known for its bars and restaurants, the downtown blocks of Franklin Street are also home to some of the best shopping Chapel Hill has to offer. Clothing, hand-crafted furniture, jewelry and books can all be purchased along this historic corridor. Follow the signs to park at one of the town lots – no need for quarters, they take plastic – and spend an afternoon wandering under the tree-lined streets of downtown Chapel Hill. *downtownchapelhill.com*

FOR KIDS OF ALL AGES (AND THEIR PARENTS):

The Carolina-blue fire engines aren't the only thing to delight Chapel Hill's youngest visitors. Playgrounds and parks are situated in nearly every neighborhood and annual street fairs draw families downtown for fried foods, live music and local art.

- **Kidzu** – In the middle of the hustle and bustle of Franklin Street, tucked between a Starbucks and a favorite college pizza joint, is 2,700 square feet of magic. The Kidzu kids museum features rotating exhibits perfect for the 1-to-7-year-old in your life. Toddlers can explore the tot lot while older kids can construct vast cityscapes, cook complex meals or conquer an elaborate ball maze. *kidzuchildrensmuseum.org*
- **The Carolina Tiger Rescue** – Originally founded as a research lab and breeder of exotic cats, the Carolina Tiger Rescue is now home to 72 of the fiercest carnivores around. These animals, many of which have been rescued from private homes, live out their lives in the comfort of the most natural surroundings the volunteers at the rescue can create. The only way to see these big cats is by reserving a private tour. For a once-in-a-lifetime treat, schedule your visit on a Saturday night to watch these predators dine. *carolinatigerrescue.org*

PART III: DURHAM & CHAPEL HILL/CARRBORO

- **Morehead Planetarium** – The Morehead was one of the first planetariums in the South. Built in 1949 with a bequest from a UNC alumnus, this scientific wonder is rich with history – nearly every astronaut from 1959 to 1975 trained here – and is a treat for any budding astronomer. Nightly shows and weekend matinées in the 68-foot domed star theater send spectators on an out-of-this-world journey. *moreheadplanetarium.org*
- **Festifall** – Featuring displays from nearly 100 artists, this street fair is creative fun for the whole family. Occupying the West End of Franklin Street, this October event is an ideal place to engage in hands-on art projects or boogie to local bands. Celebrate the changing seasons and chow down on some funnel cake while wandering through this popular event. *ci.chapel-hill.nc.us*

FOR SPORTS LOVERS:

Collegiate sports aren't the only athletic offering in Chapel Hill and Carrboro. An extensive network of greenways connect the towns, parks and gardens. Visit campus to see the UNC Tar Heels score a touchdown or 3-point shot, or head down to Finley Golf course for some quality time on the links.

UNC Tar Heels

Chapel Hill might be more famous for its brain than for its brawn, but overlooking the sporting life of this ACC powerhouse would surely be a mistake. Although basketball is the heart of UNC's athletic program, Division One football is its soul. Gameday on campus is electric: even if you don't have tickets it's worth a stop to see the revelers gear up for the game.

- **Football** – Although they rarely show up in the AP Top 25, the Tar Heel Football team is a worthwhile Saturday ticket. With a schedule that includes some of the top teams in college football, these boys in blue turn out the crowds at Kenan Stadium for their gridiron battles. Counting Giants Hall-of-Fame linebacker Lawrence Taylor among their famous alumni, the Tar Heels have a strong tradition. Arrive early for the game and take in Tar Heel Town in the UNC student union. *tarheelblue.cstv.com*

- **Basketball** – Five-time national champions, these ballers are the hottest ticket in town. Sellouts are frequent, especially as the season wears on, but there's always a seat for former UNC guard Michael Jordan, who can sometimes be seen in the crowd, rooting his alma mater to victory. Traffic can be tricky getting to the Dean Smith Center near game time, so try the park-n-ride at University Mall. For a season preview, pick up a $10 ticket in October to Late Night With Roy, the celebrated first practice of the year. *tarheelblue.cstv.com*

OUTDOOR ADVENTURES

- **North Carolina Botanical Garden** – More than 800 acres of native wildlife await in this riparian paradise just off Chapel Hill's main drag. Dirt paths meander through the garden's offerings – which span from botanical to sculptural – offering a welcome retreat. Check out the dozens of species of rosemary in the herb garden or take on a challenger in a game of chess on the garden's 12-foot-square board. Don't miss the collection of carnivorous plants; North Carolina is the only place in the world where the Venus Flytrap grows naturally. *ncbg.unc.edu*

- **UNC Finley Golf Club** – This 18-hole course is known for its meandering design and well maintained greens. Once named the 11th best collegiate course in the country by Golfweek magazine, the Finley Golf Club is the ideal place to relax for few hours and test out your skills on new turf. A 42-tee driving range is

PART III: DURHAM & CHAPEL HILL/CARRBORO

available, as are tee times any day of the week. *tarheelblue.cstv.com/finley/unc-finley.html*

From the country's best chefs to face-painting sports fans, these little towns have it all. Whether you are looking for an evening out or a weekend adventure, a stop in Carrboro and Chapel Hill should be on your map. For more information, check out *visitchapelhill.org*

PART IV

INTERVIEWS

In this section you will hear from 19 people (or couples) who moved to the Raleigh area over the past few years. You will learn how they chose the municipality in which they live, if they would make that same choice again, and why. They will tell you who they think would like their part of the Raleigh area, and who would not. And finally, they will tell you what they do for fun!

The names of most of the interviewees have been changed to protect their privacy.

CHAPTER 20

BRANDON & ALICIA DONLEY

TO DOWNTOWN RALEIGH FROM ALISO VIEJO, CALIFORNIA

Tell me a little bit about yourself and what brought you to the area?

Alicia and I are both originally from the Midwest. Alicia's from a town in Michigan just outside of Toledo, Ohio, and I grew up near Chicago. We were living in Orange County, California before we came to Raleigh. Alicia works in the GIS (Geographic Information Systems) department at NC State, and I'm a freelance writer, video professional and marketing consultant.

What made you choose the Raleigh area to relocate to?

We were both a little tired of California. We liked the climate and the ocean, but the traffic was terrible and the cost of living was outrageous. We didn't want to go back to the Midwest winters, but we wanted to be within a day's drive of our families. We started doing some research, and the Triangle was one of the places that kept popping up. Of all the places we looked at, the Triangle had the strongest economy and the lowest cost of living. So we visited for a long weekend, and really enjoyed it.

Did you consider any other areas or was the Triangle area the only one?

We narrowed our search down to three places: the Triangle, Nashville, TN, and Austin, TX. We visited Raleigh first and were sold. The economy and the opportunity to further our education were two factors that set Raleigh apart. We felt like the other two cities were closer to peaking, economically, than Raleigh.

How long have you lived here?

We've been here a little over 2 years.

Why did you choose your particular municipality in the Raleigh area?

We live in the Cameron Village neighborhood on the west side of downtown; it's situated between downtown Raleigh and NC State University. When we first moved here we sublet a townhouse in West Raleigh. It was okay, but after doing some exploring we decided we wanted to be closer to downtown. We enjoy walking, and we wanted to be in a neighborhood where we could walk to restaurants and the grocery store. Where we live now, Alicia can even walk to work.

If you had to do it over again, would you choose the same area?

Absolutely. We plan on staying in this area for a long time.

PART IV: INTERVIEWS

What have you liked about the area that you didn't realize before you moved here?

The abundance of live music options, restaurants and outdoor activities has been a surprise. We've been here over 2 years, and we're still discovering new bands, new neighborhoods, new restaurants and new things to do on the weekends.

What have you not liked about the area?

The Interstate system could use some work. The signage can be confusing, and some of the entrance and exit ramps are not designed too well.

What are your favorite things to do here?

We like to go up to Falls Lake or Umstead Park and run or hike, or walk around downtown Raleigh and try new restaurants. We go to a lot of the concerts and outdoor festivals that take place in Moore Square and elsewhere.

What are your favorite restaurants here?

We like the Irregardless Café, Raleigh Times (great burgers), the Red Dragon, Tir Na Nog (great shepherd's pie), and The Pit for barbecue.

What are your favorite things to do on weekends?

Since we've moved here, we've visited the Outer Banks, Charleston, Asheville, Smoky Mountains National Park, Charlotte and Topsail Island. My favorites were Charleston and Asheville. They're great towns for walking, eating and live music.

Who do you think would like this area?

Our neighborhood is filled with a lot of young professionals, but there are also families, retirees and graduate students. There are a lot of folks who have relocated from the Midwest and Northeast, and plenty of native North Carolinians too. For us, Cameron Village is the perfect compromise between the city and the suburbs. Neither one of us wanted to live in a community where we had to drive everywhere, but we did want a little bit of outdoor space as well. Cameron Village provides that. Raleigh is a good spot for someone who wants the cultural offerings of a big city without the crowds and the costs.

Who do you think would not like this area?

If you like really big, fast paced cities, then this probably isn't the place for you. If you have a negative attitude about the South, then don't bother moving here, though many think that Raleigh is not a very Southern city.

Do you feel that Raleigh is a "true" representation of North Carolina?

North Carolina is a pretty big state, and there is a lot of variety. Like anywhere, you have to live in a place for a while to really get to know it, and we're still getting to know Raleigh and North Carolina. I don't know if Raleigh is representative of all of North Carolina, but because of the universities and RTP it attracts people from all over the state, the country and the world. I don't think you can overemphasize the impact of the three large research universities on the area's culture.

Many people move here for a better "quality of life." Do you feel this area offers that?

It does for us. I'm not sure we knew exactly what we were looking for when we moved to Raleigh. We knew we wanted a small city with a

PART IV: INTERVIEWS

strong economy and plenty to do, but Raleigh has exceeded our expectations in many ways. We plan on staying here for a long time.

Was it hard to meet others when you moved here?

We hit it off with a few of our neighbors right away, and some of our friends from college moved down here after we did. We have barbecues and watch football games. Some of our friends have young children and some don't. We've found plenty of things, like going to Durham Bulls games, that are fun for everybody.

How's the weather?

September through June is great. July and August can get a little steamy, but we've gotten used to it. Spring and fall are my favorite seasons here. The seasonal changes are more gradual compared with the Midwest.

Do you feel like locals resent people from other parts of the country moving here?

Some do, but that goes for anywhere. There will always be some people who long for the way things were "back in the day". We haven't experienced any kind of personal resentment since moving. The locals we have met have been nothing but friendly and welcoming.

The area is experiencing unprecedented growth. Do you think that Raleigh is booming too fast?

I know it's hypocritical, but I sometimes find myself hoping that the growth will slow down, even though I've only been here for 2 years. But in terms of land and infrastructure there is still plenty of room for growth, and I don't think there will be any negative impact on quality of life anytime soon. A traffic jam in Raleigh is not the same as a traffic jam in Chicago or Los Angeles or New York.

What else can you tell me that would help others moving here?

There are a lot of cool neighborhoods and towns in the Triangle. Take your time to check out the options and get a feel for the lay of the land, and find out which areas you like best.

CHAPTER 21

HEIDI MCCORD

TO DOWNTOWN RALEIGH FROM SAVANNAH, GEORGIA

Where did you move here from?

I moved here with my now-husband, Keith in 2000 after we graduated from Savannah College of Art and Design in Savannah, Georgia. After a brief stay with my mother-in-law, who lived on the east side of downtown Raleigh, we knew we wanted to stay nearby.

How did you go about choosing where you wanted to move to?

I love North Carolina, but I'd never been to Raleigh. I had a relative and friends who lived here, and they told me it was a good area. I had heard from my friend who went to college with me that the whole Triangle was a really cool place to live.

What made you choose the Raleigh area over other areas you were looking at?

We thought about Chapel Hill, but we couldn't find jobs there. We looked at Durham briefly, but, frankly, we didn't care for it. We ended up staying in Raleigh because there are more job opportunities and amenities here. Things just fell into place for us here. We had strongly considered Asheville [in western NC] – I love it there – but we couldn't make it work because it's really expensive over there and also, the jobs that are there are only service-type entry-level jobs. We loved this area for the music scene. Also, there are plenty of opportunities to work as an artist because there are more high-income people here who can buy art.

What was your opinion of Raleigh before moving here?

I didn't know very much about Raleigh at all. I had heard a lot about the cultural amenities and with three cities together here I thought there would be three times the amount of jobs and amenities. I though that it would be clean and I had read that it had a high education level and I figured there were a lot of intelligent people. I thought it would have more of a cosmopolitan feel than Garner. All true.

Why did you choose your particular municipality in the Raleigh area?

We work in Raleigh and we do business here and we wanted to be in biking distance of where we work. It was important to us to stay near the people we knew. We have a studio that is open to the public at Artspace, and we wanted to be able to come and go from that easily.

What other areas did you consider?

We enjoy living on the East side of downtown Raleigh. However, I loved Oakwood and Boylan Heights and Mordecai, and I looked at those neighborhoods but was priced out. I wanted to live inside the Beltline – that was my thing. We looked at all the historic neighborhoods but we were priced out. I really wanted a historic house and I even looked closer to the center of downtown but we thought that neighborhood seemed like a place we would be afraid to live in.

PART IV: INTERVIEWS

If you had to do it over again, would you choose the same area?

I would absolutely buy here again. But if I had a second choice , I would probably say Durham, just because we wanted a historic house. We love Chapel Hill but we wouldn't be able to afford any kind of house there.

Have you moved since you've been here? What prompted that move?

Previously, I was renting in the same neighborhood that I am in now. We moved three blocks when we bought our house in 2003. I wanted to stay here because I like the Longview neighborhood for the older homes, big trees, bigger property lots and proximity to downtown.

What have you liked about the area that you didn't realize before you moved here?

I guess, I was surprised that the traffic isn't really that bad. Inside the Beltline the traffic never gets that thick, even at rush hour. I was also surprised at how easy it was to meet people and make friends here.

What have you not liked about the area since you moved here?

Definitely the walk-ability that we had in Savannah we don't have here. You can't walk to anything; you have to drive everywhere. The public transit could be better, too. There should be a train connecting the three cities of the Triangle. I hate driving down I-40. There should be a better way to get from city to city. Also, I wish that Raleigh had a really big main library downtown. I miss that about living in my hometown of Jacksonville, Florida; they had a really great library.

THE GUIDE TO RALEIGH NORTH CAROLINA AREA REAL ESTATE

What sort of people do you think would like this area, or not like it?

I think anyone would like Raleigh because I feel like there is something for everybody here. And if it isn't in Raleigh then Durham is right there. Anyone from a college student to a wage slave to a self employed person would thrive here. The economy is pretty good. There are a lot of people living in Raleigh who are from other places. This is not your typical southern town. It's rare to meet someone who is actually from Raleigh. There are so many people from different walks of life in my neighborhood. It's great for anyone who wants to live near downtown in an older house with a wood floor on a large lot. This neighborhood in the last few years has really come into its own. I always see people out walking dogs, younger families out with their children.

People who have allergies wouldn't like living in Raleigh because it is extremely bio-diverse. People who don't like nature wouldn't like it here. People who don't have cars wouldn't like it here either – you have to drive everywhere.

What are your favorite restaurants?

Neomonde on Beryl Road. I love their hummus and baba ghanoush. They make their own pita bread and it's the best pita bread I've ever had. I crave their falafal. My second one is Udupi in Cary because I love Indian food and I'm vegan and their buffet is a really good way to introduce yourself to Indian food without having to learn the names of everything. It's got a home-cooked feeling to the food and it feels authentic.

What is your favorite way to spend a weekend here?

I love to go out to Lake Johnson and go hiking. I like to go to the thrift store – there are lots of good thrift stores around here. I like to garden, visit friends go to art shows and spend time with my family.

PART IV: INTERVIEWS

If you could, is there something you would change about Raleigh?

 I would get rid of the cookie-cutter growth that's happening with the subdivisions. I don't like neighborhoods with two spindly trees and all the houses look the same. I would put more stuff on the East side of Raleigh. We need more retail and more amenities over here. I feel like everything is on the west side of town.

CHAPTER 22

LANE NEWGARD

TO NORTH RALEIGH FROM LOS ANGELES, CALIFORNIA

What made you choose the Raleigh area?

I wanted to relocate after my divorce and I had family living here. I was coming home.

How did you choose the subdivision Bedford at Falls River [in North Raleigh off Falls of the Neuse Road, north of 540]

Being a single woman, I was looking for a good, safe area to live that didn't have too much maintenance. I had looked around a lot and had started to buy a different home but then decided the yard was too big. The townhome I found in Bedford was low maintenance, safe, and had plenty of neighbors.

What do you like most about your community?

It's a beautiful area and everything I want is within a five-mile radius. The nearest grocery store is just two and a half miles away and there are many walking trails nearby.

PART IV: INTERVIEWS

Other than family, what made you choose the Raleigh area over other areas that you were looking at?

Coming from California, I'm used to living in a place with lots to do. In Raleigh, it's like living in California but on a smaller scale. I like that I can live a quiet lifestyle but have plenty of opportunities nearby – like the arts and athletic events. The closest beach is only 2 hours away. For me, Raleigh offers all of the possibilities of California but on a smaller scale.

What other areas of Raleigh did you consider?

I looked in Rolesville and Wake Forest. I ended up choosing my home because I loved being close to the lake and hiking trails. They're building a new Mountains-to-Sea Trail and it will cut through Falls Lake where I do a lot of hiking. If you want to hike, it's the perfect place to live!

If you had to do it over again, would you choose the same area? What would your second choice be?

Definitely. I don't have obligations to small children and I'm fortunate not to have to work. However, if I did need to work I know there are plenty of opportunities to find a good job in Raleigh. If I didn't live in Raleigh, my second choice would be out-of-state – probably Smith Mountain Lake, Virginia.

What do you like about the area that you didn't realize before you moved here?

I didn't realize that Raleigh had all these nice parks and greenways. The area has so many wonderful playgrounds for small children, too. The city has done a lot to make sure it's family friendly.

How do you find the weather here?

Coming from California, the best part about the weather is that when it does snow, it only stays a few days. One thing I missed while in California were the summer thunderstorms that we have here – as well as the four seasons.

What are your favorite restaurants here?

I don't eat out a whole lot since I'm single. But one of my favorite hangouts is Pipers Tavern *[near the corner of Falls of Neuse Road and 540]*. It has great food and there are lots of locals there watching games. As for cultural activities, there are lots of wine tastings and other activities. Raleigh is very multicultural and it's nice to see that here.

Have you been disappointed in anything about the area since you moved here?

I wanted a slower pace of life and when I get on the highway – it's slow! I'm used to California aggressive drivers. But, it's what I asked for and I need to accept it.

Do you feel like Raleigh is the real North Carolina?

Raleigh isn't what it used to be. When my family moved here in 1974 it was a true Southern town. I think it's growing for the better and is coming out of its bubble and becoming more accepting of others. I think being surrounded by all these transplants and new cultures have benefitted Raleigh.

What kind of people do you think would like this area, or not like it?

Anyone interested in a good town to raise a family. It's also a great place to retire – especially for people coming from the Snowbelt that still want the four seasons.

CHAPTER 23

MANDY & JASON HOLLOWELL

TO RALEIGH FROM DAYTON, OHIO THEN TO MELBOURNE FLORIDA AND BACK TO NORTH RALEIGH

Why did you choose to move to the Raleigh area?

We actually moved to Raleigh twice – both times out of our own choice, not for jobs or family – and we plan to stay here as long as possible. The first time we came to Raleigh, in 1993, we were straight out of college and looking for a place to settle down together. I was from Michigan and Jason from New York, and we were looking for a warmer climate and a lower cost of living. We initially considered Atlanta, but were steered toward the Raleigh area. I was still in college and waiting tables and a lot of people recommended coming to RTP (Research Triangle Park).

Why did you choose the specific location to which you moved in the Raleigh area?

I had a cousin who was leaving her home in Raleigh before her lease ran out. So we moved into her home into an area closer to downtown known for its ancient trees and stately, historic homes – most of which are meticulously preserved. Our home, however, stood out. It was a tiny brick ranch in the middle of all these beautiful homes.

We stayed in Raleigh 13 years, and ended up building two homes in North Raleigh – the second was our "dream home" – until Jason was drawn to Florida by a job offer. When that job didn't work out, we didn't hesitate: There was not even a question in our mind that we would return to Raleigh. You don't know how good you have it until you move away.

Tell me about your second move to the Raleigh area.

By the time we were ready to escape Florida, the economy had taken a turn for the worse. In our conversations with friends and family across the country, it seemed Raleigh was doing better than most other places. Raleigh was somewhat sheltered from what was happening in other areas of the country.

Since we had lived in Raleigh before, we knew more about the different areas where we could settle. We considered Cary and a few other areas of Raleigh, but were pretty much convinced from the beginning that we would settle in North Raleigh. I like the conveniences that are within North Raleigh so that I don't need to leave North Raleigh if I don't want to. I like how visually beautiful it is compared with, say, south Raleigh. I also felt safer out in North Raleigh. Jason didn't have a job yet when we were looking, but I wanted to be close to my church and the Franciscan School where my daughter went before, because I wanted her to go back there. We also wanted to be close to the airport in case my husband's job required him to fly a lot.

PART IV: INTERVIEWS

What surprised you about the Raleigh area in a positive way?

One thing is the natural environment here. Before we moved here, we had never been to Raleigh or North Carolina, and I was surprised by how visually beautiful it is here. We love the hills, the lakes, the trees, just how beautiful it is. I grew up between Detroit and Ann Arbor, where it is flat and ugly and gray.

We're impressed by the quality of medical care available in the Triangle. I realized just how renowned some of the area's doctors are when my daughter's doctor in Florida referred me to a specialist back here in Raleigh. We absolutely love our pediatrician here, and we are very lucky to be here for that reason because that group is the most recommended worldwide.

While my experience in the area applies mainly to people with young families, I think other age groups also enjoy Raleigh. Our landlord is in his late 70s, maybe 80, and he says he's lived everywhere; he started out in New Jersey or New York once upon a time. He made a concerted effort to stay in Raleigh. He says it's just as good if not better than other areas of the country for people his age.

Anything disappointing about Raleigh?

The lack of nightlife. The first time we moved here, we were just out of college, and wanting to go out to bars and have fun. When we moved here in 1993, I think it was a dry county until just before we moved here. There were no bars. We always felt like when our relatives came in from out of state, it was kind of boring.

The second time we moved to Raleigh, the school system presented a challenge. Wake County is one of the largest and fastest growing school systems in the nation, and its policies call for balancing student enrollment so that no single school has too many low-income students. The result is the frequent redrawing of school attendance zones and, for parents, confusion. Living in a smaller city down in Florida, the public school system was much easier to navigate. We never rezoned. That's a definite minus here. You're constantly wondering if your kids are going to be at that same school the next year. We are hopeful all that will improve now after the recent school board elections [*during which several "neighborhood schools" advocates were elected*].

I say most people would enjoy moving here, but maybe not people who want an urban lifestyle, city people. I have friends that live in Chicago or New York City and I can't imagine them living here. Yes, you can go downtown and thank God there are more things to do now. If someone wanted more of a "city feel" (and us if we were still a young couple and didn't have kids) should be looking at North Hills [*a newly-revitalized area with shopping, restaurants, and condo buildings at the intersection of 440 and Six Forks*] or a downtown area condo.

A lot of people, though, would like this area, including people who have kids. There are great schools and great colleges very close, which is another reason we wanted to come back. I'd love for my children to go to UNC-Chapel Hill, and there are other very strong colleges nearby, too.

CHAPTER 24

JOHN & PATRICIA SOUTHWELL

TO RALEIGH FROM ROCHESTER, NEW YORK

How did you go about choosing where you wanted to move?
We moved here because our daughter and her family were here.

How long have you lived here?
We've been here for 11 years; since August of '98.

What other areas did you consider?
We had vacationed in North Carolina and this was our only choice for relocating.

What have you liked about the area that you did not realize before you moved here?
Everything is relatively new. We have watched Raleigh grow in the eleven years we have been here. When we first moved here, everything was spread out. The city is still spread out, (yet) everything you need is

nearby because you have clusters of communities. You don't have to go downtown, ever.

The medical facilities are excellent. We found that out once we got here. There are more churches than you can shake a stick at. This is the Bible belt. If people are concerned about church, we have gazillions of them.

I don't know whether you want to talk about money, but when we were in Rochester our property taxes were three percent of market value. In Raleigh, they are one percent of market value.

What have you not liked about the area since you moved here?

In July and August, the heat and humidity have been dreadful. It's like you don't want to go outside. On the other hand, you don't have the snow.

What sort of people do you think would like this area, or not like it?

I think this is a good area for about everybody. There are a lot of good jobs for college educated people, good jobs for people in various trades—construction for example. The schools need a lot of teachers. So, if you are a qualified person, a registered person and you have skills, then I think you can find a good job here.

Just think about the opportunities at Research Triangle. Think about all the positions in the medical field, bio-medicine, and in computer software. If you are the type of person who can deliver and produce, I think you will be rewarded here.

What are your favorite restaurants?

We like to go to the Angus Barn. We know the owner. We like the food. We like the gun collection. It's very interesting, guns from the past

100 years or 200 years. We like Sullivan's (Steakhouse), but we can't afford to go there a lot.

What do you do for fun?

Sometimes we go to the symphony. We like to go to the summer symphony series in Cary. We sometimes go to a hockey game. We take our grandchildren bike riding and to ball games and we go walking. We like the beach. We were at Atlantic Beach recently. From here, you can go to the Outer Banks and Wilmington. Also, we have been to the mountains a couple times.

How did you decide on a house?

When we moved down here we rented a home. We decided we wanted to rent and looked around. Then we saw a new home for rent and we liked it. It was a new home that didn't sell. The reason it didn't sell was that the driveway was one-hundred-fifty feet straight up hill. Renting gave us a feel for living in a home here. The homes are different up North. For example, they have basements. Down here, there aren't very many.

One day, we were walking and we walked through a development where they were putting up new homes, and one kind of caught our eye; and that was the one we ended up buying. We knew that was where we should be. The real estate agent for the house we wanted to buy lived across the street from the house we were renting. He was a young guy who needed a mother and he liked my wife.

CHAPTER 25

DANNY & ELISABETH AGOSTINI

TO RALEIGH FROM ATLANTA, GEORGIA

Where were you before moving to the Raleigh area?

We moved from Atlanta in March 2009 after 20 years in Atlanta. We really had roots there. We had family there. I played tennis and had a huge tennis community. I had a network for work where I felt like I could find a job anywhere.

How did you go about choosing where you wanted to move?

My husband Grant's company got bought out by a Raleigh company. We were given the option to move to Raleigh or stay in Atlanta. I didn't want to leave Atlanta. I had a lot going on there. But now that we've made the move, I'm never going back to Atlanta. It was very difficult, but once I went through the door I was 100 percent positive I made the right decision.

PART IV: INTERVIEWS

What made you choose the Raleigh area over staying in Atlanta?

This choice is very fresh: We visited here last September and January, and moved here in March. When we visited we came specifically to meet with schools. My daughter is a special-needs student and we felt her needs weren't being met in the Atlanta school system. When we talked to the people at the schools in Raleigh something just clicked. If it wasn't for my daughter's needs, I think we would have just stayed in Atlanta. It was like a bad boyfriend – I knew it was not right but it was comfortable.

What was your opinion of Raleigh before moving here?

My husband had looked at living here 10 years ago. At the time I was afraid Raleigh was turning into Atlanta north – I feared a huge increase in traffic and uncontrolled fast development. When we came here it wasn't what I expected at all – Atlanta had gotten so big and unmanageable that Raleigh by comparison was manageable.

Why did you choose your particular municipality in the Raleigh area?

We live in North Raleigh in a neighborhood off Leesville Road. We love this area – it has a small-town feel to it. Not everything on every corner is developed. There isn't a gas station or CVS on every corner. There are a ton of trees – old trees – here. No vacant lots that have been clear cut and abandoned due to lack of financing.

What other areas in the Triangle did you consider?

We Looked heavily in Cary. But it turned out Cary was the place we moved from in Atlanta. It was completely overdeveloped. Where are the trees? There are shopping centers on every corner. We pulled out of a subdivision where we were looking at a house and saw a sea of cars.

THE GUIDE TO RALEIGH NORTH CAROLINA AREA REAL ESTATE

If you had to do it over again, would you choose the same area?

Yes, we definitely would. This house, for us, is perfect. It takes three minutes to get to school. Everything is pretty close. Everything I need is in this general area. I think it's pretty. We joined a nearby tennis club and we love it there. We can go from our driveway to sitting down in a movie theater in five minutes.

What have you liked about the area that you didn't realize before you moved here?

I like our neighborhood a lot. I like that we're in a part of town that we see a lot of people walking and exercising. I see people I know whereever I go, even just walking down the road. I shouldn't know anybody yet; I've only been here a few months. It took me years to know this many people in Atlanta.

The people here are very, very friendly and very outgoing with us. Everyone is very accepting and they've welcomed us completely. It's a very accepting place. People are friendly with open hands and open arms.

I also like that I don't have to wait for stuff – comparatively – at the bank they apologize profusely after making me wait for five minutes. I don't have to wait to get a doctor's appointment or wait too long at the doctor's office. It just has a smaller feel to it while being a capital city. Here there are a ton of trees and I like that I don't see billboards. I also like that Raleigh is two hours from the ocean. I didn't know that before I moved here.

What don't you like about living in Raleigh?

I haven't found any restaurants I like yet. But we haven't been going out much yet. It turned out housing was more expensive here, so we don't have as much money to go out to eat. We sold our house in Atlanta for $157,000 and this house is $370,000 and it's a just a little bigger. Another thing I'm not quite sure I like is the school calendar. Both kids are on year-round and I'm not quite sure what I feel about that yet. I really don't have any complaints yet. We're still in a honeymoon phase.

What sort of people do you think would like this area, or not like it?

I think people who would like Raleigh are people like us – people tired of sitting and living in their cars. People who just want to enjoy the benefits of a city and yet feel like they are part of a community. I never felt like that in Atlanta. In 20 years I always felt like my shoes were on the wrong feet. People who wouldn't like it here would be uptight people because it's just too laid back. Also it wouldn't be good for people who love basements – I miss basements.

How would you describe the personality of Raleigh?

I would call it established and understated. There's a lot here – it's the capital – and yet it's a quiet secret. It doesn't have the feeling of a big, hustle-bustle capital city.

If you could, is there something you would change about Raleigh?

I would transplant from Atlanta the restaurants and also the performance venues. I miss big concerts. There are a lot of people who don't play here and go to Charlotte instead. Bruce Springsteen didn't come here, and I can think of a few other shows that passed us by.

What is your favorite way to spend a weekend here?

We have traveled a lot, but when we are here, Friday nights we usually watch a movie. Saturday go to the pool at the Tennis club, we cook out Saturday night. We go to church Sunday, which is new here. We found a great deal more Episcopalian churches in this area and had no trouble finding one we really liked. The weather here is pretty good, so we spend some time working outside in our yard on the weekends as well.

CHAPTER 26

FRANCO & KARLA LUCIANO

TO RALEIGH FROM ITALY

Tell me about yourself. Where did you move here from?

My husband and I moved here from Italy and we have two sons – ages four and five. We've lived here a year and a half.

How did you choose this area to move to?

We chose this area because it's safe, has a good climate and good schools. My husband and I went to the website *www.findyourspot.com* which asks questions and guides you to where you need to be. We wanted a safe area with good public schools that's close to the airport since we have family in Canada and Italy.

What made you choose your current community over others you were looking at?

We live in the Long Lake subdivision in Raleigh [in North Raleigh, off Glenwood, between 440 and 540]. We chose it because it's very clean,

PART IV: INTERVIEWS

well organized and well maintained. We have a beautiful community pool and the backyard lot on our house is nice and big.

What other areas did you consider?

Anything in central North Raleigh. Our goal was to stay in that area for my job since I didn't want to commute more than 15 minutes.

Have you moved since you've been here? What prompted that move?

We originally had a rental apartment in Cary for a few months until we figured out where we wanted to end up. It was too far for me to commute.

What have you liked about the area that you didn't realize before you moved here?

That it's very green and there are lots of stores. Everything is very convenient.

How do you find the weather? What are Triangle winters like?

I love the weather. For me, it's the perfect climate. Triangle winters are perfect because it snows a couple of times a year and it's always above zero degrees. There's enough snow for the kids to play in for a few days and then it goes away.

What are your favorite restaurants here?

We love Brixx pizza in Brier Creek [a popular golf-course community and outdoor shopping area near the intersection of 540 and 70]. It's awesome! We're from Italy and it's hard to find the pizza that we're used to. Brixx is the closest we've found. We also love McCormick & Schmick's for seafood. Also, PF Chang's and Pei Wei.

What about other things to do?

There are lots of parks for my kids. They love to be able to ride their bikes – that's really important to us. We moved here from a place that had nothing but natural beauty, great food and beaches. Here we have everything else – bowling, mini putt-putt. Everything we need to entertain ourselves is just 15 minutes away.

What have you not liked about the area since you moved here?

The healthcare system. We lived in Connecticut for a few years before we moved to Italy. It was night and day better – less copayments, no deductibles. For us, it cost less to have decent healthcare there than it does in North Carolina.

Do you feel that Raleigh is "true" North Carolina?

Yeah, I do. I guess because I work in a high-end hair salon and deal with the public everyday. People say that the area has grown tremendously but there's still a definite Southern culture here.

Many people move here for a better "quality of life." Do you feel this area offers that?

Except for the healthcare, yes. I think the schools are better – and it's not as much of a rat race. The cost of housing is less so you're not as stressed to pay your mortgage but you do have other costs. It is definitely better than the North.

Was it hard to meet others when you moved here?

We didn't know anyone and had never even visited. It was very easy to meet people because most people are from other places. We get invited to so many things that we can't say yes to everything. People are very welcoming and it's easy to make friends.

PART IV: INTERVIEWS

What sort of people do you think would not like this area?

I think people that are from more Southern areas may find this area too cosmopolitan – that it's trying too hard to be too modern. For people who really like a big city like New York, there may not be enough quality restaurants because things can seem watered down here.

How did you find the job climate when you moved here?

I moved here at a time when things were a little slower so it did take some time to build my clientele. People from the South don't like change – they're more loyal.

What can you tell me that would help others moving here?

Get a GPS! Some streets change names halfway down. It's hard to backtrack and find your way home. I find driving on the highway a little bit confusing. If I'm anywhere around Durham I don't even want to go there unless I have a GPS. But I've lived so many places; I find it relatively easy to live here.

CHAPTER 27

TRAVIS & OLIVIA DRURY

TO RALEIGH FROM ROCHESTER, NEW YORK

Tell me a little bit about yourself?

I was born and raised in Rochester, New York. My wife is also from Rochester. I teach language arts to sixth, seventh and eighth graders in Johnston County. My wife and I are expecting our first child.

Congratulations! What made you choose the Raleigh area to relocate to?

My wife's brother was a police officer in Durham and we had come down here to visit. We started visiting probably four to five times a year and would come down every chance we could get. We chose Raleigh because we liked the city better than Durham and it was closer in size to Rochester. It seemed like a good place to raise a family, so we decided to make a go of it.

PART IV: INTERVIEWS

Did you consider any other areas or was the Triangle area the only one?

We also considered Atlanta and possibly Florida. But since we had been here so much, it made us more confident about moving here.

What about work? Did you have a job lined up down here?

I was a professor in New York and my wife was working at a daycare. She got a job down here first and then I came down here and looked for a job.

So, you moved here without having a job lined up. Would you recommend that other people do the same?

I would never recommend that someone make a big life decision without a job – but it can be done. I was pretty confident that I wouldn't have a hard time. I knew this was a developed area and that they were building schools and needed teachers. In New York they were closing schools, which meant less teachers, and colleges were pumping out teachers so the job market was getting flooded. At the time I was 27 and still young enough to make the move.

Was there anything holding you back?

Friends and family were the only things really keeping me in New York. But being that it's only 600 miles away, I can drive it in a day or catch a cheap flight. I have friends in Atlanta, Hilton Head and Florida so it's a good place to meet up.

Did you buy a home right away when you got here?

We rented for about two years in Six Forks Station Apartments [*near intersection of Strickland and Lead Mine*]. We really liked it at first. Then it was sold to another property management company and went downhill pretty fast. We actually got robbed. So we left to buy our first home.

Where did you buy your home?

We bought in Sunscape in March 2009. It's located near Millbrook Road and Glenwood Avenue. We like it a lot. It's a small community that's very well taken care of. It has plenty of mature trees and it doesn't feel too close to major roadways (Glenwood and Millbrook). Our neighborhood is dog-friendly and there are always people walking around outside. It feels very safe here.

Sunscape is also in a very central location. We're four miles from Route 440 and four miles from Route 540. We have easy access to Brier Creek [*the County Club and the large shopping center*] and Crabtree Valley Mall.

As far as residents, it seems like more young professionals live there, but there are some single older people as well. The complex has been around since 1983 so there are some people who have lived there from the beginning.

What things about the area you didn't expect?

This is kind of funny. When we first came down to visit we'd go to this country bar called the Longbranch Saloon [*www.longbranchsaloon.com*]. We'd hang out with my brother-in-law and his friends who were born and raised here. It gave me the impression that this was a really Southern place.

But now you feel otherwise?

Living in North Raleigh, I realize what a melting pot this area is. It's rare to find someone that was born and raised here.

That leads me to my next question. Do you feel that Raleigh is "true" representation of North Carolina?

I guess I do in a funny way. North Carolina has a lot to offer and there's something for everyone. You can go to the mountains, you've got

PART IV: INTERVIEWS

big cities like Charlotte, and you've got the Outer Banks. Raleigh is right in the middle of everything so it makes sense that it's a diverse melting pot with a lot of newcomers, rather than true North Carolinians. It's pretty far away from some of the stuff it's known for – like bootlegging liquor. It's more up-to-date.

Many people move here for a better "quality of life." Do you feel this area offers that?

I do. I love where I'm from and like to go back and visit but the economy has gone downhill which makes times a lot tougher there. A lot of big companies in Rochester have been affected. But then you come down here and RTP is like a rebirth. It's a good place to start over.

It sounds like you really like the area. Is there anything in particular that stands out?

The malls are very well taken care of inside and out. In Rochester, we didn't have outdoor malls but here I find them interesting to visit. We love going to the Streets of Southpoint [*an indoor/outdoor shopping complex in Durham www.streetsatsouthpoint.com*] and North Hills [*an upscale shopping area in North Raleigh www.northhillsraleigh.com*].

We also like to go to Falls Lake and Shelley Lake to walk our dog. We're also right next to Umstead Park. It's nice that there are so many little lakes in the area. Where I grew up in New York, we spent so much time on Lake Ontario and many of the Finger Lakes. Although the lakes here are much smaller, they're still a nice addition to the area.

Also, there are plenty of golf courses at different price ranges in the area. I get to play at Brier Creek because I'm a part-time employee but there are plenty of well-maintained courses that are cheap to play in the area. Also, we're close to some excellent private clubs, including Prestonwood Country Club where I've seen the Seniors play twice.

You said that friends and family were the only things keeping you in New York. Was it hard to meet new people when you moved here?

I grew up in a neighborhood with a lot of people my age. Those people are still my closest friends. Here, I've met people at work that I'm friends with now. My wife and I both work part time at Brier Creek Country Club [www.briercreekcountryclub.com] and we've become friends with a lot of members and coworkers. We also joined a kickball league with Tri Sports [www.trissc.com]. They have pub-crawls and co-ed sports like Corn Hole and Volleyball. Each season there's something different.

What are your favorite restaurants here?

I really miss the food in Rochester. There are certain foods that are just better in upstate New York. I found this place called Blinco's [www.blincos.com) that has authentic New York Zweigle's Hots, a Rochester term for hot dogs. They serve red hots and white hots and it's within walking distance from my house.

Speaking of food, how do you find the Southern cuisine?

Working in Johnston County, I've had real collard greens, okra and East Carolina BBQ. I've never had anything like that In New York. The food at the State Fair (*held in Raleigh every October, www.ncstatefair.org*) is a pretty good representation of North Carolina. I like learning about different cultures. If I go to another city, I want to eat something from that area to get the whole experience.

What about Raleigh's cultural activities? Do you feel like there's a lot to do?

I've gone to Marbles Kids Museum [*www.marbleskidsmuseum.org*] and the IMAX theater. I haven't been to the history museum but my wife says it's an awesome place to go [*www.ncmuseumofhistory.org*) We've also

PART IV: INTERVIEWS

gone to Moore Square Park for the free music in the summer to see "Downtown Live," the free concert series on Saturdays in the summer [*www.raleighdowntownlive.com*]. We've been to Lincoln Theater [*www.lincolntheatre.com*] and to the Koka Booth [*www.boothamphitheatre.com*]. We've gone to the Durham Performing Arts Center [*www.dpacnc.com*] and they did an awesome job with it. We've even gone to Charlotte and Ashville to see shows. It sounds like we've done a lot!

Another thing we like is the Carolina Brewing Company in Holly Springs *[www.carolinabrew.com]*. If you go there on a Saturday at 1:00 they have free tastings. You get a pint glass and they pour free beer. You can probably get two or three beers. Then they talk about their whole process as to how they make the beer. It's amazing that in one little building they make this much beer for the state!

What about the weather? A little milder than Rochester?

It's awesome! You can't beat the weather here. It's not far from being sunny everyday. There's something about the blue sky that makes you feel better. One year we went back to upstate New York for Christmas and were there for nine days and didn't see sun once. That's how I grew up. It would be tough to leave this area.

What have you not liked about the area since you moved here?

I don't like that people don't signal when they change lanes. I don't like the traffic on Capital Boulevard. Really, there's a lot that I do like here. So the things that I don't, really don't matter.

Do you feel like locals resent people from other parts of the country moving here?

I do at times. Less so in Raleigh only because there are so many people that aren't from the area. I feel it more in Johnston County where I work. There's definitely a "good ole boy" philosophy there.

The area is experiencing unprecedented growth. Do you think that Raleigh is booming too fast?

I know some people, especially those from this area, feel like it is. At the same time, if the area will support it, and if people want to be here, then let it be.

What else can you tell me that would help others moving here?

Give it a little time. When you move to a new city, you need to give it a chance. Sometimes it takes a little while to feel at home. For me, it's a world away from upstate New York and I knew I wouldn't go right back if I wasn't happy. There were times when I was lonely but there's a whole city – or two or three [*Raleigh, Durham, Chapel Hill*] – out there and there's always something to do.

CHAPTER 28

LARRY & CLAIRE SCHUYLER

TO EAST RALEIGH THEN ROLESVILLE, FROM CENTRAL PENNSYLVANIA

Tell me a little about yourself and what brought you to the area?

My wife, daughter and I moved to the Raleigh area in the fall of 2007 from central Pennsylvania. My wife and I are both professionals in the Raleigh area and my daughter is a 7th grader at Heritage Middle School. We ended up in Raleigh because my wife got a job transfer and I was able to do the same thing. It worked out really well.

How did you choose where you wanted to live?

We are very much Pennsylvania Dutch people. We don't like to do a lot of driving and city life doesn't suit us. So that led us to the Southall Subdivision [in East *Raleigh*]. We picked this area because my wife wasn't used to driving long distances and wanted to be close to her office.

Did you consider any other areas to live?

We made about five or six trips from Pennsylvania to the Triangle area. We looked at everything from Cary to North Raleigh to Wake Forest to Garner to Fuquay-Varina. There was no area that we left unturned. Places like Fuquay-Varina and Garner didn't suit us because the commute was unbearable. Cary is heavily populated and that didn't suit us either. You get a feeling just hanging out if it feels right.

Have you moved since you've been here? If so, what prompted that move?

We didn't like East Raleigh at all. The crime was pretty pervasive in the area that we originally moved to. We were victims ourselves. After living there for 13 months we moved to Rolesville.

What made you choose Rolesville?

We ended up picking the Village of Rolesville subdivision *[off 401/Louisburg Road]* because we got to know the area and my wife was more comfortable driving further. We wanted something in the country like what we were used to. This month, we will have lived in Rolesville for one year.

What have you liked about the area that you didn't realize before you moved here?

I like the people. For the most part they're very friendly. There is quite a bit to do compared to living in Central Pennsylvania. You can get downtown to the arts. You've also got stadiums that are close by, like the Hurricanes. There's plenty to do without driving too far.

How about the Triangle weather?

This is our second summer and both were drastically different. It was a lot hotter this summer than last. It's a nice benefit certainly for my wife and daughter – they don't like the cold weather. The only downside is that the summers tend to be humid, and along with the heat, it can be unbearable. But I'd take that over negative 20 degrees and 2 feet of snow.

What about dining out? What are your favorite restaurants?

The Angus Barn. Also Shuckers Oyster Bar & Grill. It's a seafood place and it's just great.

What about other things to do in the area?

My daughter has always been into soccer which is big in this area. We like to go to Hurricanes games, NC State basketball and the Carolina Mudcats. We like more of the sporting events.

Is there anything you haven't liked about the area since you moved here?

I will say that aside from the few restaurants we've found, we don't care for the food at all. We're born and bred Pennsylvania Dutch and the food we grew up on is much different.

Do you feel that Raleigh offers the true Southern experience or is it more multicultural?

It's definitely multicultural. In both subdivisions we lived in, I would say over half of the people we knew in our neighborhood were from out of the area. The neighbors to the left, right and across the street from us are from Florida, New Jersey and Oklahoma. I don't feel like I'm getting the Southern culture. I travel through North and South Carolina for business so when I'm down closer to Fayetteville I see more of the typical Southern culture. I definitely don't think you see any of that in the Triangle area.

Many people move here for a better "quality of life." Do you feel this area offers that?

It's a different quality of life – not necessarily better. This is actually a faster pace of life than what we were used to in Pennsylvania. My neighbors who are from North Jersey chuckle – they think they've died and gone to heaven. It has caused us to live a slightly different lifestyle.

What sort of people do you think this area is best suited for? What about retirees?

Younger couples that don't mind a drastic change in lifestyle and culture. It's not well suited for people from the North that are looking to retire. A lot of people will come here thinking they're entering into a slower, Southern lifestyle. It's very much a city atmosphere. If you are expecting a slow lifestyle, then it's not a good move.

Do you think that the area is growing too fast?

Yes, I do. They have no way to control that. The infrastructure is not in place to support the continued growth. The transit system is a disaster – I used to travel 90 miles in about 2 hours in Pennsylvania. Here, most days it takes an hour to travel 19 miles from Rolesville to Cary.

What about employment in the Triangle? Would you recommend moving here without finding work first?

In this climate, I definitely wouldn't move here without a job unless you're in a few key sectors like healthcare. My neighbor is a nurse and found a job within a week. If you're an electrician moving here from Boston, I'd be careful.

CHAPTER 29

TINA FRANKLIN

TO RESEARCH TRIANGLE PARK
THEN EAST RALEIGH, FROM SACRAMENTO, CALIFORNIA

Tell me a little bit about yourself. What brought you to the Triangle area?

Well, I moved here two years ago from Sacramento, California. I'm single and don't have a family which is a little odd here. I wanted to move from California for a combination of reasons – real estate and crime being two of the biggest. I really wanted to buy a home and at the time $250,000 would only buy you a shack in California.

What made you choose the Raleigh area to relocate to?

Someone had mentioned this area to me and I decided to start researching it online. Everything just seemed so perfect – the price of real estate, the mild weather, the job opportunities. Just everything I read made me want to move here.

Did you consider moving to other areas of the country?

I didn't know where I wanted to go, but because this area was recommended it was all that I researched. So no, this was really the only area that I looked at.

Have you moved since you've been here? If so, what prompted that move?

I initially lived in the RTP area [Research Triangle Park] where I sub-letted an apartment. It was really great to be in the middle of the Triangle – especially since I work in sales. About a year and a half ago, I bought in the Hedingham subdivision [*in East Raleigh, several miles east of 440*]. I'm a little more ostracized but I like my location for other reasons. It's a nice golf community and I want to start playing golf.

What things do you like about the Triangle area that you didn't expect?

Everything is better than I imagined. Things are more beautiful. There are so many hiking trails and parks available which was surprising and awesome. I had huge expectations and most were met!

As a single woman, was it hard to meet other people when you moved here?

I'm not having a hard time meeting people at all. I've met a lot of my current friends through work. And I'm constantly meeting new people through them. I moved here not knowing a soul, and that's definitely not the case now. I like getting involved in a lot of things out here – and want to get involved with classes to meet even more people. There are so many networking meetings that it's easy to meet others.

PART IV: INTERVIEWS

What about in your subdivision? Is it mostly families or also young professionals?

People kind of keep to themselves but there do seem to be some young professionals. It seems like a lot of the people are busy but the community puts some activities together. I haven't gotten involved in a lot of that stuff yet.

What are your favorite places to go for entertainment?

I love Sullivan's Steakhouse [*located on Glenwood Avenue in Raleigh's trendy "Glenwood South" neighborhood*] and lots of music venues like a little place called the Berkeley Café [*in downtown Raleigh*] – it's a hole in the wall but they have really great Open Mic Jams on Wednesdays. I like the 42nd Street Oyster Bar [also *in Glenwood South*] and Oliver Twist [near the intersection of Creedmoor [route 50] and 540]. I still haven't been to a ton of places since there are so many new ones popping up – and I like to check out spots that I haven't been.

What about Raleigh's cultural attractions? Have those met your expectations?

I moved here for the culture that the museums have to offer and actually haven't been to any yet. I have been to some art festivals in downtown Raleigh and Durham a few times. I'm dying to get to museums though!

Where do you find out what's going on in the area?

The Independent Weekly [www.indyweek.com] is one of my favorite ways to find things to do. It offers all sorts of information on movies, plays and festivals.

The area is experiencing unprecedented growth. Do you think that Raleigh is booming too fast?

No way. There are still so many areas still left to grow – and so much land right outside of Raleigh that I think there's room for growth. Although I do have a fear that one day our beautiful trees will be knocked down for housing.

Many people move here for a better "quality of life." Do you feel this area offers that?

Yeah, I do. It's not the rat race and there are plenty of business opportunities. For me, it's nice and stress-free.

Speaking of business opportunities, what about jobs? Would you recommend moving here without finding work first?

I moved here without work. I knew I had enough experience in sales and property management and I had never had a problem finding a job before. So I had the confidence that I could find something. Now it may be more difficult – but I'm still looking for part-time opportunities and I see there are tons available. I definitely don't think it's as bad as other parts of country. I'm actually looking to open a home staging and redesign company here in the near future.

What sort of people do you think this area is best suited for?

It all depends on what you're looking for. If you're really young and want stuff happening 24/7 it may not have enough nightlife. But I think it offers plenty. I would tell everyone to come here because it's fabulous!

What about that Southern culture. Do you feel that Raleigh is the "true" North Carolina?

Yes, and I think it's awesome. I grew up saying "please" and "thank you." It's been lost for years and I came here and found Southern hospitality and common courtesy. It seems like a bunch of people who are coming to this area are conforming to that as well. People open doors! I love the diversity too – people from all over the world.

Do you feel like the locals resent people from other parts of the country moving here? Like it's watering down their culture?

I ask people that all the time and I think they're mixed. Some people are a little fearful that it will change what they're so proud of. I do hear comments about Yankees but it's mostly embraced. Overall it seems like most are pleasantly surprised.

Is the cost of living lower in the Raleigh area?

It's pretty similar to other areas of the country. It's not dirt-cheap here but it's comparable and probably less than certain metro areas. I've found that the salary you can get is comparable, if not more. Even checking on what I'd make in California it's pretty much the same– but it's cheaper for me to live here.

What about the weather?

I love the four seasons. Living in Sacramento it would get a lot hotter out there. Summers would regularly be 100 degrees. I'd rather see snow once or twice a year like we have here.

Is there anything that you don't like about the area since you moved?

Honestly, no! My allergies are a tad worse than I expected in the spring and fall. Other than that, I love the area so much that I can't think of anything.

Any funny stories or anecdotes to share?

I went to a music venue for the Derek Trucks Band in downtown Durham. After the show they hung out at the Marriott and I got to hang out with them. That was pretty cool!

What else can you tell me that would help others moving here?

Just do your research on the areas that you want to move to. There's an abundance of areas to choose from. I used the web and checked out blogs on what people said about visiting here, read reviews on restaurants, looked at craigslist.org and read the MLS listings to look at real estate [*go to www.reganco.com, and click "Search the MLS"*].

CHAPTER 30

JAMES & KRISTEN TUGOOD

TO WAKE FOREST FROM WILMINGTON, NORTH CAROLINA

How did you go about choosing where you wanted to move to?

We chose Wake Forest because we wanted to be away from the congestion of Raleigh. I like the small town feel, but we also wanted to be near the things we need. Growing up in Garner, I knew I liked the small town feel with proximity to the big city.

What was your opinion of Wake Forest before moving there?

I was familiar with it as we have close friends who lived here. I knew I liked it. I liked the school system, the coziness and the cleanliness. It feels like a small town but it's really close to Raleigh. The preconception was that it was a little farther out of our comfort zone of where we go. Once we got here and we were looking, we noticed there were plenty of roads and the ease of traffic going to Raleigh wasn't so bad.

What other areas did you consider?

We considered looking in the Falls of Neuse, Bedford, Wakefield and North Hills area. We found a house we really liked in Wake Forest and we got more bang for our buck here as far as price per square foot.

If you had to do it over again, would you choose the same area (What would your second choice of municipality be)?

Oh yes, easy, definitely. Once we got here, we just love our house, we love our neighborhood, we love our neighbors. We like the amenities our neighborhood has. It's a place we want stay. Our second choice would have been North Hills [intersection of 440 and Six Fork in North Raleigh) because it's closer to my wife's family, but we are in the right spot here.

What have you liked about the area that you didn't realize before you moved here?

I didn't realize there was as much to do in Wake Forest. I always pictured traveling to Raleigh for everything as far as eating out and going to the movies. But it has everything so we don't have to travel into Raleigh as much as I expected.

What have you not liked about the area since you moved here?

The traffic on Capital Boulevard can get bad at certain times. You just have to know when not to go to Capital Boulevard to avoid getting stuck.

What sort of people do you think would like this area, or not like it?

I think families, anyone with small children would really like it. There are lots of activities here for small children. The Factory, a great sporting complex is up there, there's baseball fields and tons of parks and

PART IV: INTERVIEWS

playgrounds. People who wouldn't like Wake Forest, I would say would be singles and newly married that still like to enjoy a nightlife lifestyle. It's far away from a downtown scene with the nightlife. It's definitely more geared for a family.

What are your favorite restaurants?

I like Chili's, I can bring the kids there. Really, I like anywhere I can bring my kids. I like Steak and Shake. And I like La Foresta, they have good, really good pizza. Mellow Mushroom is also a good place to go.

Where is your favorite place locally to shop?

Probably Kohl's I guess. Also, I like Target. For other stuff, Wake Forest is close enough to the Triangle Town Center mall – 15 minutes away. I like that because it's far enough away that you avoid the congestion but close enough that you can get something you need pretty quickly.

What is your favorite way to spend a weekend here?

Just hanging out with my kids going to the park. Me and my son play golf – we live right on the golf course. I also like getting out and riding bikes in our neighborhood.

If you could, is there something you would change about Wake Forest?

I wish there was easier traffic flow on Capital Boulevard and an easier route to get to the Beltline, to I-540. An easier way to get outside our area would help me, as my job has me driving all over the Triangle.

189

CHAPTER 31

RON & DANIELLE CASEY

TO DURHAM, THEN WAKE FOREST, FROM NEW YORK

Can you tell me a little bit about yourself?

Ron: We met in Wilmington, North Carolina. We've been married for seven years and have two daughters - ages two and four. I grew up in upstate NY and moved to Wilmington for a job. I stayed there for six years and moved here.

Danielle: I had gone to NC State (North Carolina State University) but moved to Wilmington after graduation.

What brought you to the Raleigh area?

Ron: My job brought us here six and a half years ago. I work for Cree (a market-leading innovator of LED lighting and semiconductor solutions for wireless and power applications). At the time Danielle didn't have a job. She's a teacher and could work anywhere.

What neighborhood did you originally move to?

Ron: We lived in a neighborhood in Durham called Magnolia Place for six years (located North/West of the Raleigh/Durham border off of

PART IV: INTERVIEWS

US-70/Glenwood Avenue *www.magnoliaplace.us*). It's next to RTP (Research Triangle Park) by Brier Creek. It's a nice little community with a pool.

What made you choose that location?

Ron: Mainly because it was in close proximity to my job. When we lived there I had a 10 minute drive to work. Danielle drove about 25 minutes. At the time we choose the house, Danielle didn't know where she'd work.

Are you still living in Durham? If not, where do you live now?

Ron: We live in Wake Forest in the Dansforth subdivision (located at the intersection of Burlington Mills Road and Linslade Way). We've lived here for less than a year. It's pretty good. It has a neighborhood pool and a clubhouse.

What made you move to Wake Forest?

Ron: We essentially moved because of the schools and to get a bigger house.

Danielle: I teach up at Wakefield High School so I wanted to be close to school and be more active in extracurricular activities, as well as have the kids near where I work. It takes about 10 minutes to get to work. For Ron, it now takes about 30 minutes.

What are the differences, if any, between Magnolia Place and Dansforth?

Ron: Dansforth is similar to the other neighborhood but the homes are a little bigger and it has more families. We choose it because it was a step up from other neighborhood. With young kids, we wanted to live where there were other children.

191

And what about the difference between Durham and Wake Forest?

Ron: Wake Forest has that small town feel. (Located in northern Wake County, Wake Forest is a progressive community of over 26,000 residents.) We're right near Capital Boulevard but we live so close to the town of Wake Forest that it feels like a smaller town. In Durham, Brier Creek is on the border of Wake and Durham counties. We lived close to the line and felt safer in Wake County than Durham. Everything we needed to do such as grocery shopping, stores, and extracurricular activities we did in Wake County.

Are there any differences from a financial perspective?

Ron: The higher taxes in Durham County are not worth it. We've noticed that the cost of living is a little cheaper in Wake Forest compared to the area that we lived in before. Also, Durham County has significantly higher taxes than Wake County. But Wake is a more desirable area to live in.

How so?

Ron: In Durham, there are less attractions, less security, and less desirable things to do compared to Raleigh. I'm paying 30% less in taxes to live in Wake County. You're a fool to live in a higher tax zone!

Can I quote you on that?

Sure, go ahead.

Was it hard to meet new people when you moved here?

Ron: No, I think we were fortunate enough to have jobs and met most of our friends through work and a few in the neighborhood. I don't think we had any trouble meeting new people. We don't get out as much

PART IV: INTERVIEWS

as we used to because of our young kids. If we were kidless, we wouldn't have any trouble meeting people since there's so much to do here.

Speaking of things to do, what are your favorite restaurants here?

Ron: With kids, we don't eat out as much as we used to. We do a lot of boating at Falls Lake though. With young kids, we're more involved with their activities, like soccer and gymnastics.

What about Raleigh's cultural activities? Do you feel like there's a lot to do?

Ron: When we lived in Durham, we belonged to the Museum of Life and Science (located at 433 W Murray Avenue in Durham *www.ncmls.org*). It's great for kids, they can go exploring and learn things there. We have not yet gone to the similar museum in Raleigh. (The North Carolina Museum of Natural Sciences is located at 11 West Jones Street in Raleigh. The museum's goal is to enhance the public's understanding and appreciation of the environment in ways that emphasize the natural diversity of North Carolina and the southeastern United States and relate the region to the world as a whole. *www.naturalsciences.org*)

In the six and a half years since you've been here, have you noticed any changes in Wake County?

Danielle: The population has grown and it's gotten a little more crowded. With all the redistricting, I've noticed big changes at Wakefield High School.

When you say big changes do you mean in the population or the diversity of students?

Danielle: It's an entirely different population of students. This is my seventh year there. With busing, there are now different people from

193

different parts of Raleigh. Since the population has grown, now Wakefield is one of the largest high schools in the state.

Do you feel that Raleigh is "true" representation of North Carolina?

Danielle: I don't know if it's representative of North Carolina. I would say that Raleigh is more of a melting pot of people from all different areas. When I think of North Carolina itself I'm used to the Eastern part of the state where it's more rural. As you get to the outskirts of the Triangle, I feel a little more of that. For example, in Wake Forest and Youngsville (located 25 miles north of Raleigh, Youngsville is a growing community in Franklin County) it gets more of a down home kind of feeling.

Ron: I definitely don't think it's representative of the state. It's the fastest growing region in North Carolina and is a melting pot of the rest of the country. Raleigh definitely does not represent the rural areas of North Carolina.

Do you feel like locals resent people from other parts of the country moving here?

Ron: No, I haven't gotten that impression. Most of the people we interact with aren't locals, they're from out of the area. The subdivisions seem to be mostly people from other parts of the country.

Would you say it's more cosmopolitan than the rest of the state?

Ron: I'd say it's more metropolitan.

Many people move here for a better "quality of life." Do you feel this area offers that?

Ron: Yes, I think it's a better quality of life. It's a very good area for jobs, especially in high tech. It's got RTP (Research Triangle Park is the largest research park in the nation) yet it's not urban with a high cost of living and some of the bigger urban problems. But, I guess if the population keeps growing we'll get there eventually.

Speaking of RTP, how is the job climate here?

Ron: I feel like it's one of the best areas to come to. I'm at a company that's booming so much that we're setting records. We may be an exception to the rule, though. I think this area is good for jobs and growth compared to the rest of the country.

What about the weather?

Ron: Being from New York State, I love it. I didn't like six months of cold weather and snow on the ground. Here, it might snow once year and give you some flurries. For the most part, you have the change of seasons, but it's not too extreme in the winters.

Tell me about your feelings on the school system.

Danielle: It's pretty crazy. I feel like there's a lot of growth and we're getting a lot of extra students. Now that we're looking at our daughter starting school next year, you do start paying attention to the constant redistricting and the bussing. All these things are very concerning. Also, with all the budget cuts this year, the class sizes are extremely large.

The area is experiencing unprecedented growth. Do you think that Raleigh is booming too fast?

Ron: Yes, I'm starting to feel that way after being here for almost seven years. In that time, the growth in the amount of strip malls and subdivisions has been really fast compared to where I grew up. In New York State, a new house wasn't built in 20 years but here new subdivisions seem to go up every year. The area is growing too fast for the local water supply - especially with Falls Lake being the reservoir. Traffic is pretty horrible sometimes. Yeah, I think it's growing too fast.

What else can you tell me that would help others moving here?

Danielle: Definitely make sure you see the area before you decide where you want to end up. I think that's one of the biggest things. Don't rush into buying a house. It seems like the Raleigh Durham area has so many different parts - like Cary, North Raleigh and Wake Forest. Each area has its own positives and negatives.

Ron: Do not settle. Make sure you write a detailed list of what you want and don't want - and don't settle for less. Get yourself a darn good person who knows the area, either a friend or a real estate agent before you buy a home.

Are you happy with your decision to relocate here?

Danielle: Overall, we've been very happy here. We talked about moving to other places in North Carolina, and other states, but we've been very happy here and there seems to be a lot that Raleigh offers.

CHAPTER 32

JANE MITCHELL

TO CARY FROM HOWARD COUNTY, MARYLAND

Tell me a little about yourself. What brought you to the Raleigh area?

I've been a single mom for the past ten years. I moved to North Carolina from Maryland in November of 2006. I had been living in Howard County, Maryland for 30 years and was ready for something different.

In what part of the Triangle do you live?

I live in Oxxford Hunt in Cary. It's right off of West Chatham Street and Cary Parkway. I've been in the same place since I moved here.

That sounds like a convenient area.

It is. I'm pretty much near everything – Apex, Holly Springs, Fuquay-Varina and, of course, Raleigh.

Were there any other areas in North Carolina that you were considering?

Wilson [*located about 50 miles east of Raleigh*] was one of the first places I looked. I knew someone who lived there and they said it was quiet and laid back. However, when I went there and looked it seemed to be really difficult to find a career where I could thrive. I also considered Chapel Hill but I was a little leery of having two kids at home and living in a college town. The housing was more expensive in Chapel Hill, too.

What stood out about Cary in particular?

Cary just seemed to have convenience and more opportunities for work than Wilson. When I moved here, the housing was extremely affordable. Cary was rated well in Money Magazine too.

Have you moved since you've been here?

No, but lately I've been considering moving out of Cary because it's very restrictive in some respects. The HOAs [*Home Owner Associations*] are extremely persnickety. In fact, one of my neighbors actually got a ticket on her trashcan because it wasn't on the side of her house. It is controlling with lots of rules and regulations. I guess that can be a benefit too, but it bothers me.

Was it hard to meet others when you moved here?

When I arrived, I didn't know one person. At first I met people through my kids. Then after a year I needed health insurance and got a job at Starbucks. I worked there for about a year and that's how I met a lot of people. It's hard to meet people if you don't work outside the home. I have a friend here that's new and works out of her home. She has to go online and join interest groups to meet people. There are plenty of nice people around here.

PART IV: INTERVIEWS

What do you like about the area that you didn't expect before you moved here?

I like that, for the most part, it's well kept and nicely landscaped in common areas. I like the convenience of everything. When I moved here, I wanted my kids to be able to walk places – and there are shopping areas that are close by. Also, there are parks everywhere. Bond Lake is practically in our neighborhood.. In Bond Park there are boat rentals, trails, a playground, baseball fields, a senior center, and an amphitheater. They also have events there – for example, during the election Bill Clinton was at the senior center giving a speech.

What are your favorite activities here?

I feel like it's pretty typical of a suburb. The parks are probably the things that set it apart a little more than most suburbs. As far as activities, my kids like to go out in paddleboats and also swim. That's one thing I like about this area – a lot of the neighborhoods have pools and tennis courts. There are a lot of great places to do yoga also. My daughter started taking yoga classes at Triangle Pilates and is now majoring in Traditional Eastern Arts in college.

What about the arts and cultural events in the Triangle?

The festivals have been really popular with my kids. Bond Park has an arts and crafts festival. In old Cary they have an arts festival. The addition of the Durham Performing Arts Center and having concert venues close by like the Koka Booth Amphitheater have been great.

How do you find the weather here?

The winters are quite mild. As for the snow, we actually get enough to make me not miss it. It's here for a couple of days and it's fun – then we're back to the 50s. The only thing I don't like is trying to drive with people who have no experience driving in bad weather. The first year we were here they were predicting snow – nothing had fallen and school was closed. It snowed from 9-11 AM and had melted before the kids would have been out of school. It's kind of entertaining!

Is there anything you don't like about the area?

I really don't like how crowded it has gotten, especially regarding the schools. My son has been at the same school since he graduated 5th grade. This year they've started busing in other kids which resulted in him being redistricted. Luckily I was able to negotiate that he stay, but he now has no transportation. So I have to drive him to and from school everyday. It seems to be a pretty big problem here – keeping up with growth. Also, the roads are terrible most of the time. Again, they're struggling to keep up with massive growth. The growing pains make it difficult at times.

Do you feel that Raleigh is "true" North Carolina?

It doesn't really feel like the South. You can drive an hour west and feel like you're in a whole different state. My friends in Maryland used to tease me about moving to the South. Then they came here and it felt just like home. I ran into a lady yesterday and she said 'the Yankees are taking over and we can't stop it'.

Many people move here for a better "quality of life." Do you feel this area offers that?

Yes, actually I think it does. When I go back to Maryland, as soon as I cross over the Wilson Bridge, I feel my blood pressure rise. It's easier here to relax.

Any specific reasons why you think that?

It's just the overall atmosphere here – the way people move around the area.

PART IV: INTERVIEWS

Who do you think would like this area – or not like it?

It's really difficult to live here without at least a Bachelors degree. I've seen that even menial jobs require that. I think you probably should be educated if you relocate to this area. The Triangle area is actually rather diverse and I think really anyone could find a place to fit in and feel comfortable.

What about the job climate here? Would you recommend moving here without finding work first?

No, absolutely not. I don't think this is the place to come to look for a job. I've been unemployed since January and I can't find a job. Now I'm trying to get my license to practice real estate. I could probably find work at a restaurant, but not at a major corporation without knowing someone or having a really advanced degree. I've never had a harder time earning an income than I have here.

Many people claim that the cost of living is lower in the Raleigh area compared to other parts of the country. Do you feel this is true?

The housing costs are lower but everything else is as much, or more than, what I'm used to. I almost fainted when I got my first water bill. It was $90 for one month! We're also taxed on groceries and cars – these are things that I didn't look into because I got distracted by housing. That was huge motivator, but I do wish I had looked more at the little things.

CHAPTER 33

DAVIS & SIMONE CANTON

TO CARY FROM MEMPHIS, TENNESSEE

Where did you move here from?

We moved from Collierville, Tennessee, which is a suburb of Memphis, and relocated with my husband's company.

How long have you lived here?

We've lived here for thirteen months. We are both originally from Greensboro, so we were excited to come back to North Carolina.

What have you liked and disliked about the area?

We were definitely excited to come back to North Carolina and have both the beach and mountains so easily accessible. It's nice to get away for weekend – this weekend we went to the mountains. And we can go to the beach for a day. There's a nice change of scenery – from mountains to the beach.

PART IV: INTERVIEWS

This area has much more of a bigger city feel. One thing I don't get here versus Tennessee – we don't get the quaint feeling of smaller town in your area. My husband had to drag me back. He was the one leaping across mountains to get here. Traffic is a minus. In Cary, especially, the way the roads are set up, you don't go from Point A to Point B; there's not a normal grid pattern. Roads are the most confusing thing here.

One of the pluses is having colleges nearby and some of the performing arts. We have season tickets to the Durham Performing Arts Center and to the Durham Bulls games. We've also gone to a few things at RBC, most recently the Cirque Dreams show.

Why did you choose your particular municipality in the Raleigh area?

We chose Cary solely based on the schools. We have a 10th grader, 5th grader, and a 3-year-old. We moved from a much smaller town, but knowing what I know now –the schools were number one priority. We've moved a number of times, and schools are the biggest factor in the kids' lives and our lives. While there are things about Cary I don't adore, they're in good schools.

What sort of people do you think would like this area, or not like it?

I don't know how to tell people what to choose. When people move here – they know what they're looking for in home life. The great thing about Raleigh is that there's so much to offer for so many different people. Cary is great for families. Raleigh is a great fit for singles and young married couples. There's a lot of diversity. It's easy to find something to interest anyone.

THE GUIDE TO RALEIGH NORTH CAROLINA AREA REAL ESTATE

How do you like the neighborhood and home you've chosen?

Long-term, we got a good value for our money in a house. We absolutely love the neighborhood that we're in. It's all new construction. We're pleased with the builder, and it's a great neighborhood with tons of kids and a nice pool and playground. There's also a nice mix of couples with no kids and also older couples. It's becoming an active neighborhood with a lot of social groups. We've found a lot of new people and made friends in the neighborhood and with our kids' friends' families.

What are your favorite restaurants?

There's definitely a better restaurant selection here. We like Stonewood Tavern in Cary, and going into Raleigh, we like Solas and The Red Room.

CHAPTER 34

DAVE CREAGER

TO APEX FROM ST PAUL, MINNESOTA

Tell me a little about yourself and what brought you to the area?

I've lived in Apex for 13 years now and own two businesses – Neighbor Boy Inc, which is a residential lawn maintenance company, and also a Christmas tree lot that I run every year. My business really determined where I would live. It really blossomed in the Apex area, and that's where I ended up settling.

Where did you move here from?

I grew up outside of St. Paul, Minnesota, near Bald Eagle Lake. After going to school in Wisconsin, my wife at the time and I moved to the Triangle so she could go to Duke for grad school. I first lived in Cary, which was a great experience, but I noticed that almost everyone was a transplant from the Northeast. I really wanted to live among North Carolinians, and lived briefly in Angier, which was great. I worked doing pig pickings for a while and it gave me a great sense for that part of North Carolina's culture. I found that people down here are really open, which was refreshing. Once my work really took off in the Apex area, I moved there.

Who do you think would like this area, or not like it?

The Raleigh area in general is great because it's just not intimidating, the way Chicago or New York might be. Everyone is really friendly, and the city is small enough that it feels manageable. You have more privacy here and definitely less of the hustle and bustle of a really big city. Apex, in particular, is great for people who love to be outdoors. We are so close to Jordan Lake, and there are lots of hunting and fishing opportunities here. There are also lots of golf courses in the area, which is great if you are a golfer – they are gorgeous courses and fun to play. It's also very family friendly, with lots of schools and housing and tons of stores that are just a few minutes away.

Why did you choose Apex in particular? If you had to do it over again, would you choose the same area?

I loved Apex from the start. It has that small-town feel but also has all the conveniences of a big town. It's much less congested than other areas in and around Raleigh. Holly Springs and Fuquay-Varina were other options for me, because they are somewhat similar to Apex – they also are quieter and more small town-ish. But, because of my business and the overall appeal of Apex, that's where I settled.

What have you liked about the area that you didn't realize before you moved here?

I did not expect that Apex would grow as quickly as it has. For me, this has been terrific because as the residential areas grow, so does my business. This has been a great boon for me. I didn't at all expect it when I first settled here, but it's been a good thing for the area. I also discovered that my neighbors, and most everyone in Apex, are just really good

PART IV: INTERVIEWS

people. They have good values, similar to my own and have made this a really welcoming place to be.

Do you have any favorite local restaurants?

I don't go out to eat too much – I really enjoy cooking for myself and my girlfriend, so we stay in and cook a lot. There is one really good Mexican restaurant that we like, La Rancherita. The food there is always good, and it's locally owned. Another little place we sometimes go is Daniel's, which is an Italian restaurant with just really good food. There are chain restaurants here too, but those two are locally owned.

What are your favorite things to do here?

I am at Jordan Lake nearly every weekend, just enjoying the open air and everything they have to offer, It's sort of become my "church". Coming from Minnesota, I grew up playing hockey, so I love going to Hurricanes games. I've become really involved in coaching a youth hockey league and playing in a league myself. We also love the mountain biking around the area. There are tons of trails in both Raleigh and other parts of the Triangle and we've had fun exploring them.

What activities do you like on weekends, any areas close by to visit for fun?

Outside of what I've already mentioned, the golf around here is fantastic. I have been a member of the Preserve at Jordan Lake for some time, and love to get out and play whenever I can. There are golf courses and clubs all over the area, so there are lots of opportunities for new challenges and experiences. Since being here, my handicap is just a 2!

What else might people be interested in knowing about Apex?

It just really has a homey feeling to it – many of the businesses are family owned and have been in the families for multiple generations.

They know your name when you walk in, and really look out for you. Apex has great housing and education, but also a fantastic quality of life. Even though it's getting bigger, it still maintains that small-town feel. It's just good living.

CHAPTER 35

KEN & SHELLY CAMP

TO HOLLY SPRINGS FROM DUXFORD, MASSACHUSETTS

Tell me a little about yourself.

I'm a 36 year-old woman originally from Duxbury, Massachusetts. I'm married and have three daughters – ages four, two and two.

Why did you choose to move to the Raleigh area?

My husband and I were tired of the high cost of living and long winters in Massachusetts. I worked for Fidelity Investments and they were relocating employees to the Raleigh area. My husband applied for a job and within six months we had been relocated here. We liked that the Raleigh area had mild winters, affordable real estate and family-friendly amenities.

Why did you pick the town of Holly Springs?

We came down to the area for two house hunting trips and kept being drawn to Holly Springs. We loved that the community still has that small-town, rural feel but is just 20 minutes from downtown Raleigh. From a real estate perspective, we liked that Holly Springs offers us more for our money. Since it's a growing town we felt it would be exciting to be part of a community that is "up and coming."

If you had to do it all over again, would you pick Holly Springs or would you consider another area?

I don't regret one thing about moving to Holly Springs. We love the town and the Sunset Oaks subdivision that we live in. Having moved here knowing just about no one, we like how easy it is to meet others. We now have friends who hail from all over the United States. I would move here all over again! In fact, if we found ourselves financially able to upgrade, we'd probably stay right in the Sunset Oaks subdivision and buy a more custom home.

What do you like most about the Raleigh area?

From the very first trip I took to Raleigh, I was amazed at how "easy" it was to live here. The area has so much to offer its residents – from family-friendly events like Bug Fest to outdoor recreation at Umstead State Park to upscale shopping at North Hills and Cameron Village. There really is something for everyone. Having lived in Boston for five years, I actually prefer Raleigh. It's got big city amenities with a small town sensibility.

What disappoints you about the Raleigh area?

That's a tough one. Our kids are not old enough for public school yet, but it concerns me that there's so much overcrowding and I'm disappointed that these issues haven't been worked out yet. I'm also a bit dissatisfied in the job market. I quit a great job as a copywriter to move here. I've been freelancing for the past two years but I'm disappointed that there aren't more opportunities for me. In fact, the Triangle has a very weak ad agency presence which is surprising based on its high concentration of creative residents.

PART IV: INTERVIEWS

What are your favorite restaurants and things to do here?

Well, I have three preschool-aged children so fine dining isn't something we do much of. However, when we do go out we like Humble Pie, Battistella and Red Room. One of my favorite places to visit is the Raleigh Farmer's Market to pick out fresh produce and meet true North Carolinians. I also like visiting the North Carolina Museum of Art, jogging around Lake Pine, and exploring Glenwood South and Five Points.

What type of people would like the Raleigh area? Which areas are better for which people?

The beauty of living in the Triangle is that there is a community that's right for people in every stage of life. For example, my single sister-in-law lives in Brier Creek and loves the reasonable apartment rents and close proximity to shopping. Growing families enjoy towns like Cary, Wake Forest, Apex and Holly Springs since they have the suburban amenities. Empty nesters can downsize to condos downtown or in the vicinity of Raleigh. So, I think this area is perfect for everyone – with the exception of people who want 24/7 amenities and nightlife that big cities like NYC offer.

Do you feel that Raleigh is "true" North Carolina?

Since there are so many transplants here, I feel that the Raleigh culture is somewhat watered down. I hear the true North Carolina accent rarely and usually find myself meeting people from New York, California and Massachusetts. I don't feel like my children will grow up with the true sense of Southern culture that I had hoped for.

What is the biggest challenge that the Raleigh area faces?

I think the area needs to be careful about not growing too fast. Every time I drive into downtown Raleigh I'm amazed at how much construction is going on. The same is true for suburban areas like Apex and Holly

Springs. I hope these areas are smart in their development and retain their culture before the area turns into "Anyplace, USA."

Many people claim that the cost of living is lower in the Raleigh area compared to other parts of the country. Do you feel this is true?

I think this is one of the biggest misconceptions about the Raleigh area. When we were researching moving here, I kept hearing how much cheaper it was. While we were able to get more for our money in terms of real estate – I think the cost of groceries and gas is just as expensive, if not more, than the Boston suburb we moved here from.

CHAPTER 36

BRIAN & SAMANTHA JARMAN

TO FUQUAY-VARINA FROM WASHINGTON D.C.

Tell me a little bit about yourself.

I'm 31 years old and have been married for going on nine years. I have two children, ages three and one month. I'm an artist and a graphic designer, an adventurous type.

Are you from the Raleigh area?

No, I was born and raised in Cleveland, Ohio. I went to school at Pratt Institute in New York City. It's an art and design college. I've lived in Los Angeles, New York and Washington D.C. That's where we moved here from.

What made you move from D.C. to the Triangle?

About two and a half years ago, my wife and I went to a family reunion in Winston-Salem [*located about 75 miles west of the Triangle*]. We really liked the family aspect of North Carolina and the friendly people.

THE GUIDE TO RALEIGH NORTH CAROLINA AREA REAL ESTATE

We also liked that it wasn't as crowded as some of the areas that we previously lived. In the Triangle, you have a lot of areas to see, there's not just Wake County, you have Chapel Hill, Durham, and other outlying areas.

Where in the Triangle did you move to?

We live in Fuquay-Varina in the Park Grove subdivision, which is off of Route 55 and Old Powell Road.

Was Fuquay-Varina the only town you looked at?

It's a long story but when we first came here we saw a lot of homes in the Cary and Durham areas. We bid on a house in Preston [*near Cary Parkway and Davis Drive in Cary*] but someone came in with cash and bought it. We gave up and then saw the house in Fuquay-Varina and bought it.

How do you like Fuquay? Do you find it a far commute to other parts of the Triangle?

We like Fuquay-Varina because of its small town atmosphere. It's a nice in-between area. I work at the United Way of the Greater Triangle. We have outreaches in Wake, Durham, Orange, and Johnston Counties. So, living in Fuquay-Varina is a nice place to access those areas. My wife works at SAS, and we work close to each other. It's good for our children because there's not a lot of mileage between home and work.

Did you consider any other areas or was the Triangle the only one?

We also considered Charlotte and some other areas. We landed in Wake County because the schools are good and once we visited it we found it to be really nice.

PART IV: INTERVIEWS

Speaking of visits, how many times did you come down here?

We came down five times to visit and got to know the area a little bit too well.

How so?

Well, you start to know where you want to live and either it's out of your price range or not the right house. We saw something different every time we came back.

Did you have your job lined up from the United Way when you moved here?

No, we didn't have jobs for a year. It was very stressful. I thought it would be easier since the area is ranked one of the best places to live. It takes a little longer to get employment here than in a bigger city.

That must have been incredibly stressful. Would you recommend that others find work before they move here?

I would probably recommend having a job if you can. However, North Carolina is very family and friend-oriented. If you know people you can live with during the job search, then come down. I also think North Carolina is a great place for independent businesses. I had my own business coming here to supplement our income while I was looking for a regular job. I did murals and paintings and it was very lucrative because there are a lot of families in the area.

Did you know anyone in the area before you arrived?

My wife has cousins in Cary that showed us around which helped. You can get a lot of assistance from people that know the area and they can guide you to different places.

THE GUIDE TO RALEIGH NORTH CAROLINA AREA REAL ESTATE

Was it easy to make friends here?

One of the easiest things to do here is meet people. It's important to extend friendship first and not be shy because a lot of people here have a lot of history. They were either born and raised here, moved away and came back, or people like me who heard a rumor that this is the place to live.

How would you describe real estate in this area?

There are a lot of different options for families. There are condominiums, townhomes, 1-story houses, some with basements. Depending on where you live, you can have a lot of land. Some people want that because of the American Dream. As far as housing, it's a little cheaper but still up there with the norm. It's slowly creeping up – I feel that in about five or six years it will be very expensive to live here.

Did anything surprise you about the area?

This area is more spread out than you might expect, so make sure you have a good car! Also, people think it's a lot of Southerners. Most people you meet aren't from here; it's a lot of different cultures. Also, you can get an urban experience here. A lot of things here feel like they did in New York and LA.

Really? Like what?

The youth, the urban landscape – especially in Downtown Raleigh and Durham. Progressive people are moving here and businesses and restaurants are marketing to younger people.

Speaking of restaurants, what's your favorite in the area?

Red Hot and Blue is good. [Located at 6615 Falls of Neuse Road and 1900 Hillsborough Street in Raleigh *www.redhotandblue.com*.] A lot of the local restaurants are very good and beat out the chains. It's a mix here – a lot of variety like great pizza, Thai, Chinese and Indian foods.

So, do you like the Southern cuisine?

Well, the Southern cuisine is great, of course. I'm still not sure about the BBQ, but otherwise it's great.

What about culture in the Triangle?

For kids, Marbles Kids Museum [*www.marbleskidsmuseum.org*] is very nice. The $1.50 movies are great by NC State. [The NCSU Campus Cinema offers $1.50 movies for NC State students and $2.50 for non-students. Located where Cates Avenue ends at Dan Allen Drive on the NC State campus]. Pullen Park is also very nice. [Founded in 1887, Pullen Park features a carousel, train ride, lake, theater and more. It's located at 408 Ashe Avenue in Raleigh.]

What about the area's natural resources?

Oh yeah, in your backyard is nature which is what draws a lot of people here. I remember being in New York and wanting to see a tree! There are so many places to find a park or a lake or pond. They're very clean and accessible too.

Many people move here for a better "quality of life." Do you feel this area offers that?

Yes, I definitely do. In recent years though it's starting to feel more of a metropolitan type of city, which I think is happening with a lot of cities across the United States. The whole gentrification and making everything look the same.

THE GUIDE TO RALEIGH NORTH CAROLINA AREA REAL ESTATE

What about the weather here?

It's cold but dry in the winter. There's maybe one day of snow. I see people running with shorts on in the winter. In the summer, some days are hot but there are places to go to get out of the sun. It's not unbearable.

Do you feel that Raleigh is "true" representation of North Carolina?

I think it is the true North Carolina but also feel that what makes North Carolina appealing are the different aspects of it. There is the city but down the street you might have a farm. I think it's a mix, which is great. You still can get the local customs and local foods.

That leads me to my next question. Do you feel like locals resent people from other parts of the country moving here?

No, actually. I think people coexist pretty well. There's enough room for different sections of society to live in.

The area is experiencing unprecedented growth. Do you think that Raleigh is booming too fast?

I attended a Rotary Club meeting where a guy from the planning committee spoke about the growth of Raleigh. He said they have a 20-year-plan so I think they anticipate the growth here and are making a lot of long strides. I think they're preparing adequately.

What else can you tell me that would help others moving here?

Make sure you can afford your lifestyle so you can enjoy what's here. I know some people buy a big house and all they have is the house. It might be great to start off small and then have extra income to enjoy other things about the area. The weather is good so you can be outside. Be friendly to people because they're friendly here. Just enjoy life here. It's as good as it gets.

CHAPTER 37

BOBBY UPSHAW

TO GARNER FROM WILMINGTON, NORTH CAROLINA

Tell me a little about yourself and what brought you to the area?

I'm a North Carolina native – I grew up near Lumberton and then spent some time in Wilmington before finally moving to Garner for work. Now I work for a moving and storage company in the area, and have been here since 1994. I have actually lived in Garner twice, with a brief stint in the Brier Creek area in between.

How did you go about choosing where you wanted to move?

It was just luck that brought me to Garner the first time around, but when I moved here last year it was because I knew my realtor through work. Garner was one area that we decided to target because it is so convenient to everything. It feels like living in town, but with a bit of country feel to go with it.

How long have you lived here?

I moved back to Garner in December of 2008, but I've been in the Raleigh area since 1994. It's great to be back in Garner.

What other areas did you consider?

I did look in Holly Springs and Durham, because I wanted to be close to my work. I never really considered the city, because I knew I wanted more of what the outlying areas had to offer – more privacy, a quieter lifestyle. Garner just felt right to me.

Why did you choose Garner in particular? If you had to do it over again, would you choose the same area?

I love Garner, and would definitely choose it again. It is just so convenient – I can get to any restaurant or store that I need to without going into Raleigh. Shopping is so convenient, it's an easy commute to work, it just really is the right fit. Apex was my second choice, because it's a growing area with some great neighborhoods, but I would still pick Garner if I had it to do over again.

What have you liked about the area that you didn't realize before you moved here?

It seems like a small thing, but Garner is planning an extension of Timber Drive, one of the big throughways in the area. Once complete, everything will be just that more convenient to get to. Garner has just proven to be so accessible to everything I need and the home prices are so reasonable. Living here has been a great experience.

What have you not liked about the area since you moved here?

When I first moved here in 1994, the biggest negative was the cost of water – it wasn't until the city of Raleigh took over providing water that the rates went down, and now they are nearly half what they once were. Now, I can honestly say that I don't see any downsides to living here.

PART IV: INTERVIEWS

What sort of people do you think would like this area, or not like it?

Garner is not really a country-club type of community. It is largely blue collar, just down home people. So those who prefer a more upper-class feel might not feel as at home here as I do. But the home prices here are very reasonable and the people here are great. Those who want a place outside the city with all the conveniences of one might enjoy Garner.

What are your favorite restaurants?

I head down to the White Oaks shopping center to eat out usually – there are all the usual chain restaurants there such as TGIFriday's and O'Charleys. I also love the Garden Gate Café, which is locally owned. It's a great spot if you want to go watch the game at a bar or grab a meal with your family.

What are your favorite things to do here?

Lake Benson has lots of activities throughout the year. I love their fireworks on July 4th – it's a non-alcoholic event, so it's terrific for families. Fishing is also really big at Lake Benson. Jordan Lake is also very convenient, and they nearly always have events. It's a wonderful place for picnicking, if you aren't into fishing and things like that.

What is your favorite way to spend the weekend?

I do occasionally get back to Wilmington. I love the Azalea Festival every year. And the beach is only a few hours away, so that makes a nice getaway some weekends. Greensboro is also fairly close, and they have great shopping if you are a sportsman, with Gander Mountain. There is also a Bass Pro shop in Concord that I'll sometimes go to on the weekends. When I have the time, I do like to fish, so being here so close to the lakes is a definite plus.

If you could pick out one thing that you particularly love about Garner, what would it be?

The convenience. I love my home, but having everything I need within easy reach has really been the best part about living here. I have everything I need without having to travel for it, so it's been ideal for my situation.

CHAPTER 38

DEREK TYBOROWSKI

TO ZEBULON FROM NEW YORK CITY

Tell me a little about yourself and what brought you to the area?

My family and I had been living in New York City, where I had a fantastic job with great pay and benefits, but the hours and everyday commute were killing me. We realized that the money I was making wasn't worth the quality of life we were experiencing. My wife's sister already lived in the Raleigh, so we were familiar with the area and had visited so many times. We liked it so much here that we decided to move, and in 1998 we took the plunge.

What was it that you liked so much?

The people here are so nice, to begin with. We really felt at home. The climate is fantastic – we definitely don't miss the New York winters! And, honestly, the low crime rate here is a big draw. Although we didn't live in a bad area in New York, here we really have the security of knowing we aren't going to wake up in the morning and find our car missing.

Who do you think would like this area, or not like it?

Zebulon is not for those who really want a city life, who want to have something going on all the time. It's a pretty quiet area. Although we love that the homes here often come with an acre or more of land, if you don't enjoy gardening and yard work, this may not be the place for you. If you want to know all your neighbors and enjoy a nice, quiet lifestyle, it's the perfect place for you.

How did you go about choosing where in the Raleigh area you wanted to move?

We had been visiting my wife's family for years, and initially bought a home in northeast Raleigh. As time went by we noticed the neighborhood shifting away from what we loved about it, and after 5 years all our neighbors had changed at least twice. We wanted to live in a neighborhood with less turnover, and Zebulon was where we ended up. Here, we know all our neighbors. Families are well established and don't move in and out much. In fact, one family owns a lot of the land around here and we love that - the families here are truly invested in the neighborhood.

How long have you lived here?

We have been here since 1998, and moved just once. Zebulon was the perfect fit for us and we haven't felt the need to move again.

What made you choose the Raleigh area over other areas you were looking at?

We honestly didn't look at many other areas because we enjoyed Raleigh so much from our past visits. This was the place we wanted to be. Of course we had also visited other southern cities, but Raleigh has a unique character that those didn't offer. You see many unique homes here. Raleigh just didn't have that cookie-cutter feel and we love that.

PART IV: INTERVIEWS

Why did you choose Zebulon in particular? If you had to do it over again, would you choose the same area? (What would your second choice of municipality be)?

Zebulon has so many good qualities. We love that people have been settled here for generations, and in practical terms, we got an unbeatable price for the size and location of our house. We couldn't have found anything like this in the city. Youngsville was our second choice, but Zebulon was just a better fit for us overall. It is so convenient to the city and to Wake Forest – everything is less than 10 minutes away, and we have the added benefit that there isn't much traffic coming through every day.

What prompted your move to Zebulon?

We had really outgrown our house in Raleigh. My business here was taking off and we needed extra storage space – and we really loved the idea of having this larger property only 12 miles from the city.

What have you not liked about the area since you moved here?

There can be lots of traffic during commute times, as people come and go from Raleigh, and the school system has some negative points as well. The community is not as invested in the schools here as in other places I have lived. But overall, the good here truly outweighs the bad.

What sort of people do you think would like this area, or not like it?

This is a great place for families or those who want land and privacy, with easy access to the city. But we do spend a lot of time on yard work, because we have so much land – so those who really dislike home maintenance may not enjoy the area as much.

What are your favorite restaurants?

We don't go out to eat much, so I haven't found any great places in Zebulon that I can let you in on.

What are your favorite things to do here?

We love to go biking. There is no traffic to worry about, so we can take our kids with us. Lots of the families here do the same.

What activities do you like on weekends, any areas close by to visit for fun?

We frequent Wake Forest for shopping, and being so close to Raleigh is great for taking advantage of the activities there. There are so many cultural opportunities there, and it's great to be able to take the kids into the city, or just spend a day there. Everything is so easily accessible from our home that we really could do anything on the weekends. It's been fantastic.

PART V

THE NEWCOMER'S GUIDE TO THE RALEIGH AREA

CHAPTER 39

GETTING SETTLED

GETTING SETTLED

So, you've joined the Triangle-bound migration that has made Wake County, North Carolina one of the fastest growing counties in the country. Thousands before you have been drawn here by the region's climate, economy and attractions. Before you can establish roots in your new home, though, you'll need to take care of basics such as hooking up utilities, getting your car registered, and finding a doctor.

UTILITIES

Wake residents have some choices to make when it comes to the basic utilities they use in their homes. While electricity and natural gas options are few, the number of companies offering local and long distance telephone service and Internet access has mushroomed, increasing both the competition for customers and the potential for poor business practices.

In North Carolina, the N.C. Utilities Commission oversees and sets rates for electric, natural gas, phone, water and sewer service. Contact the commission for general utility questions at 919-733-7328 or www.ncuc.commerce.state.nc.us. For complaints about utility services, you should first try to resolve the dispute with the company in question. If you are still not satisfied, contact the commission's Consumer Services Division at 866-380-9816.

Electricity

Unless you are renting a home where utilities are included, your first step will likely be to hook up the juice, so to speak. Despite several attempts, North Carolina has not adopted proposals to guarantee competition among electric companies, as many states have. As a result, you likely won't have a hard time choosing who to pay for electricity.

The largest provider of electricity in the Triangle is Progress Energy, 800-452-2777, *www.progress-energy.com*, which serves most of North and South Carolina. The company charges a monthly fee of $6.75 plus 10.634 cents per kilowatt hour from July to October and 9.634 cents per kilowatt hour from November to June. After you have lived in your home for a year, you may be eligible for a program that allows you to pay a flat rate each month based on your previous power usage.

You may also choose to use the electricity cooperative Wake Electric, 800-474-6300, *www.wemc.com*, that serves much of the county. One of a group of organizations formed decades ago when larger utility companies did not serve rural areas, these organizations are membership-based. You pay to join, but you also have some say in how the cooperative is run.

Natural Gas

If your home uses natural gas for heating, cooling or to operate a gas range or other appliances, you will need to contact PSNC Energy, 877-776-2427, *www.psncenergy.com*, the only gas company in the area, to set up service. The company charges a flat monthly fee of $10, plus about a dollar per therm of usage.

PART V: THE NEWCOMER'S GUIDE TO THE RALEIGH AREA

TELEPHONE

AT&T provides local telephone service to most Wake County homes, but you can also choose to work with a variety of long-distance carriers, including those listed below. These companies will contract with AT&T for local service so that you only receive one bill. Prices generally start at about $20 a month for local service. Plans with unlimited long distance are becoming more common, and usually cost about $40 a month.

- AT&T, 888-757-6500, *www.att.com*
- Time Warner Cable, 800-892-2253, *www.yourtwc.com*
- Verizon, 800-483-4000, *www.verizon.com*

As broadband Internet access has become more common, a number of companies have started offering low-cost telephone service using a broadband Internet connection. Some of the most established Internet phone services are Vonage, 800-519-4007, *www.vonage.com*, and Net2phone, 973-438-3111, *web.net2phone.com*. These plans can cost as little as $25 a month, but keep in mind that if you choose one of these companies for phone service, your phone won't work when your Internet is down.

Area Code

The area code for Wake County and the rest of the Triangle is 919. That includes Durham, Orange and Johnston counties. To the east, it changes to 252. To the west, it will be 336 throughout the Greensboro and the Triad area.

Cell Phones

Both AT&T and Verizon, listed above under "telephone," offer cell phone service. In addition, here are some of the many companies that offer wireless service and phones.

- Verizon Wireless, 1-800-922-0204, *www.VerizonWireless.com*
- Sprint, 888-211-4727 , *www.sprint.com*
- T-Mobile, 800-T-MOBILE, *www.t-mobile.com*
- VirginMobile, 888-322-1122, *www.virginmobileusa.com*

Cell phone service will start at about $30 a month for a single phone, and the prices will go up from there as you add services, phones and minutes. A family plan with two phones and 200 minutes will run about $60 a month with most companies. This is an increasingly popular option, as some families choose to give up their home phone in favor of using cell phones. Many companies offer free or low-price phones when you sign up for their service.

Another increasingly popular option for people who don't use their cell phones much is the pay-as-you-go plan. Under these plans, you pay about $20 for 200 minutes. Usually you have to add minutes to the phone every month in order for the minutes to roll over, or every three months to keep the same phone number. VirginMobile has a variety of pay-as-you-go options, as does AT&T and smaller companies such as BoostMobile, 866-402-7366, *www.boostmobile.com*.

INTERNET

Time Warner Cable, the area's largest provider of cable television, dominates the market for high-speed Internet service as well. Time Warner also offers bundled cable TV, high-speed Internet and telephone service with unlimited long distance starting at about $150 a month. Each is more expensive separately.

AT&T is starting to offer a similar package for as low as $100 a month in some areas. EarthLink high-speed Internet is also available through Time Warner for about $45 a month, slightly cheaper than unbundled Time Warner cable Internet.

PART V: THE NEWCOMER'S GUIDE TO THE RALEIGH AREA

High-speed wireless Internet providers are starting to arrive in the Triangle, most notably Clearwire, 866-599-8559, *www.clearwire.com*, whose portable Internet access plans start at $30 a month. So far, however, these Internet services are not as reliable as cable.

Slightly slower and slightly less expensive is DSL service, which is offered by AT&T in the Raleigh area for as little as $20 a month. Earth-Link, 800-EARTHLINK, *www.earthlink.net*, offers dial-up Internet access in the area starting at $10 a month. Dial-up is also available through AT&T and Verizon, which offers a list of access numbers on its Web site.

WATER AND SEWER

The City of Raleigh, 919-890-3245, *www.raleighnc.gov*, provides water and sewer service to most of Wake County, including the towns of Garner, Knightdale, Rolesville, Wake Forest, Wendell, and Zebulon. The towns of Apex, Cary, Fuquay-Varina, Holly Springs, Knightdale and Morrisville operate their own water and sewer systems. Outside of these municipalities, most residents will use well and septic systems.

New Raleigh water customers must pay a $50 nonrefundable fee to hook up water service. Water charges are calculated based on usage and meter size, while sewer customers pay a flat monthly fee of $6.80 a month for Raleigh residents and $10.63 for customers outside Raleigh.

Water restrictions are common throughout the Triangle in times of drought, usually limiting outdoor watering to evenings and mornings on certain days of the week. In 2008, Raleigh adopted voluntary water restrictions that will apply throughout the year to all of its water customers. Under these rules, customers using sprinkler and other irrigation systems may water their lawns from midnight to 10 a.m. on Tuesday, Thursday and Saturday for addresses ending in an odd number and on Wednesday, Friday and Sunday are for addresses ending in an even number. Hose-end sprinklers can be used from 6 a.m. to 10 a.m. and 6

233

p.m. to 10 p.m. on the same days for odd and even addresses. Violators receive a warning on the first violation, fines of $50 and $200 for second and third violations, and cancellation of service on the fourth violation. Check with your town government to get a list of its water restrictions.

Wells and septic systems are regulated by the county, which also offers a list of people licensed to repair wells and septic systems. Wake will also test well water for bacteria and inorganic compounds for a fee at its Human Services Lab, 919-250-4441, *www.wakegov.com/water/wells.*

GARBAGE AND RECYCLING

The City of Raleigh picks up garbage and recyclable items one day a week from homes throughout the city. The city's Solid Waste Services, 919-996-6890, *www.raleighnc.gov,* issues standard rolling trash cans and green recycling bins for trash and recycling collection. The department also offers smaller garbage cans and help getting them to the street for elderly and disabled residents. Larger items such as rocks, building materials and appliances can be dropped of for free at the South Wake Municipal Solid Waste Landfill, 919-856-6196 in Apex, 6300 Old Smithfield Road, or picked up for a fee. The city also picks up yard waste, which is used to make mulch and compost that is for sale to the general public.

The towns of Cary, Fuquay-Varina, Garner, Holly Springs, and Zebulon run their own solid waste departments. Some unincorporated areas of the county contract with private garbage collection agencies. In other parts of the county, residents bring their trash and recycling to one of 11 county-run convenience centers. A complete list of refuse collection services and convenience centers throughout Wake County, as well as a listing of where various materials should be disposed of, is available from Wake County at *www.wakegov.com/recycling.*

PART V: THE NEWCOMER'S GUIDE TO THE RALEIGH AREA

DRIVING IN NORTH CAROLINA

Getting a license and registering your car seems to require a new sheet of paper every few years, and has almost always required a bit of waiting in line. But you might want to make it a priority to get yourself and your car set up for North Carolina soon after you arrive. You can be ticketed for having an out-of-state license or registration after you've been in North Carolina more than a month. To drive legally, you will also need to buy insurance.

Driver's Licenses, State IDs, and Automobile Registration

Getting set up to drive will mean spending some quality time at the N.C. Department of Motor Vehicles, 919-715-7000, *www.ncdot.org/dmv*. You can find a DMV office or see a full list of the types of identification that are accepted to get a driver's license or register a car at the DMV Web site. To save some time, you can also download the forms you will need so that you can fill them out before you get to the office.

Driver's Licenses and State IDs

To get a North Carolina license, you will have to prove your residency, age, identity and U.S. citizenship or legal residency through a combination of documents. Most commonly, applicants bring a license from another state, a social security card and a utility bill showing a North Carolina address. If you don't have another license yet, a birth certificate will serve as your identification.

The same documents are required to obtain a state ID card, which works only for identification purposes and does not make you eligible to drive a car. A social security card or other proof of legal residency in the United States is now required to get a driver's license or state ID. You will also have to prove that your car is insured.

Drivers as young as 15 who have taken a driver's education course are eligible for a learner's permit, though anyone younger than 18 is considered a provisional driver and is subject to certain restrictions. Young drivers go through tiered rules that become less strict the longer they drive without any violations.

Licenses are issued for a period of five to eight years, and cost $4 a year. Learner's permits are issued to new drivers at a cost of $15 for 18 months. ID cards cost $10. All applicants for driver's licenses will have to pass a vision screening and a written test covering road signs and driving knowledge. First-time applicants will also have to pass a road test. A driver's handbook is available in English and Spanish at the DMV Web site and all offices.

Automobile Registration

Be sure to have all of the documents you need when you show up at the DMV. To register your car, you will first need to have North Carolina driver's license or ID card. To use an out-of-state license, you'll need documentation showing that you are in the military, a student or one of a few other exceptions that an be found on the website or by calling the DMV. The registration fee is $28.

You should have your car inspected in North Carolina before taking it to be registered. Most mechanics and dealerships perform inspections, which can cost anywhere from $6 to $30. A DMV Web page, *www.ncdot.org/DMV/moving/newnc/emissions.html*, offers an explanation of fees and allows you to search for inspection stations. Bring proof of inspection, along with your title, to register your car. If your car is less than 10 years old, you will also need to either produce an odometer statement from when you bought the car or sign one as part of the application. If you owe money on the car, you'll also need a lien release.

PART V: THE NEWCOMER'S GUIDE TO THE RALEIGH AREA

Automobile Insurance

All cars registered in North Carolina must carry at least $20,000 for bodily injury insurance for one person, and $60,000 for two or more people, as well as $25,000 in property damage coverage.

Parking

Parking is ample and mostly free throughout the suburban areas and small towns that surround Raleigh. Downtown Raleigh is a different story, so knowing the ropes can prove helpful.

Metered street parking is available throughout the city at a cost of 50 cents for the set time limit that is marked on each spot, usually one or two hours. Pay stations take credit cards as well as cash. Metered parking spaces are free before 8 a.m., after 5 p.m. and on holidays.

If you wish to stay in the same place longer than a couple of hours, you will have to choose one of the parking lots scattered throughout the city. The indoor and outdoor lots are city-run, and charge $1 an hour or an $8 daily maximum. Available lots will charge a flat $5 fee after 5 p.m. for special events.

Note that some lots are reserved for people who pay for parking by the month. Reserving a monthly spot is likely your best bet if you work downtown. A parking information brochure with a list of available downtown lots is available from Park Raleigh, 919-828-1020, *www.parkraleigh.com*, or by navigating to the "Parking" page from *www.raleighnc.gov*.

Violations, Towing and Theft

Tickets for parking violations are $20. A form to appeal a parking ticket is available at *www.parkraleigh.com* or by calling Park Raleigh at 919-828-1020. An unmovable boot will be attached to a car that has three outstanding parking tickets. If the boot remains on your car for 24 hours, you may be towed. Other reasons for towing include parking in a tow-away zone or a reserved space.

If your car is towed and you have outstanding tickets, call Park Raleigh. If you suspect your car has been towed, but do not know by whom, call the Raleigh Police Department non-emergency number, 919-996-3335.

If you suspect your car has been stolen or broken into, call 911 immediately.

BROADCAST AND PRINT MEDIA

Television

Television reception is spotty in the Triangle if you don't subscribe to cable or satellite service. Most households can expect to get all the major networks without an antenna. With the purchase of an antenna from an electronics store, a household can receive up to 20 stations. For access to the hundreds of stations available these days, you'll have to purchase cable or satellite service.

Cable access: Only two companies offer it in Wake County:
- AT&T, 888-757-6500, *www.att.com*
- Time Warner Cable, 800-892-2253, *www.yourtwc.com*

Satellite service is the other way to buy access to more channels. Those companies include:
- Direct TV, 919-233-0675, *www.directv.com*
- Dish Network, 919-341-1161, *www.dishnetwork.com*

Wake County Television Stations
- UNC-TV (Statewide public television), Channel 4, *www.unctv.org*

PART V: THE NEWCOMER'S GUIDE TO THE RALEIGH AREA

- News 14 Carolina (24-hour local news for Time Warner Cable customers), 919-882-4040, *www.news14.com*
- WRAL (CBS affiliate), Channel 5, 919-821-8555, *www.wral.com*
- WTVD (ABC affiliate), Channel 11, 919-683-1111, *www.wtvd.com*
- WNCN (NBC affiliate), Channel 17, 919-836-1747, *www.nbc17.com*
- WLFL 22 (CW affiliate), Channel 22, *www.wlfl22.com*
- WRAZ (Fox affiliate), Channel 50, *www.fox50.com*
- WRDC (MyTV affiliate), Channel 28, *www.wrdc28.com*

Radio

Wake County radio listeners can access a wide variety of local and national programming through stations based in Raleigh and beyond.

- WSHA 88.9 FM. Shaw University, 919-546-8430, Jazz
- WRSN 93.9 FM, Raleigh, 919-876-1061, Soft Rock
- WSRC 1410 AM, Durham, 919-477-7999, Religious
- WTIK 1310 AM, 919-220-3226, Country
- WTRG 100.7 FM, 919-876-1007, Alternative Rock
- WUNC 91.5 FM, Chapel Hill, 919-966-5454, News, Local and Syndicated Talk and Music shows, National Public Radio
- WXDU 88.7 FM, Durham, NC 27708, 919-684-2957, Progressive
- WXYC-Chapel Hill, 919-962-7768, Rock, Progressive
- N.C. News Network, Raleigh, 919-890-6111, News
- WNNL 103.9 FM, 919-848-9736, Gospel
- WKNC 88.1 FM, Raleigh, 919-515-2401, N.C. State University, Rock, Progressive
- WPJL 1240 AM, Raleigh, 919-834-6401, Christian
- WPTF 680 AM, Raleigh, 919-876-0674, Talk

- WQDR 94.7 FM, Raleigh, 919-876-0674, Country
- WRAL 101.5 FM, Raleigh, 919-890-6111, Adult contemporary
- WRDT 570 AM, Raleigh, 919-855-9383, Christian
- WRDU 106 FM, Raleigh, 919-876-1061, Classic Rock, Adult Contemporary
- WRTP 1530 AM, Durham, 919-471-1530, Contemporary Christian

Newspapers and Magazines

The News & Observer, 919-829-4500, *www.newsobserver.com*, is the region's largest newspaper, with a circulation of about 200,000. Based in Raleigh, it covers the Triangle region with a particular focus on state government. In addition to its news site, it also offers an informational site at *www.triangle.com*. The N&O is also affiliated with a series of local publications owned by the same national company, The McClatchy Co., including:

- The Cary News, 919-460-2600, *www.carynews.com*
- The Eastern Wake News, 919-269-6101, *www.easternwakenews.com*
- The Midtown Raleigh News, 919-829-4538, *www.newsobserver.com/midtownnews*
- The North Raleigh News, 919-829-4538, *www.newsobserver.com/nrn*

Wake County has also spawned a wide variety of local newspapers and magazine that includes:

- The Apex Herald, 919-362-8356, *www.theapexherald.com*
- Fuquay-Varina Independent, 919-552-5675 *www.fuquayvarinaindependent.com*
- Garner News, 919-772-1166, *www.garnernews.net*
- The Raleigh Telegram, *www.raleigh3.com*

PART V: THE NEWCOMER'S GUIDE TO THE RALEIGH AREA

- Raleigh Downtowner Magazine, 919-821-9000, *www.raleighdowntowner.com*
- Triangle Free Press, 919-286-2056, *www.trianglefreepress.org*
- Holly Springs Sun, 919-552-5675, *www.hollyspringssun.com*
- The Independent (a free Durham-based Triangle weekly), 919-286-1972, *www.indyweek.com*
- The Wake Weekly, 919-556-3182, *www.wakeweekly.com*
- The Garner Citizen News & Times, 919-521-5849, *www.garnercitizen.com*
- Carolina News Wire (aggregates state news), 919-788-2090, *www.carolinanewswire.com*

Spanish Language Newspapers

- Que Pasa, 919-645-1680, *www.quepasamedia.com*
- La Conexion, 919-832-1225, *www.laconexionusa.com*

Local Magazines

- Business Leader, 919-872-1590, *www.businessleader.com*
- Carolina Woman, 919-852-5900, *www.carolinawoman.com*
- Cary Magazine, 919-674-6020, *www.carymagazine.com*
- Wake Living, 919-870-1222, *www.wakeliving.com*
- Boom! Magazine, 919-462-0141, *www.boomnc.com*
- Women's Edge, 919-345-9847, *www.womensedgemagazine.com*
- Fifteen501, 919-870-1722, *www.fifteen501.com*
- Women in the Triangle, 919-872-7077, *www.businessleader.com*

Blogs

A number of blogs (that's Web logs to the uninitiated) are cropping up where people discuss all kinds of local issues. These tend to come and

go pretty quickly, but here is a sampling of what's available at the moment:
- Raleigh Philosophical Society, *raleighphilosociety.blogspot.com*
- New Raleigh, *www.newraleigh.com*
- GoGo Raleigh, *www.gogoraleigh.com*
- Wake MyNC.com, *www.mync.com*
- WNCN Blogosphere, *blogs.wncn.info*
- News and Observer Blogs, *blogs.newsobserver.com*
- Raleigh Eco News, *www.raleigheconews.com*
- Outdoor Adventure, *www.takeitoutsidenc.com*

OFFICIAL DOCUMENTS

Voter Registration

Gone are the days when voters were out of luck if they hadn't registered a month before Election Day. In North Carolina, new voters can register and vote during the One Stop Absentee Voting period, which starts 19 days before Election Day and ends three days before. To use this option, show up at any designated One-Stop voting site in the county where you live with photo ID and proof of your name and address.

For a more traditional voting experience, you still must register 25 days before in order to vote on Election Day at your assigned precinct. You can register at any DMV when you get your North Carolina driver's license. Or you can pick up a form at a local library, high school or other location. The N.C. Board of Elections, 919-733-7173, *www.sboe.state.nc.us*, is the place to find all the information you need about elections, including polling and one-stop voting places, upcoming election dates and sample ballots.

In North Carolina, you must be registered as a member of a political party (Democrat or Republican) in order to vote in the primary election for that party. Residents who register as independents can vote in the general election, which includes many local candidates, but not in any race that will determine who a particular party's candidate will be for the general election.

Library Cards

Wake County operates 19 libraries throughout the county, including locations in Cary, Zebulon, Wendell, Wake Forest, Holly Springs and Fuquay-Varina. Most offer computer access, children's activities such as weekly story times, classes for adults, and other activities. A full list of libraries and the activities they offer are available from Wake County, 919-856-6868, *www.wakegov.com/libraries*.

You can apply for a library card at any library, and the card is good for all Wake County library locations. To get a card you will need to bring a photo ID that has your current address or a photo ID with a bill, lease or other document to prove that you live in the county. Residents from outside Wake can still get a card for a $25 annual fee. Once you have a card, a lot of library business can be done online, including requesting and renewing books, using a four-number PIN that you choose when you apply. Books can be returned to any location.

The library system also offers a telephone reference service where librarians answer questions that require short, factual answers. To reach them, call 919-856-6868.

The university libraries at N.C. State University and other area institutions are also available for research, though most will not allow you to check out materials unless you are a student there.

Passports

"Think ahead" should perhaps be your mantra these days when you're preparing for international travel. With the process for obtaining a U.S. passport getting ever stricter, you will need to allow at least 6 weeks to get a passport, and at least three weeks if you pay an extra $60, plus shipping, to expedite service.

The U.S. State Department, 877-4-USA-PASSPORT, *www.travel.state.gov/passport*, issues passports from its 15 regional offices. The closest office to Raleigh is in Washington, D.C., but you can also apply in person at some area post offices. Forms are available at these locations and at the passport Web site:

- Cary Post Office, 150 Wrenn Drive, Cary, 919-468-7182
- Cameron Village Station, Raleigh, 919-833-4918
- USPS Capital Station, 311 New Bern Ave., Raleigh, 919-833-1604
- Westgate Postal Retail Store, One Floretta Place, Raleigh, 919-420-5335
- Apex Post Office, 501 W. Williams St., Apex, 919-362-0395
- Garner Main Post Office, 267 Timber Dr., Garner, 919-779-7331
- Holly Springs Post Office, 112 Third St., Holly Springs, 919-557-3508
- Fuquay-Varina Post Office, North 131 Judd Parkway NE, 919-552-8593
- Wake Forest Post Office, 224 E. Holding Ave, 919-556-8421
- Wendell Post Office, 40 Hanor Lane, 919-365-0657
- Zebulon Post Office, 139 E. Vance St., 919-269-0361

You must apply in person if you are applying for the first time, are under 16 (or were when your current passport was issued), lost your passport or suspect it was stolen, or your name has changed. Otherwise, you may send the forms and documents by mail. Generally you will need to provide a birth certificate and picture ID for a new passport, as well as two passport photos. Contact the passport office for alternative forms of ID if you don't have these handy.

PART V: THE NEWCOMER'S GUIDE TO THE RALEIGH AREA

PETS

Your dog, cat, or more exotic pet will likely find Wake County as hospitable a home as you do, as long as your landlord or neighbors are welcoming. You'll also want to know the ropes to keep your pet legal or safe in its new home. Keep in mind that for truly unusual pets, you might want to check with the local animal control to see if any specific laws pertain to your out-of-the-ordinary friend.

Licensing and Pet Laws

Dogs and cats over four months of age in Raleigh must be registered, and must have a rabies vaccine to register. The cost of a dog or cat tag is $7 each for spayed or neutered animals and $14 for fertile animals. Call 919-738-3463 or visit *www.raleighnc.com* for more information on the tags.

The city's leash law prohibits dogs and cats from roaming unattended within the city limits, though this law is rarely enforced unless there is a specific complaint. Roaming dogs and cats will be brought to the Wake County Animal Shelter, 250-1475, *www.wakegov.com/pets*. To report a roaming animal, call 919-831-6311 or 919-996-1449.

Local laws mandate that pets receive adequate food, water and shelter. Pet owners are also required by "pooper scooper' laws to clean up after their dogs and cats.

Spay/Neuter and Rabies

Low-cost spay/neuter services are available through the local nonprofit Snap-NC, 919-783-SNAP, *www.snap-nc.org*, which also offers mobile services throughout the region. The shelters below in the "Acquiring a Pet" section also offer information on having your pet vaccinated and spayed or neutered. The Wake County Animal Shelter also offers rabies shots for $5 at periodic clinics.

Acquiring a Pet

There are no shortage of rescue groups and shelters where cats, dogs, or even rabbits and birds await new owners. Even pure-bred dogs are available, largely through rescue groups who focus on particular breeds. Most will charge an adoption fee of about $100 that covers vaccinations and spaying or neutering. A good place to start any pet search is with these local shelters, where knowledgeable staff can find your pet of choice or point you to another source:

- SPCA of Wake County, 919-772-2326, *www.spcawake.org*
- Wake County Animal Control and Adoption Center (also the place to find a lost pet or more information on pet ownership, including a list of pet-friendly apartment complexes), 919-212-PETS, *www.wakegov.com/pets*

Pet Recreation

Raleigh and the surrounding towns run several parks where dogs can roam free for a spell without running afoul of local leash laws.

- Millbrook Exchange Dog Park, 1905 Spring Forest Road, Raleigh, 919-872-4156
- Oakwood Dog Park, 910 Brookside Drive, Raleigh, 919-872-4156
- Carolina Pines, 2305 Lake Wheeler Road, Raleigh, 919-831-6435
- Cary Dog Park, 2050 Northwest Maynard Road, Cary, 919-469-4064
- Flaherty Dog Park, 1226 North White Street, Wake Forest, 919-554-6180

PART V: THE NEWCOMER'S GUIDE TO THE RALEIGH AREA

CRIME AND SAFETY

Raleigh, like any urban area, has its share of high-profile crimes. In recent years, the Triangle region has also seen an uptick in gang activity in both urban and rural areas. But generally, the crime rate in the Triangle is below average for its size. That doesn't mean you shouldn't take precautions such as being aware of your surroundings and avoiding poorly lit, solitary or otherwise dangerous situations. If you want to know how often certain crimes occur in certain areas, the Raleigh police department keeps an online mapping system that allows you to search reported crimes: *imaps.co.wake.nc.us/imaps/main.htm?mservice=ralcrime&msize=425*.

Should you need to contact law enforcement, Wake County is served by a variety of agencies that cover every inch of the county and will cooperate on major cases. To find them during an emergency, though, use only one number: 911. For all other matters, here is a list of the non-emergency numbers and jurisdictions for each department:

- Wake County Sheriff's Office, 919-856-6900, *www.wakegov.com/sheriff*, covers rural areas of the county. As a rule of thumb, any area not covered by another agency is under the sheriff's jurisdiction.
- Raleigh Police Department, 919-996-3335, *www.raleighnc.org/police*, covers the city and is broken down into units based on region and type of crime.
- N.C. Highway Patrol covers state highways, 919-733-4400
- Capital City Police covers the state capital area downtown, 919-733-4646
- N.C. State University Police, 919-515-3000
- Apex Police, 919-362-8661
- Cary Police, 919-469-4016
- Fuquay-Varina Police, 919-552-3191
- Garner Police, 919-772-8810
- Knightdale Police 919-217-2267

- Rolesville Police, 919-556-7226
- Wake Forest Police, 919-554-6150
- Wendell Police, 919-365-4444
- Zebulon Police, 919-269-7455

CHAPTER 40

THE JOB MARKET

More often than not relocating to a new city is a life-changing decision, one that can affect your family, your day-to-day lifestyle, and especially your job. The quality of job opportunities tops the priority list for most people looking to relocate, and as such, a city or region's job market weighs heavily on magazines' and Websites' "Best Places to Live" or "Best Places to Relocate" lists and ratings.

Raleigh and the greater Triangle area have consistently ranked as one of the best places to "live, work, and play." And when it comes to the "work" aspect of that equation, experts say Raleigh's job market has two defining characteristics that make it an appealing one for families and single professionals alike: stability and diversity.

Experts point to Raleigh's large public-sector base as one of the reasons it's such a stable job market; its wide base of government employers provides protection from economic slumps. Moreover, unlike other regions that also have strong public-sector presence – namely Washington D.C. – the Triangle has a much more diverse economy. In addition to the numerous local, state, and federal agencies that employ thousands of workers, there are also dozens of large corporations (and many more smaller ones) that employ workers in the areas of pharmaceutical manufacturing, biotechnology, financial services just to name a few.

While Raleigh's public-sector presence and diverse economy make for an overall stable and strong job market, that's not to say it's a job seeker's paradise either. No region is truly recession proof, and though Raleigh has fared considerably better than many comparable metropolitan areas, it's best for each potential job seeker to get the lay of the land and evaluate opportunities relative to their strengths, experience, and professional aspirations. Below is a collection of statistics and figures to help you become familiar with the opportunities that Raleigh may offer.

WHAT JOBS ARE OUT THERE

In January 2008, Forbes.com named Raleigh No. 9 on its list of "Best Cities for Jobs." And while the city has certainly lived up to its expectation, there are a number of industries and occupations that have found themselves to be the best in this "Best City."

Though Hickory and High Point take the cake as the furniture manufacturing centers of North Carolina (and arguable the United States), Raleigh can confidently step forward as the High-Tech City of North Carolina. High-technology companies in fields such as pharmaceutical manufacturing, biotechnology, information technology, and materials sciences and engineering, have made quite the niche for itself in the Triangle (namely Research Triangle Park), and as a result, scientists, engineers, and technologists have been welcomed with open arms in Raleigh.

But for those of you who may not consider yourself quite that tech savvy, there are still a wide range of career opportunities in the Triangle especially in the finance, healthcare, education, construction, and public administration industries. What follows are a series of graphs highlighting the most popular industries and occupations for men and women in Raleigh.

As you look through the data, don't forget the occupations and industries included are only a small representation of Raleigh's overall job

PART V: THE NEWCOMER'S GUIDE TO THE RALEIGH AREA

market. If you prefer to evaluate job opportunities by employer, a section on the area's largest employers follows.

MOST COMMON INDUSTRIES FOR MEN, 2007

- Professional, scientific, and technical services (12%)
- Construction (11%)
- Accommodation and food services (7%)
- Educational services (7%)
- Computer and electronic products (5%)
- Public administration (5%)
- Administrative and support and waste management services (4%)

Raleigh is quite the land of opportunity for professionals in high-technology and other associated industries such as biotechnology. In 2008, AeANet.org ranked Raleigh No. 12 on its High Concentration of Tech Workers list, and it's easy to see why so many tech workers have flocked to the area. With Research Triangle Park and some of the best research institutions in the country headquartered in and around Raleigh, those in scientific and technical services industries are at home in the Triangle.

MOST COMMON OCCUPATIONS FOR MEN, 2007

- Other management occupations except farmers and farm managers (7%)
- Computer specialists (6%)
- Other sales and related workers including supervisors (6%)
- Sales representatives, services, wholesale and manufacturing (4%)
- Electrical equipment mechanics and other installation, maintenance, and repair occupations including supervisors (3%)
- Retail sales workers except cashiers (3%)

- Engineers (3%)

Computer specialists, engineers, and other high-tech-related professionals will without a doubt feel welcome in Raleigh. With multinational companies such as IBM, Nortel, GlaxoSmithKline, and Cisco Systems dotting the potential-employer landscape, there are a wide range of opportunities for those already in high-tech fields, such as computer specialists, or those looking to break into these quickly growing occupations.

MOST COMMON INDUSTRIES FOR WOMEN, 2007

- Educational services (14%)
- Health care (11%)
- Professional, scientific, and technical services (11%)
- Public administration (7%)
- Accommodation and food services (7%)
- Finance and insurance (6%)
- Social assistance (4%)

Raleigh has often been recognized for having one of the most educated populations in the country so it's no surprise that the area offers a wide range of career opportunities for those in educational services. Duke University, the University of North Carolina Chapel Hill, and North Carolina State University are some of the largest employers in the area. In addition to higher education institutions, the Wake County Public School System employs more than 18,200 staff and faculty members.

MOST COMMON OCCUPATIONS FOR FEMALES IN 2007

- Other management occupations except farmers and farm managers (6%)

PART V: THE NEWCOMER'S GUIDE TO THE RALEIGH AREA

- Other office and administrative support workers including supervisors (6%)
- Preschool, kindergarten, elementary and middle school teachers (5%)
- Other sales and related workers including supervisors (4%)
- Secretaries and administrative assistants (4%)
- Information and record clerks except customer service representatives (3%)
- Registered nurses (3%)

According to *Chief Executive Magazine*, North Carolina is the second best state to do business in. Corporations, large and small, continue to relocate to the Triangle in order to take advantage of the region's business environment. With the influx of corporations, Raleigh's job scene is chock full of management, administrative support, and administrative assistant opportunities. Some of Raleigh's heavy-hitter employers such as Progress Energy and Blue Cross & Blue Shield of North Carolina may steal the spotlight, but don't forget about the many other "smaller guys" that have settled down in this business-friendly town.

IN-DEMAND JOBS

With the undeniable presence of healthcare companies, biotechnology companies, and high-tech corporations in the Triangle's job market, it's no surprise the jobs that are in most demand are very closely linked to these industries. The list below includes some of the "hottest" jobs in the Triangle:

- Senior software developer
- Software project manager
- Senior network engineer
- IT project manager
- Pharmaceutical project manager

- Biotech research scientists
- Healthcare professionals

WHERE TO FIND JOBS

Research Triangle Park

Research Triangle Park, *www.rtp.org*, is considered one of the major cornerstones of the Raleigh job market. (It's likely second only to the State of North Carolina, which is the city's largest employer.) Research Triangle Park – or RTP as it's often known – encompasses 7,000 acres and is dedicated to being an epicenter for high-tech research and development. Since its founding in 1959, RTP has grown to be the largest research park in the United States and now stands as the country's fourth oldest research park.

More than 170 companies have offices and/or headquarters in RTP. Though IBM, GlaxoSmithKline, and Cisco are some of most well-known residents of Research Triangle Park, established multinational corporations, government agencies, and small startup companies happily coexist. Collectively, these companies and agencies employ 42,000 full-time employees and an estimated 10,000 contract employees.

In addition to being one of the largest sources of employment in the Raleigh area, RTP also has the advantage of being located in the center of the Triangle. Nearly equidistant from the Triangle's three major cities – Chapel Hill, Durham, and Raleigh – Research Triangle Park is an easy commute for almost anyone in Wake County.

DISTRIBUTION OF RTP COMPANIES, BY INDUSTRY

- Life Sciences   29%
- Information Technology   21%
- Professional Business Services   15%
- Materials Sciences and Engineering   13%

- Scientific Associations and Institutes   11%
- Environmental Sciences   5%
- Retail Amenities and Service Providers   4%
- Financial and Insurance Activities   2%

Source: Research Triangle Foundation of North Carolina, RTP At a Glance Brochure

RALEIGH'S LARGEST EMPLOYERS

In addition to the government agencies (at both the state and federal levels) that have made their home in Raleigh, a number of corporate powerhouses have also established roots in the Triangle. Thanks in part to Research Triangle Park and Raleigh's lower cost of living compared to other metropolitan areas, a long list of worldwide business giants have set up shop in Raleigh, and they've brought thousands of jobs with them.

Below is a selection of the area's largest employers. The list includes government agencies and organizations as well as private corporations. As of the writing of this book, many of the area's public universities were officially under a hiring freeze, but that does not mean these institutions are not hiring. A hiring freeze simply means an organization or company will hire new employees to fill open spots, but they will not create new openings. However, when economic conditions do improve, it is likely these organizations will again be a great source for job hunters.

- **The State of North Carolina**, *www.ncgov.com*, employs more than 10,000 people in Raleigh and the surrounding areas, making it the largest employer in the region. Because Raleigh is the state capital, its residents reap the benefits of having many of the state's agencies headquartered or based in Wake County. To browse current job opportunities and to submit your resume for an opening, visit the State of North Carolina's human resources Website *www.osp.state.nc.us/jobs* or call 919-807-4800.

- **Duke University and Duke Medical Center**, 2138 Campus Drive, Durham, 919-684-8111, *www.duke.edu*, has grown to be one of the largest employers in the entire state. According to its human resources department, Duke has an employee base of more than 30,000 people, which is comprised of staff and faculty members at Duke University and the thousands of staff and healthcare providers that run Duke Medical Center and other associated facilities. For more information on potential employment opportunities, visit *www.hr.duke.edu/jobs* or call 919-684-5600.
- **University of North Carolina**, CB 9100,103 South Building, Chapel Hill, 919-962-2211, *www.unc.edu*, is the oldest state university in the United States and was recently named one of "Great Colleges to Work For" by *The Chronicle for Higher Education*. The University of North Carolina Chapel Hill employs more than 11,500 faculty and staff members. For more information about potential employment opportunities, visit *hr.unc.edu/jobseekers/* or call 919-843-2300.
- **IBM**, 3039 E Cornwallis Road, Research Triangle Park, 919-558-0075 *www.ibm.com*, employs 386,000 employees worldwide. Of those 386,000 employees, 14,000 are based in IBM's Research Triangle Park facility. RTP is the global headquarters for a number of the company's groups and divisions including the Networking Hardware and Retail Store Systems divisions; the Personal Systems Group; and human resources. Moreover, the Triangle is also headquarters to IBM's national university relations and recruiting operation. For more information on potential employment opportunities, visit *www.ibm.com/employment/us/*.

PART V: THE NEWCOMER'S GUIDE TO THE RALEIGH AREA

- **Wake County Public School Systems**, 3600 Wake Forest Road, Raleigh, 919-850-1600, *www.wcpss.net*, is the largest school system in North Carolina. The school district is comprised of 156 schools and serves nearly 138,000 students. WCPSS employs more than 18,200 people, half of whom are full-time teachers. For more information on job opportunities, visit *www.wcpss.net/employment.html* or call 919-850-1800.
- **North Carolina State University**, 1210 Varsity Drive, E. Carroll Joyner Visitor Center, 919-513-1200, *www.ncsu.edu*, is one of the three most visible education institutions in the Triangle. NC State employs nearly 8,000 people, which include staff and faculty for its graduate and undergraduate academic programs and the Centennial Campus Research Park. For more information on potential job opportunities, visit *www7.acs.ncsu.edu/hr/* or call 919-515-2135.
- **UNC Healthcare**, 101 Manning Drive, Chapel Hill, 919-966-4131, *www.unchealthcare.org*, employs more than 6,800 employees in industries ranging from nursing, information systems technology, and support services. The UNC hospital system includes North Carolina Children's Hospital, North Carolina Memorial Hospital, North Carolina Neurosciences Hospital, and North Carolina Women's Hospital. For more information on potential job opportunities, visit *www.unchealthcare.org/site/humanresources* or call 919-966-5226.
- **GlaxoSmithKline**, 5 Moore Drive, Research Triangle Park, 888-825-5249, *www.gsk.com*; Research Triangle Park is the U.S. headquarters for pharmaceutical giant GlaxoSmithKline, makers of well-known products, such as Nicorette, and brands including Panadol, Aquafresh, and Lucozade. It employs 5,850 people through the Triangle. For more information on potential job opportunities, visit *www.gsk.com/careers/index.htm*.

- **Wake Medical Center**, 919-350-8000, *www.wakemed.org*, is a hospital system based in Raleigh. It has 810 beds across its facilities and has medical facilities throughout Wake County. WakeMed says it employs 7,000 registered nurses, technologists, medical professionals, and support staff in addition to another 1,000 medical staff employees. For more information on potential job opportunities, visit *www.wakemed.org/topnav.cfm?id=346* or call 919-350-8140.
- **SAS Institute**, 100 SAS Campus Drive, Cary, 919-677-8000, *www.sas.com*, provides business analytics software and services and is a leading company in the business intelligence market. Though it is a multinational company, SAS Institute locally employs 4,300 to staff its headquarters in Cary. For more information on potential job opportunities, visit *www.sas.com/jobs*.
- **Blue Cross and Blue Shield of North Carolina**, 5901 Chapel Hill Road, Durham, 800-250-3630, *www.bcbsnc.com*, was founded in 1933 and has grown into a company comprised of more than 3,800 employees. In recent years, it was named one of the Top 100 Best Companies by *Working Mother* magazine. For more information on potential job opportunities, visit *www.bcbsnc.com/content/careers/*.
- **Rex Healthcare**, 4420 Lake Boone Trail, Raleigh, 919-784-3100, *www.rexhealth.com*, is a private, not-for-profit health care provider. Its facilities include an acute care hospital, four wellness centers, two skilled nursing facilities (focused on rehabilitation and long-term nursing care), freestanding outpatient diagnostic, urgent care and surgery center. It employs 4,400 people and has a volunteer staff of 1,200. For more information on potential employment opportunities, visit *www.rexhealth.com/Staff_and_Volunteers/Careers/* or call 919-784-3169.

PART V: THE NEWCOMER'S GUIDE TO THE RALEIGH AREA

- **Progress Energy**, 410 South Wilmington Street, Raleigh, *www.progress-energy.com*, is the main electricity provider for the Carolinas and parts of Florida. Headquartered in downtown Raleigh, Progress Energy is a Fortune 500 company with $9 billion in annual revenue. The company was recently named by *Carolina Parent* magazine as one of North Carolina's most family friendly companies. For more information about potential employment opportunities, visit *www.progress-energy.com/aboutus/employment/index.asp*.
- **Wake County Government**, *www.wakegov.com*, employs 4,000 people in Raleigh and the surrounding areas, making it the 31st largest employer in all of North Carolina. For more information on potential employment opportunities, visit *www.wakegov.com/employment/*.
- **NORTEL Networks**, 4001 E. Chapel Hill-Nelson Highway, Research Triangle Park, 919-992-5000, *www.nortel.com*, is a well-recognized leader in high-tech communications technology. One of six U.S. offices, Nortel's Research Triangle Park facility is home to 3,000 RTP-based employees. For more information on potential job opportunities, visit *www.nortel.com/employment/*.
- **Verizon Communications**, 6501 Weston Parkway, Suite 150, Cary, 919-606-1122, *www.verizon.com*, is likely one of the most familiar names in IT communications among consumers. In addition to its many retail stores and offices across the U.S., Verizon employs 3,000 workers to staff its facilities in Cary. For more information on potential job opportunities, visit *www.verizon.com/careers*.
- **Cisco Systems**, 7025 Kit Creek Road, Research Triangle Park, 919-472-2000, *www.cisco.com*; Cisco Systems employs 65,545 workers worldwide, 4,500 of whom are based in RTP. Cisco is a world leading Internet networking company. For more for

information on potential job opportunities, visit *www.cisco.com/web/about/*.

- **Fidelity Investments**, 5411 Page Road, Durham, 877-236-9340, *www.fidelity.com*, provides numerous financial services including investment management, retirement planning, brokerage, and benefits outsourcing services. Its Raleigh-Durham location is one of 15 Fidelity U.S. offices. For more information on potential job opportunities, visit *jobs.fidelity.com*.

TRIANGLE HEADQUARTERS

Although the employee statistics for Raleigh's largest employers are indeed impressive, it's important not to forget some of the not-so-little "littler guys" that have chosen to headquarter their operations in Raleigh.

Those companies include:

- **First Citizens Bank**, 4300 Six Forks Road, Raleigh, 919-716-700; provides financial services to 200 communities throughout North Carolina, Virginia, and West Virginia; employs 5,000 people
- **Red Hat**, 1801 Varsity Drive, Raleigh, 919-754-3700, *www.redhat.com*; develops enterprise IT solutions based on open-source technology; employs 2,800 people worldwide
- **Tekelec**, 5200 Paramount Parkway, Morrisville, 919-460-5500, *www.tekelec.com*; supplies network switching solutions and diagnostic systems; employs 1,100 worldwide
- **PRA International**, 4130 Park Lake Avenue, Suite 400, Raleigh, 919-786-8200 *www.prainternational.com*; provides outsourced clinical services for pharmaceutical and biotech drug development; employs 3,200 people worldwide
- **Headway Corporate Resources**, 421 Fayetteville Street, Suite 1020, Raleigh, 919-376-4929 *www.headwaycorp.com*; provides

PART V: THE NEWCOMER'S GUIDE TO THE RALEIGH AREA

recruitment and staffing resources in addition to managed workforce programs

RALEIGH BY THE NUMBERS

When Forbes.com ranks its "Best Cities for Jobs," a number of indicators are factored into the rankings: median household income, unemployment rate, income growth, cost of living, and job growth. It's these factors that many economists and industry observers use to evaluate the health of a particular job market and/or local economy.

Setting all accolades aside, it's only reasonable for potential job seekers to ask: How does Raleigh fare in terms of these indicators? And the answer is: Quite well.

MEDIAN HOUSEHOLD INCOME

In 2007, Wake County had one of the highest median household incomes in the entire state, "out earning" the state average by $17,000 dollars. Moreover, the median household income for Wake County also outpaced the U.S. average by more than $10,000.

But what do stats like the median household income mean when it comes to things like the "Best Cities for Jobs" ranking? Median household incomes are calculated by adding the income received during a calendar year by all of a household's members (15 years old and over) and then finding the average of that figure across a particular region. This figure is considered to be a general indicator of economic well being of households in that particular region. As a result, through an expert's eye, Raleigh's households as a whole are likely faring much better than their state counterparts.

THE GUIDE TO RALEIGH NORTH CAROLINA AREA REAL ESTATE

Region	Median Household Income, 2007
United States	$50,740
North Carolina	$44,772
Wake County	$61,706
Travis County (Austin, TX)	$53,209
Fulton County (Atlanta, GA)	$58,052
Charleston County (Charleston, SC)	$47,297

Source: www.ers.usda.gov/Data/Unemployment/

UNEMPLOYMENT RATE

Since the economic fall out in 2008, Raleigh's job market has weathered the storm quite well. Even in the face of a volatile economy, Raleigh managed to continue to add new jobs at a rate of 4% during the last five years.

In May 2008 and June 2008 unemployment stood at 4.6% and 5.0%, respectively. In May 2009 and June 2009, unemployment rose sharply to 8.9% and 9.1%, respectively. According to industry experts, the increase in unemployment is expected in light of the significant growth trends Raleigh had experienced during the last five years, but good times are on the horizon, experts say 2010 and 2011 are expected to bring Raleigh's job market back on the upswing.

Even with this seemingly inevitable downturn, Raleigh's unemployment rates still fall below the national average (9.4% in May 2009 and 9.5% in June 2009), demonstrating Raleigh's economic resilience.

PART V: THE NEWCOMER'S GUIDE TO THE RALEIGH AREA

COST OF LIVING

The cost of living in Raleigh is probably one of the city's best attributes. The Triangle offers many of the amenities of larger metropolitan areas, but falls near or just above the national average cost of living. In a way, residents get some of the city perks without the city costs. As such, this relatively low cost of living makes Raleigh an ideal place for families, couples looking to retire, and even businessmen setting out to start up new companies.

According to statistics from CarolinaLiving.com, the cost of living in Raleigh is 0.7% below the national average. Comparatively, Durham falls well below the national average (10.2% below) and Chapel Hill is slightly above the national average at +2.7%. When comparing Raleigh to many other parts of the country, however, it's much easier to see the cost-of-living advantages Raleigh offers.

City	Cost of Living Compared to National Average
Raleigh, NC	-0.7%
Durham, NC	-10.2%
Chapel Hill, NC	+2.7%
Ashville, NC	-0.4%
Tucson, AZ	+0.3%
Wilmington, DE	+7.1%
Orlando, FL	+3.4%
Atlanta, GA	-3.9%
Richmond, VA	+6.4%

Source: www.carolinaliving.com/financial_matters/cost_of_chart.asp
* National Average = 0

A number of other organizations have produced similar cost-of-living figures. The ACCRA Cost of Living Index takes into account the variances in the cost of consumer goods and services for each region and is considered one of the dependable stats on cost of living in U.S. metropolitan areas. According to the ACCRA, the Triangle's composite cost-of-living index is 99.1 (National cost of living = 100), which is considered relatively low for the U.S.

City	Cost of Living Index
Raleigh, NC	102.6
Chapel Hill, NC	101.2
Durham, NC	93.5
Austin, TX	95.5
Denver, CO	105.0
Richmond, VA	104.2
Chicago, IL	112.5
Las Vegas, NV	107.9
Orlando, FL	101.0

Regardless of which data is used, the bottom-line is the same: When compared to other large metropolitan areas in the United States, Raleigh's cost-of-living advantage is clear. While this advantage may not be as prominent with some of the more mid-sized cities in the Southeast, Raleigh still maintains a competitive level when it comes to cost of living.

Combine this cost of living with the other advantages Raleigh has to offer, and it creates an area that bodes well for a wide range of people and lifestyles. For example, Raleigh's affordability, its temperate climate, job opportunities within "industries, professions, and occupations are particularly age-friendly," and quality healthcare make it a great option for retiring couples and singles.

Affordability also plays a key roll in where businesses decide to set up headquarters and satellite offices, and Raleigh's affordability makes it an appealing city in which to do business. According to Forbes.com, Raleigh's combination of strong job growth, low business costs, and a highly educated workforce make it the top place to do business in the United States.

HOW TO LOOK FOR JOBS

Now that you've read about what kind of jobs are out there and what companies are likely to offer those jobs, a more important question remains: How do you find those jobs? With the pervasiveness of the Internet, "hitting the pavement" has been replaced by "hitting the search engines."

Nearly every major corporation these days posts job openings on their corporate Websites. Others may choose to use online job-posting sites such as CareerBuilder.com or Monster.com to get the word out about open positions. As a result, a lot of job-hunting footwork can actually be done by your fingers. Here are some of the best resources for sniffing out job openings in and around the Triangle:

- **Corporate Websites** are some of the best resources for job posting, especially if you have a particular company in mind for which you would like to work. Employment opportunities are usually posted under the human resources sections of companies Websites. Some companies only advertise job openings on their Website so it's a good idea to regularly check company sites to see if anything has opened up.
- **CareerBuilder**, *www.careerbuilder.com*, is one of the largest online job-posting sites available today. According to CareerBuilder, more than 300,000 employers post more than 1 million jobs on the Website. Job seekers can browse job openings for free and can even post their resumes for recruiters to review.
- **Monster**, *www.monster.com*, is another popular online job-posting site. Since its launch in 1994, Monster has become well known as a go-to place for potential job opportunities. Like

CareerBuilder, job seekers can search the site for free and post their resumes for potential employers to review.

- **CraigsList**, *raleigh.craigslist.org*, probably best known as the go-to place to post online ads to get rid of your unwanted junk, is a great source for job opportunities, both big and small. CraigsList has become a main source for job leads as many employers prefer to avoid the costs associated with posting jobs on sites like Monster and CareerBuilder. Job postings on CraigsList can be hit or miss, but if you have the motivation and time to sift through the postings, it's likely you'll find a great job lead.
- **Indeed.com**, *www.indeed.com*, is a great resource if you're not too keen on searching through dozens of job postings on CareerBuilder, Monster, and CraigsList. Indeed.com is essentially a search engine that pulls information down from job-posting sites and puts them into one free, searchable database. Indeed.com doesn't always catch every post, but it can be a great time saver if you're in a time crunch.
- **The News & Observer**, *www.thenewsandobserver.com*, is Raleigh's hometown newspaper, which hosts an online job bank, *www.trianglejobs.com*. The selection and quality of job posting on TriangleJobs.com will likely fall very short of the selection on CareerBuilder and Monster, but there are occasionally diamonds among the rough from local companies that prefer to use local services to advertise an available position.

CHAPTER 41

CHILDCARE AND EDUCATION

For families with children, one of the highest priorities when moving to a new city is finding quality childcare and quality schools. The task can be a daunting one when moving to the Triangle because, like many other quickly growing areas, there are hundreds of childcare options and a large number of public schools and private schools from which to choose.

Childcare and education options can significantly influence where you and your family purchase your home, especially if you're choosing to enroll your children in a public school where location determines which school your child will attend. As such, it's advisable to begin researching childcare and education options as early as possible. Below is a collection of resources that can be valuable in your research. They include a number of local and national agencies and other Websites that provide tips and suggestions, maintain comprehensive directories, and/or operate helpful hotlines in addition to other services.

Please note that the inclusion and/or mention of businesses, schools, agencies, and other service providers in this chapter are not an endorsement of any kind. To ensure your child receives the best care and/or education, never underestimate the value of thoroughly researching childcare centers, agencies, and schools.

CHILDCARE

When it comes to childcare in Raleigh and the surrounding areas, families are not without their options, and more often than not, it's not finding quality childcare that's the issue, but rather it's narrowing down the options and then picking the "right" option that can be tricky and overwhelming.

Luckily, there are some great resources available to families new to the area that can help bring the daunting task down to a more manageable level. A great place to start is the **Child Care Services Association** (CCSA), 319 Chapanoke Road, Suite 114, Raleigh, 919-779-2220 *www.childcareservices.org*, which is a nonprofit organization focused on helping families find affordable, high-quality childcare. The CCSA offers a free searchable online database of childcare centers and providers called the Online Child Care Search. Wake County residents can also call the CCSA's Wake County offices, 919-779-2220, to speak with a Family Support Counselor for assistance in finding and considering the right childcare options.

DAYCARE

Whether you're considering a family daycare home, a childcare center, or a church-organized daycare, there are numerous options in and around Raleigh. For a comprehensive list of businesses offering childcare services, look under "Child Care Services" and "Day Care Centers & Nurseries" in the Yellow Pages.

Carolina Parent magazine, 919-956-2430, *www.carolinaparent.com*, also has a comprehensive directory of local daycares and childcare centers on its Web site. The directory includes nearly 300 providers of all types that serve the Triangle.

PART V: THE NEWCOMER'S GUIDE TO THE RALEIGH AREA

WHAT'S HERE

The Triangle offers a number of different types of daycare options ranging from small-group environments to preschools to more typical childcare centers. The Child Care Services Associations classifies these childcare options in the following ways:

- **Family Childcare Homes** are operated out of a childcare provider's home. As per state law, the maximum "capacity" for a licensed family childcare home is five preschool-age children and three school-age children.
- **Childcare Centers** include two types of daycare centers: (1) home-based centers in which six or more preschool-age children are cared for or (2) center in which three or more children are cared for in a building that is not the childcare provider's home. The latter definition is what most people envision when they think of a daycare. Wake County is home to numerous privately owned childcare centers as well as national "chain" childcare centers such as Appletree Day Care, *www.appletreenc.com*; Bright Horizons, *www.brighthorizons.com*; and Kindercare Learning Centers, *www.kindercare.com*. Branches of the local YMCA, **The YMCA of the Triangle**, *www.ymcatriangle.org*, also offer a variety of nursery and preschool programs.
- **Centers and Homes with a Notice of Compliance** are daycare programs and centers that are organized by churches and other religious organizations. These childcare facilities can choose not to be licensed, but they must meet typical childcare regulations and safety regulations. For more details about these programs, contact your local church.

QUESTIONS TO ASK

Regardless of what type of daycare center you're considering, there are basic questions you'll want to ask to evaluate the quality of care your children will receive and whether it's the right fit for your child and your family.

- **Childcare provider and/or the childcare center manager**: The Child Care Services Association has put together a list of questions (*www.childcareservices.org/fs/checklist.html*) to ask potential childcare providers. The list includes questions related to child-teacher ratios, how staff members communicate with parents and families, and daily activities planned for children in their care. Also look (or ask for if necessary) for the center or home's star rating. All licensed centers and family childcare homes are required to have their licenses displayed; these licenses include a star rating, indicating the quality of the program. A one-star rating signifies the center or home has met the minimal licensure requirements. Centers or homes can achieve up to a five-star rating by meeting higher standards for care.
- **Other parents**: Don't be afraid to ask other parents what their experiences have been like. Ask questions about what they like and dislike about the center's program and procedures, the dependability of the childcare provider, and whether they and their children feel comfortable at the center or home.
- **Yourself**: You are first and foremost looking for a childcare option that fits what your family and your child need. Make sure you carefully consider how your family's schedules and, more importantly, values fit into the structure of the childcare center's programs.

NANNIES

Families who choose nannies as their primary childcare providers often point to the one-on-one attention and flexibility that's commonly associated with having a nanny (as compared to daycare centers or other group settings) as some of the most important reasons behind their choice. But this one-on-one attention does come at a price.

According to a 2009 survey released by the International Nanny Association, a private non-profit organization, full-time live-in nannies in North Carolina earned an average of $567 (for an average of 55 work hours per week); that's just shy of $30,000 per year. Actual salaries vary widely based on the region in which the family lives and the nanny's experience. In addition, families who directly employ nannies are required by federal law to pay Social Security tax and sometimes state unemployment taxes on the nanny's salary.

Nanny Placement Services

If you're a first-time nanny seeker or prefer services that help you pre-screen nanny candidates, placement agencies can help with the logistics of finding a nanny for your family. These agencies screen candidates and perform background checks. Even so, always verify the status of these checks with the agency before hiring any nanny. Agencies do require placement fees, deposits, and sometimes other fees for their services. Contact each agency directly for detailed information on their fees and requirements.

- **ABC Nannies Inc.**, 6900 Creskill Place, Raleigh, 919-872-3016, *www.ncnanniesonline.com*
- **Loving Care Nanny Service**, 4724 Windbreak Lane, Raleigh, 919-790-8412, *www.lovenannies.com*
- **Nancy's Nannies of Raleigh Inc.**, 961 Cranbrook Road, Suite 200, Raleigh, 919-571-0330, *www.nancynannies.com*
- **The Teaching Nanny**, 1307 Woodcroft Parkway, Durham, 919-321-8052, *www.teachingnanny.com*
- **Trio Nanny & Babysitting Agency LLC**, P.O. Box 6476, Raleigh, 919-828-4212, *www.trionc.com*

Finding a nanny on your own

If you prefer to find a nanny on your own, there are a number of resources at your disposal:

- **4EverythingNanny.com**, *www.4nanny.com*; provides helpful how-to articles and a classified ads section
- **Ask About Nannies**, 4724 Windbreak Lane, Raleigh, 919-790-8412, *www.askaboutnannies.com*
- **International Nanny Association**, 888-878-1477, *www.nanny.org*; provides helpful tools for your nanny search and hiring process
- **NannyAnswers.com**, *www.nannyanswers.com*; a catch-all Website for frequently asked questions about nannies

Nanny taxes

As mentioned above, families who do not use placement agencies but rather directly employ nannies are expected to pay taxes on the salaries paid to their nannies. The "Nanny Tax", as its called, includes Social Security and Medicare taxes and federal unemployment tax. You may also be required to pay state unemployment taxes and/or state disability taxes.

There are several Website and agencies that can guide you through the particulars of the Nanny Tax and help you determine how much Nanny Tax you owe. Some such resources include:

- **Internal Revenue Service**, *www.irs.gov/taxtopics/tc756.html*
- **The Nanny Tax Company**, 800-747-9826, *www.nannytaxprep.com*; provides tax-filing services
- **NannyTax Inc.**, 888-NANNYTAX, *www.nannytax.com*; provides tax-filing services

PART V: THE NEWCOMER'S GUIDE TO THE RALEIGH AREA

AU PAIRS

The terms "au pair" and "nanny" are often used interchangeably, but there are notable differences between the two. As such, while a nanny may be a good fit for one family, an au pair may be a better fit for another.

Au pairs are typically between the ages of 18 and 26 and usually remain with a family for one year. Unlike nannies, au pairs aren't necessarily seeking professional careers in childcare; their yearlong commitment provides work experience but also functions as a cultural exchange program. Families with au pairs act as "host families"; the au pair provides childcare, and in return, the host family provides room, board, use of a vehicle, and a small stipend. Host families are also encouraged to facilitate continued education of the au pair while he/she is working in the U.S. Compensation for au pairs can be considerably less than nannies, ranging from $176.85 to $250 per week (approximately $9,000 to $13,000 per year, respectively).

Agencies that can assist with au pair screening and placement include:
- **Au Pair in America**, 800-928-7247, *www.aupairinamerica.com*
- **AuPairCare Live-In Child Care**, 800-428-7247, *www.aupaircare.com*
- **Cultural Care Au Pair**, 800-333-6056, *www.culturalcare.com*
- **GreatAupair**, 775-215-5770, *www.greataupair.com*
- **InterExchange AuPair USA**, 1-800-AUPAIRS, *www.aupairusa.org*

BABYSITTERS

Babysitting is no longer just a neighborhood business; babysitting is now big business, which can be both good and bad for the newcomer families.

The best babysitters are usually ones suggested by close friends of co-workers, but if you're new to the area, those solid referrals may be hard to come by—at least at the beginning. The growth of babysitting as a fortified business segment, however, has given rise to a slew of babysitting agencies that will gladly screen potential babysitters and narrow the field for your family. This can be a great way to find a babysitter if you're new to the area.

These agencies can be helpful resources, but know that they all charge fees for their services, whether it's a one-time "finders" fee or a membership fee to browse their pool of potential babysitters. Contact each agency for specific details on fees and memberships. Some local and national babysitter-finder agencies include:

- **4Sitters**, 651-756-8085, *www.4sitters.com*
- **River City Sitters LLC**, P.O. Box 5842, Cary, 919-244-3683, *www.rivercitysitters.com*
- **Sitter Connection**, P.O. Box 12434, Raleigh, 919-412-7499, *www.sitterconnection.net*
- **Sittercity**, 888-748-2489, *www.sittercity.com*; provides large database of local babysitters

If you prefer to avoid the added fees for these services, there are several local resources that may be able to help you find the right babysitter. Community centers such as the local **YMCA** or the **Wake County Public Libraries** usually have community boards that teens often use to advertise their babysitting services or that parents can use to advertise a babysitter opening. Churches, synagogues, or other places of worship might also be helpful resources.

And if all else fails, tapping into the Triangle's large populations of college students may prove to be helpful. **Meredith College**, **North Carolina State University**, and **Peace College** are all four-year universities located in Raleigh, and they more than likely have a number of students looking for small side jobs. Checking in with the student employment service, posting fliers around campus, or running an ad in the college paper are all ways to find potential babysitters. Remember to request references for each candidate and to conduct your own thorough interview before hiring any babysitter.

Once you've found a babysitter, now comes the all-important question of how much to pay them. **Sittercity.com** provides a simple Rate Calculator (*babysitters.sittercity.com/rate_calculator.html*), which calculates an approximate rate based on geographic location, age of the babysitter, number of children that will be cared for, and the babysitter's experience. For example, according the calculator, a 20-year-old babysitter with two to four years experience should be paid approximately $12 per hour to care for two children in North Raleigh (zip code 27614).

PARENTING PUBLICATIONS

Carolina Parent magazine, *www.carolinaparent.com*, 919-956-2430, is the Triangle's leading parenting publication. Its Website can provide a wealth of resources for parents new to the area, such as a calendar of family-friendly events, a family dining guide, and a slew of comprehensive directories for childcare, education, and other family-oriented services. In addition to its free monthly publication, *Carolina Parent* also produces three annual guides: Baby Guide, Ultimate Family Resource Guide, and the Parents' Guide to North Carolina Colleges. Copies of *Carolina Parent* can be found at Wake County public libraries, local YMCAs and YWCAs, and local businesses including Harris Teeter, Whole Foods Market, and many Food Lion locations.

SCHOOLS

Parent resources

Here are some resources with which to begin your school research:
- *Carolina Parent* **magazine**, 919-956-2430, *www.carolinaparent.com*; maintains an online directory of boarding schools, charter schools, and private day schools

- **National Association of Independent Schools**, 202-973-970, *www.nais.org*; an organization dedicated to non-public schools. The NAIS maintains a searchable database of independent private schools in the U.S.
- **NC School Report Cards**, *www.ncreportcards.org*; maintains a database of school report cards for all public schools in North Carolina. These report cards contain data such as student achievement, class size, and demographic details about schools and districts.
- **North Carolina PTA**, 3501 Glenwood Avenue, Raleigh, 919-787-0534, *www.ncpta.org*
- **Project Appleseed**, *www.projectappleseed.org*; a campaign dedicated to improving public education. Its Website includes helpful tips for evaluating public schools.
- **Wake County Public School System**, 3600 Wake Forest Road, Raleigh, 919-850-1600, *www.wcpss.net*

Public schools

The **Wake County Public School System** (WCPSS), 3600 Wake Forest Road, Raleigh, 919-850-1600, *www.wcpss.net*, is the largest school district in North Carolina. It includes more than 156 schools – 99 elementary schools, 30 middle schools, 23 high schools, and four special/optional schools – and serves nearly 138,000 students.

As the country's 18th largest school district (it moved ahead of the San Diego Unified School District in 2008), Wake County has received much recognition for its quality of public education. In 2006, *Expansion Magazine* named the Raleigh-Cary metropolitan statistical area (the area served by the Wake County Public School System) the strongest public school district among mid-sized metro areas. In addition, *Newsweek* magazine ranked **Enloe High School**, 128 Clarendon Crescent, 919-856-7918, *enloehs.wcpss.net*, one of the district's magnet schools (for explanation on what magnets schools are, see below), among the top 100 high schools in the country; it ranked #73.

Growth

As one of the fastest growing regions in the country, Wake County has seen a significant influx of new students during the last five years or so. During the 2006-07 school year, the Wake County Public School System welcomed more than 7,560 new students to the district. This influx has tempered in recent years but still remains strong. During the 2007-08 and 2008-09 school years, 5,930 and 3,704 new students, respectively, joined the district. For the 2009-10 school year, WCPSS anticipates an increase of 2,306 students.

To keep up with its growing student body, WCPSS continues to build new schools. Five new schools are scheduled to open during the 2010-11 school year, and another two are scheduled for the 2011-12 academic year. The school district has also put up more than 1,000 mobile classrooms across the district in order to accommodate additional students.

One of the most notable ways the Wake County Public School System has worked to meet the demands of its growing district is to shift schools to a year-round academic calendar. Nearly one-third of all schools in WCPSS now follow a year-round calendar, which means students at these schools follow a "multi-track" schedule. With year-round calendars, the student body is divided into "tracks," and each track has a different school break schedule following a "45/15" cycle, meaning students are in school for 45 days and then off for 15.

By using this year-round calendar, WCPSS says it can serve 33 percent more students in a building. At the end of the day that means, one less school has to be built for every three schools on a multi-track, year-round schedule. For more information on year-round schooling, visit the Wake County Public School System's Website: *www.wcpss.net/newcomer/getting-started/year-round.html.*

Registering your children

The first step to registering your child or children for a Wake County school is to determine which "base school" your children are zoned to attend. To simplify this process, use the Wake County Public School System's online School Assignment Locator: *www.wcpss.net/newcomer/getting-started/registration* or call the Office of Student Assignment, 919-850-1921. Your base school is where you will register your children.

- **For kindergarten and first-grade registration**, the following documents will be requested:
    - A certified copy of the student's birth certificate
    - Proof of residence
    - An updated immunization record
    - A completed Kindergarten Health Assessment, a form that must be completed by a doctor and turned in to the school (available through the WCPSS Website, *www.wpss.net*)
    - A completed Discipline Status Enrollment form if transferring from another school system (available through the WCPSS Website, *www.wpss.net*)
    - It will also be helpful to bring a copy of your child's latest report card and the previous year's achievement test.
- **For second-grade through 12th-grade registration**, it's best to make an appointment to register your child, though it is not required. The following documents will be requested:
    - A certified copy of the student's birth certificate
    - Proof of residence
    - Immunization records
    - A completed Discipline Status Enrollment form if transferring from another school system (available through the WCPSS Website, *www.wpss.net*)

- It will also be helpful to bring a copy of your child's latest report card and the previous year's achievement test.

Additional newcomer information

The Wake County Public School System has set up a helpful "Newcomer Info Center," *www.wcpss.net/newcomer/getting-started/*, for families new the district. The site contains links to important forms, the WCPSS Student Handbook (available in both English and Spanish), and even videos that introduce parents and students to the WCPSS.

Some important Wake County-specific policies that may differ from your previous school system include (but are not limited to):

- WCPSS will provide bus transportation to students living more than 1.5 miles from school and to students with special needs.
- Magnet programs play a key part in the Wake County education system. They provide students with non-traditional learning programs in addition to Wake County core curriculum. For more information on the Wake County magnet programs, see the "Magnet Schools" section below.
- Beginning with the 2009-10 school year, students will be dismissed from school one hour early every Wednesday. This time will be used for school-wide faculty professional development.

Magnet schools

The Wake County Public School System introduced magnet programs in 1982. Magnet schools structure the students' learning environment and curriculum based on a particular theme or on an approach to learning.

The magnet schools that your child is "eligible" to attend are determined by the location of your home in the same way your base school is determined. To find out which magnets schools are open to your family, use the Wake County Public School System's online School Assignment Locator: *www.wcpss.net/newcomer/getting-started/registration* or call the Office of Student Assignment, 919-850-1921.

Students do not need to pass any specific entrance exams or have specific test scores to attend WPCSS magnets schools (the only exception is the Academically Gifted Basics program), but they do need to submit an application during the WCPSS's February acceptance period. Students are then selected by a random lottery system.

There are 13 different types of magnet programs and magnet schools at the elementary, middle, and high school levels. For more detailed descriptions of magnet programs and a complete list of schools offering magnet programs, download the WCPSS's 2008-09 Magnet Schools Booklet available online at *www.wcpss.net/magnet/*. Some of the most notable and interesting magnet program offerings include:

- **The Museums Program** integrates activities that help students naturally learn through guided exploration and discovery. The magnet schools offering the Museums Program work closely with area museums, experts, and professionals. The Museums Program is available at the elementary and middle school levels.
- The **Early College** program is a unique program that allows high school students to earn free transferable college credits and an associate's degree from Wake Technical Community College while completing their high school requirements. The Wake Early College of Health and Sciences is located on the Wake Technical Community College campus.
- The **International Baccalaureate Programme**'s primary objective to help develop students in both the academic, social, and cultural worlds. The program emphasizes community service and begins foreign language instruction in kindergarten.
- **Enloe High School**, 128 Clarendon Crescent, 919-856-7918, *enloehs.wcpss.net*, features the **GT/IB Center for Humanities, Sciences and the Arts high school program**. The school offers a

strong college-preparation curriculum and has extensive Advanced Placement course offerings, which are high school classes specifically designed to prepare students for university-level work. The school has been recognized by *Newsweek* magazine as one of the best high schools in the U.S.

Evaluating schools

Public schools play a critical role in many families' home-buying decisions. All parents want their children to excel in school, and to be comfortable in their learning environments. The ultimate question is: how do you determine which school is best for your child?

One of the most straightforward ways to evaluate the quality of schools in your area is to look at their **NC School Report Cards**, www.ncreportcards.org. These report cards include important information such as student achievement, class size, school safety and environment, teacher quality, and demographic details about schools and districts. But a word of caution about NC School Report Cards: While the school data provided by the report cards are indeed helpful, it's important to not solely base your decision on these numbers as raw numbers don't always tell the whole story.

According to Project Appleseed, in addition to considering your family's lifestyle and your child's personality, a number of factors should be considered when evaluating a school:

- School philosophy as outlined in the school's statement of philosophy or mission statement
- Instructional approaches
- School facilities/personnel resources
- School policies
- School reputation
- School safety
- Curriculum

- Family and community involvement issues

Many of these factors can be evaluated by looking at the school's Website and by personally visiting the school you and your family are considering. Contact each individual school to discuss the options for a possible on-campus visit. Moreover, don't underestimate the value of asking neighbors, friends, family, and coworkers about their experiences in WCPSS and the schools their children attend.

Charter schools

For parents looking for a public-education alternative to traditional public schools, charter schools are a good option to consider. Charter schools are public schools with limited enrollment, and they often incorporate characteristics associated with private-school education such as smaller class sizes or rigorous curriculum for college- and university-bound students. In fact, U.S. News and World Report recently recognized **Raleigh Charter High School**, 1111 Haynes Street, Raleigh, 919-715-1155, *www.raleighcharterhs.org*, as one of the 100 Best High Schools in the country; Raleigh Charter came in at #20.

Funded with public money, charters are not required to meet all the rules and regulations of traditional public schools but are subject to accountability for producing certain academic results among its students. Because charter schools receive public money, they do not charge tuition. However, each school does have an admissions process. The particulars of the process vary from charter school to charter school, but the basic process is the same: Students and their families submit an application to the school(s) of their choice. Students meeting the admission requirements for the school are then entered into a lottery, and numbers are picked at random to determine which students will be granted available openings. For admission requirements and for particulars on each

PART V: THE NEWCOMER'S GUIDE TO THE RALEIGH AREA

school's admission process, it's best to check each school's Website for details.

In Wake County, there are charter schools at both the elementary and secondary levels:

- **Casa Esperanza Montessori School**, 2600 Sumner Boulevard, Suite 130, Raleigh, 919-855-9811, *www.cemcs.org*; preschool through grade 6
- **East Wake Academy**, 400 NMC Drive, P.O. Box 65, Zebulon, 919-404-0444, *www.eastwakeacademy.org*; grades K through 12
- **Endeavor Charter School**, 9400 Forum Drive, Raleigh, 919-848-0333, *www.endeavorcharterschool.com*; grades K through 7
- **Exploris Middle School**, 207 East Hargett Street, Raleigh, 919-821-3168, *www.explorismiddleschool.org*; grades 6 through 8
- **Franklin Academy**, 1127 Chalk Road, Wake Forest, 919-570-8262, *www.franklinacademy.org*; grades K through 12
- **Hope Elementary Charter School**, 1116 North Blount Street, Raleigh, 919-834-0041, *www.hopecharterschool.org*; grades K through 5
- **Magellan Charter School**, 9324 Baileywick Road, 919-844-0277, *www.magellancharter.org*; grades 3 through 8
- **Quest Academy Charter School**, 9650 Strickland Road, Suite 175, Raleigh, 919-841-0441, *www.questcharter.org*
- **Raleigh Charter High School**, 1111 Haynes Street, Raleigh, 919-715-1155, *www.raleighcharterhs.org*; grades 9 through 12
- **Southern Wake Academy**, 116 Quantum Street, Holly Springs, 919-567-9955, *www.southernwakeacademy.org*; grades 9 through 12
- **Sterling Montessori Academy and Charter School**, 202 Treybrook Drive, Morrisville, 919-462-8889, *www.sterlingmontessori.org*; grades K through 8

Private and parochial schools

After much consideration, some parents decide a private or parochial school is the best option for their child. There are a wide range of private and parochial school offerings in Raleigh. They include both large and small school settings and both religiously affiliated schools and those without religious ties. Below is a list of a small selection of private schools in Wake County. For a complete list that includes private schools in nearby Chapel Hill and Durham, visit *Carolina Parent*'s online directory at: *www.carolinaparent.com/resources/directories/* and click on "Private Day Schools" under the Education heading.

- **Atlas International School**, 314 Bashford Road, Raleigh, 919-623-2323, *www.atlasinternationalschool.com*
- **Cardinal Gibbons High School**, 1401 Edwards Mill Road, Raleigh, 919-834-1625, *www.cghsnc.org*; Catholic affiliation
- **Cary Academy**, 1500 N. Harrison Avenue, Cary, 919-677-3873, *www.caryacademy.org*
- **Cathedral School**, 204 Hillsborough Street, Raleigh, 919-832-4711, *www.cathedral-school.net*; Catholic affiliation
- **Chesterbrook Elementary School**, 130 Towne Village Drive, Cary, 919-319-9622, *cary.chesterbrookacademy.com*
- **Montessori School of Raleigh**, 7005 Leadmine Road, Raleigh, 919-848-1545, *www.msr.org*
- **North Raleigh Christian Academy**, 7300 Perry Creek Road, Raleigh, 919-573-7900, *www.nrcaknights.com*; Christian-based education
- **Our Lady of Lourdes School**, 2710 Overbrook Drive, Raleigh, 919-782-1670, *www.olls.org*; Catholic affiliation
- **Peace Montessori**, 2190 North Salem Street, Suite. 103, Apex, 919-363-2461, *www.peacemontessori.com*
- **The Raleigh School**, 1141 Raleigh School Drive, Raleigh, 919-546-0788, *www.raleighschool.org*

- **Ravenscroft School**, 7409 Falls of Neuse Road, Raleigh, 919-847-0900, *www.ravenscroft.org*
- **Southern Wake Montessori School**, 5108 Old Powell Road, Holly Springs, 919-577-0081, *www.swmsnc.org*
- **Thales Academy**, 3106 Heritage Trade Drive, Wake Forest, 919-882-2320, *www.thalesacademy.org*
- **Trinity Academy**, 10224 Baileywick Road, Raleigh, 919-786-0114, *www.trinityacademy.com*

Homeschooling

As per North Carolina law, families are permitted to homeschool their children. The State of North Carolina defines a homeschool as "a non-public school in which the student receives academic instruction from his/her parent, legal guardian, or a member of the household in which the student resides." Homeschools can be one - or two-household schools only.

Homeschools fall under the jurisdiction of the **Division of Non-Public Education** (DNPE), 116 West Jones Street, Second Floor, Room 2009F, Raleigh, 919-733-4276, *www.ncdnpe.org*, which is part of the North Carolina Department of Administration. It is vital that families who choose to homeschool their children carefully review the requirements and regulations set forth by the DNPE.

Below are some (but not all) basic requirements for homeschooled children in North Carolina who are at least 7 years old but not yet 16 years old. Parents who plan to homeschool their children must:

- Hold at least a high school diploma or its equivalent
- Send to DNPE a Notice of Intent to Operate a School. The notice must include the name and address of the school along with the name of the school's owner and chief administrator.

- Operate the school "on a regular schedule, excluding reasonable holidays and vacations, during at least nine calendar months of the year"
- Maintain at the school disease immunization and annual attendance records for each student
- Have a nationally standardized achievement test administered annually to each student. The test must involve the subject areas of English grammar, reading, spelling, and mathematics. Records of the test results must be retained at the school for at least one year and made available to DNPE when requested.

Another resource available to families who choose to homeschool their children is the **North Carolinians for Home Education** (NCHE), 4336-A Bland Road, Raleigh, 919-790-1100, *www.nche.com*. The organization provides tips and tools for setting up your own homeschool and deciding on appropriate curriculum; moreover, the NCHE even organizes and hosts a biannual conference for homeschool families across North Carolina. National homeschool organizations include **American Homeschool Association**, 800-236-3278, *www.americanhomeschoolassociation.org*, and the **Home School Legal Defense Association**, 540-338-5600, *www.hslda.org*.

CHAPTER 42

HEALTH CARE

The Triangle is known for its healthcare, with myriad hospitals and specialty clinics throughout – Durham is even known as the City of Medicine due to the large number of hospitals, physicians and healthcare services offered. In addition to the major hospitals and urgent care centers, each portion of the Triangle area hosts innumerable specialty clinics for neurology, orthopaedics, physical therapy and more. Your doctor will most likely refer you to a specific location if you are ever in need of specialized treatment or testing. In this chapter you'll find all the major health organizations and the hospitals that comprise them.

WAKEMED HEALTH AND HOSPITALS

WakeMed is a private health system based in Raleigh, but with satellite hospitals and clinics in Cary, Apex, Zebulon and other areas surrounding Raleigh. Overall, it has 870 beds, with 60 new acute-care beds under development. There are two main health complexes within Raleigh: WakeMed Raleigh Hospital and WakeMed North Healthplex.

WakeMed Raleigh

WakeMed's Raleigh campus is home to Wake County's only certified Primary Stroke Center, Neuro Intensive Care Unit, Pediatric Intensive Care Unit, Pediatric Inpatient Unit, Level IV Intensive Care Unit and Level I Trauma Center. A full-service facility, including a Women's Pavilion and Birthplace, WakeMed Raleigh holds 515 acute-care beds and sees more than 142,000 patients each year.

The WakeMed trauma center is the only designated trauma center in Wake County and is a complete system of services designed specifically to treat patients with life-threatening injuries. The Trauma Center includes adult intensive care units, a pediatric intensive care unit and a comprehensive outpatient physical rehabilitation program.

The Raleigh campus also holds North Carolina's only freestanding Children's Emergency Department, designed especially for meeting the emotional and physical needs of children. The department cares for more than 40,000 children a year, ranging in age from infancy to 17.

3000 New Bern Avenue
Raleigh, NC 27610
919-350-8000

WakeMed North Healthplex

The North Healthplex is not a full-fledged hospital, but it does have a 24-hour freestanding emergency department with 14 private treatment rooms. The emergency department is fully equipped for triage and offers state-of-the-art monitoring for patients that may need to be transferred to other medical facilities in the area.

10000 Falls of the Neuse Road
Raleigh, NC 27614
919-350-1300

WakeMed Cary Hospital

The only full-service hospital in Cary, WakeMed Cary opened in 1991 and holds 156 beds. It offers a Women's Pavilion and Birthplace, Sleep Center as well as surgical, endoscopic and imaging services. The emergency department is home to the hospital's nationally accredited Chest Pain Program and Primary Stroke Center.

1900 Kildaire Farm Road
Cary, NC 27518
919-350-2300

Other Healthcare Locations

WakeMed has several other locations throughout Raleigh and surrounding areas, including other healthplexes, nursing facilities and medical parks. To find out more about these locations, visit the WakeMed website at *wakemed.org*.

DUKE UNIVERSITY HEALTH SYSTEM

Comprised of three major teaching hospitals in Durham and Raleigh, the Duke University Health System is a world-class academic health care system. *U.S.News and World Report* has consistently ranked Duke University Hospital one of the top 10 hospitals in the nation for the past 20 years. Four Duke physicians have been named as "America's Top Doctors for Women" by *Women's Health* magazine. And more than 200 nurses from across the health system have been nominated for 31 Excellence in Nursing awards presented each year by the Friends of Nursing.

Duke Raleigh Hospital

Originally known as Mary Elizabeth Hospital, Duke Raleigh Hospital moved to its Wake Forest Road location in 1978. The hospital has more than 186 beds and over 500 physicians on staff. A full-service hospital, the location offers a 24-hour emergency department, and special centers for cancer, orthopedics, neuroscience and cardiovascular services. The hospital also offers outpatient imaging services, a diabetes center and a wellness center.

3400 Wake Forest Road
Raleigh, NC 27609
919-954-3000

Durham Regional Hospital

A 369-bed acute-care hospital, Durham Regional features a 23-bed psychiatric unit, 22-bed critical care unit and 18-bed Level II Special Care Nursery. The hospital also holds the Durham Regional Rehabilitation Institute and Davis Ambulatory Surgical Center.

3643 North Roxboro Road
Durham, NC 27704
919-470-4000

Duke University Hospital

A full-service tertiary- and quaternary-care hospital recognized worldwide, Duke University Hospital has been recognized by *Time*, *U.S.News & World Report* and many other publications. This teaching hospital has 924 acute-care beds and 19 psychiatric beds. In 2009 it was one of only 3 hospitals to be recognized by the American Hospital Association for leadership and innovation in quality, safety and commitment to patient care.

2301 Erwin Road
Durham, NC 27710
919-684-8111

PART V: THE NEWCOMER'S GUIDE TO THE RALEIGH AREA

Duke Children's Hospital & Health Center

Located within Duke University Hospital, the Children's Hospital is a unique center dedicated to providing state-of-the-art care for children from all over the world. It is consistently ranked among top pediatric centers nationwide by *U.S.News & World Report* and provides care in 28 pediatric specialties, including leukemia and genetic disorders as well as common allergies and infectious diseases. The Children's Hospital sees more than 176,000 children each year.

Other Healthcare Locations

The Duke University Health system also operates many urgent care centers, outpatient clinics and specialized health clinics throughout the Triangle and the state. For more information on these clinics, visit *dukehealth.org*.

UNC HEALTH CARE

The UNC Health Care system is a state-owned, not-for-profit system based in Chapel Hill and operating throughout the Triangle. Besides being teaching hospitals, the system strives to provide state-of-the-art patient care. The system is made up of many nationally recognized centers of excellence, including those in diabetes, cancer treatment, burn care, organ transplant and pediatrics, among others. The health system extends beyond the Triangle, with special clinics and outpatient services all over the state, as well as Rex Hospital in Raleigh.

UNC Medical Center

The 724-bed UNC Medical Center is the cornerstone of UNC Healthcare, seeing more than 31,000 patients each year. It is also home to the Lineberger Cancer Center, one of just a few National Cancer Institute-designated centers in the country. It also encompasses the North

Carolina Cancer Hospital, North Carolina Neurosciences Hospital, North Carolina Children's Hospital and North Carolina Women's Hospital.

101 Manning Drive
Chapel Hill, NC 2714
919-966-4131

Rex-UNC Healthcare

The Rex campus is located in west Raleigh, treats more than 34,000 inpatients each year and holds 665 beds. There are dedicated service centers for pain management, sleep disorders, diabetes education and state-of-the-art wound care, as well as cancer, heart/vascular, surgery and women's care services. Rex is also one of Thomson Reuters Healthcare's top 100 hospitals in the nation, and one of only 10 hospitals in North Carolina to receive Magnet Recognition, placing Rex's nurses among the top 2% in the country.

4420 Lake Boone Trail
Raleigh, NC 27607
919-784-3100

Other Healthcare Locations

UNC Health Care operates many other clinics, primary care and specialty physician practices throughout the state. To find out more about these locations, visit *unchealthcare.org*.

VETERAN'S ADMINISTRATION HEALTH CARE

The only Veteran's Administration hospital in central North Carolina is located in Durham, and serves both central and eastern North Carolina in either its main medical center or one of three outpatient clinics located

PART V: THE NEWCOMER'S GUIDE TO THE RALEIGH AREA

in communities around the area. Currently the hospital serves more than 200,000 veterans in the area. The VA Medical Center provides specialty surgical care, women's health services, primary care services, extended care and rehabilitation and mental health services. Social work services are also available. To learn more about VA services in the area, visit *durham.va.gov*.

508 Fulton Street
Durham, NC 27705
919-286-0411

URGENT CARE

There are dozens of urgent care clinics in the Triangle, operated both by the health systems listed above and by other private organizations. Listed below are just some of the urgent care clinics according to location.

Duke Urgent Care Brier Creek
10211 Alm Street
Raleigh, NC 27617
919-206-4889

PromptMed Urgent Care
7100 Six Forks Road North, Suite 101
Ralcigh, NC 27615
919-719-0785

Raleigh Urgent Care
2600 New Bern Avenue
Raleigh, NC 27610
919-231-3131

Accent Urgent Care & After-Hours Pediatrics
2406 Blue Ridge Road, Suite 190

Raleigh, NC 27607
919-789-4322

Reliant Urgent Care
7870-110 Alexander Promenade Place
Raleigh, NC 27617

Rx Urgent Care West
3100 Blue Ridge Road, Suite 103
Raleigh, NC 27612
919-719-2250

Rx Urgent Care North
10880 Durant Road, Suite 110
Raleigh, NC 27614
919-719-2260

Accent Urgent Care & After-Hours Pediatrics Cary
212 Ashville Avenue, Suite 10
Cary, NC 27518
919-859-1136

Duke Urgent Care Knightdale
162 Legacy Oaks Drive, Hwy 64 and I-540
 Knightdale, NC 27545
919-373-1800

Duke Urgent Care Morrisville
10950 Chapel Hill Road
Morrisville, NC 27560
919-327-1630

CHAPTER 43

PLACES OF WORSHIP

Nestled snugly in the "Bible Belt," Wake County offers a wide variety of worship opportunities for people of every faith.

BAPTIST

The name "Baptist" can be a catchall term for churches in the South. Some are affiliated with the Southern Baptist Conference, others are independent. Call your local church or visit their web site to find out more about its affiliations and beliefs.

- Apex
  - Apex Baptist Church - 110 S Salem St - (919) 362-6176 - *www.apexbaptist.org*
  - Salem Baptist Church - 1200 Salem Church Rd - (919) 362-7327 - *www.salem-bc.org*
  - Woodhaven Baptist Church - 4000 Kildaire Farm Rd - (919) 362-0127 - *www.woodhaven.org*
  - Good Hope Baptist Church - 6628 Good Hope Church Rd - (919) 467-8526 - *www.goodhopechurch.org*
  - Green Level Baptist Church - 8509 Green Level Church Rd - (919) 362-4310 - *www.greenlevel.com*

THE GUIDE TO RALEIGH NORTH CAROLINA AREA REAL ESTATE

- Fairview Baptist Church - 5608 Ten Ten Rd - (919) 779-1791 - www.fairviewchurch.org
- Olive Chapel Baptist Church - 600 New Hill Olive Chapel Rd - (919) 362-7479 - www.olivechapel.org
- Mt. Pisgah Baptist Church - 1334 Mount Pisgah Church Rd - (919) 362-7951 - www.mountpisgahchurch.org
- Mt. Zion Baptist Church - 520 Richardson Rd - (919) 362-5697
- Apex First Baptist Church - 419 S Salem St - (919) 362-7416
- Faith Baptist Church - 1004 US Highway 64 W - (919) 362-0131 -
- St. Mary's Free Will Baptist Church - 9305 Holly Springs Rd - (919) 362-0678
- New Hope Baptist Church - 581 New Hope Church Rd - (919) 362-7074 - www.newhopebaptistchurch-apex.org

- Angier
  - Angier Baptist Church - 155 Hickory St S - (919) 639-6114 - www.angierbaptistchurch.com
  - Kennebec Baptist Church - 9808 Kennebec Church Rd -(919) 639-4021 - www.angierbaptistchurch.com
  - Oak Grove Baptist Church - 851 Oak Grove Church Rd -(919) 639-9720
  - Cutts Chapel Freewill Baptist Church - 210 W Church St - (919) 639-6194
  - Neill's Creek Abaptist Church - 4200 Neills Creek Rd - (919) 639-6126
  - Black River Grove Baptist Church - 828 N Broad St E - (919) 639-6219
  - Trinity Baptist Church - 29 W Wray St - (919) 639-2495
  - Piney Grove Chapel Baptist Church - 4440A Piney Grove Rd - (919) 639-2481

- Cary

PART V: THE NEWCOMER'S GUIDE TO THE RALEIGH AREA

- Colonial Baptist Church - 6051 Tryon Rd -(919) 233-9100 - *www.colonial.org*
- First Baptist Church of Cary - 218 S Academy St - (919) 467-6356 - *www.caryfbc.org*
- Bethel Baptist Church - 1111 W Chatham St - (919) 467-6789 - *www.bethelbaptistcary.net*
- North Cary Baptist Church - 505 Reedy Creek Rd - (919) 469-8023 - *www.northcarybaptist.org*
- Westwood Baptist Church - 200 W High St - (919) 469-9393 - *www.westwoodbc.org*
- Landmark Free Will Baptist Church - 9011 Chapel Hill Rd - (919) 460-8007 - *www.lfwbc.org*
- College Park Baptist Church - 3761 NW Cary Pkwy - (919) 380-7278 - *www.collegeparkministries.org*

- Fuquay-Varina
  - Fuquay-Varina Baptist Church - 301 N Woodrow St, - (919) 552-4644 - *www.fvbaptist.org*
  - Saint Augusta Missionary Baptist Church - 605 Bridge St - (919) 552-382 - *www.staugustabaptist.org*
  - Pleasant Grove Baptist Church - 10005 Lake Wheeler Rd - (919) 552-4634 - *www.pleasantgrovebaptistonline.org*
  - Piney Grove Baptist Church - 3217 Piney Grove Wilbon Rd - (919) 552-3522 - *www.pineygrovebc.org*
  - New Providence Missionary Baptist Church - 4813 Hilltop Needmore Rd, Fuquay Varina, NC -(919) 552-3531 - *www.newprovidencebaptist.com*
  - Faith Missionary Baptist Church - 1305 S Main St - (919) 567-8173 - *www.faithmissionarync.com*
  - Baptist Grove Church - 6140 Christian Light Rd - (919) 552-8592

- Bazzel Creek Baptist Church - 1228 Wilbon Rd - (919) 552-2513
- Chalybeate Springs Baptist Church - 238 Chalybeate Rd - (919) 552-2856 - www.cspringsbaptist.org
- New Breed Baptist Church - 3900 Us 401 N - (910) 814-9202 - www.newbreedchristiancenter.org
- First Baptist Church - 105 N West St - (919) 552-9150
- Rawls Baptist Church - 10665 Us 401 N - (919) 552-6905

- Garner
  - Garner Free Will Baptist Church - 1133 Benson Rd - (919) 772-6093 - www.garnerfwb.org
  - Aversboro Road Baptist Church - 1600 Aversboro Rd - (919) 779-0434 - www.arbc-garner.org
  - New Bethel Baptist Church - 2110 Benson Rd - (919) 772-2712 - www.newbethelgarner.org

- Holly Springs
  - Holly Springs Baptist Church - 304 Raleigh St - (919) 552-2591
  - Macedonia Baptist Church - 10481 Nc Highway 42 - (919) 567-3460 - www.macedonia-nc.com
  - First Baptist Church of Holly Springs - 208 Grigsby Ave - (919) 552-6383

- Knightdale
  - Knightdale Baptist Church - 15 Main St - (919) 266-2471 - www.knightdalebaptistchurch.org
  - Green Pines Baptist Church - 1498 Hodge Rd - (919) 266-1613 - www.greenpines.org
  - Malabys Crossroads Missionary Baptist Church - 911 Old Knight Rd - (919) 266-1071 - www.malabyscrossroads.org
  - Bethlehem Baptist Church - 8400 Poole Rd - (919) 266-2486 - www.bethlehembaptistnc.com

PART V: THE NEWCOMER'S GUIDE TO THE RALEIGH AREA

- New Covenant Life Baptist Church - 3332 S Smithfield Rd - (919) 266-0573
- Shotwell Baptist Church - S Smithfield Rd - (919) 217-0064
- Good Hope Baptist Church - 4209 S Smithfield Rd - (919) 266-0217
- Morrisville
  - First Baptist Church of Morrisville - 209 Church St - (919) 467-8317 - *www.fbcmorrisville.com*
  - Sorrell Grove Baptist Church - 210 Sorrell Grove Church Rd - (919) 469-3533
  - Calvary Baptist Church of Morrisvile - 10310 Chapel Hill Rd - (919) 469-3366
  - Shiloh Baptist Church - NC 54 Hwy - (919) 469-0790
- Raleigh
  - North Raleigh
    - Bay Leaf Baptist Church, 12200 Bayleaf Church Rd, - (919) 847-4477, *www.bayleaf.org*
    - Crabtree Valley Baptist Church - 4408 Lead Mine Rd - (919) 781-5345 - *www.crabtreevalleybaptist.org*
    - Friendship Baptist Church - 5510 Falls of Neuse Rd - (919) 876-0585 - *www.fbcweb.net*
    - Trinity Baptist Church - 4815 Six Forks Rd - (919) 782-6192 - *www.tbcraleigh.com*
    - Creedmoor Road Baptist Church - 6001 Creedmoor Rd - (919) 787-3317 - *www.creedmoorroadbaptistchurch.org*
    - Wake Chapel Baptist Church - 4509 Bland Rd - (919) 872-7776
    - Loving Word Baptist Church - 1616 N Market Dr - (919) 872-3800
    - Greystone Baptist Church - 7509 Lead Mine Rd - (919) 847-1333 - *www.greystonechurch.org*

- Christ Baptist Church - 400 Newton Rd - (919) 573-5454 - *www.christbaptist.com*
- Mount Vernon Baptist Church - 7600 Falls of Neuse Rd - (919) 845-0090 - *www.mtvernonbaptist.net*
- Bethlehem Baptist Church - 7215 Six Forks Rd - (919) 847-5219

- West Raleigh
  - Haven Free Will Baptist Church - 5408 Tryon Rd - (919) 233-2233 - *www.havenfwbchurch.org*
  - South Hills Baptist Church - 6400 Holly Springs Rd - (919) 859-5915 - *www.southhillschurch.com*
  - Macedonia Baptist Church - 7100 Holly Springs Rd - (919) 851-3216 - *www.mbcnc.org*
  - Swift Creek Baptist Church - 9300 Penny Road - (919) 851-0112 - *www.swiftcreekchurch.com*
  - Ephesus Baptist Chuch - 6767 Hillsborough St - (919) 851-1928 - *www.ephesusbaptistchurch.com*

- Inside the Beltline
  - First Baptist Church - 99 N Salisbury St - (919) 832-448 - *www.fbcraleigh.org*
  - Pullen Memorial Baptist Chuch - 1801 Hillsborough St - (919) 828-0897 - *www.pullen.org*
  - Mt. Peace Baptist Church - 1601 Martin Luther King Jr Blvd -(919) 807-1194 - *www.mountpeace.org*
  - Hayes Barton Baptist Church - 1800 Glenwood Avenue - (919) 833-4617 - *www.hbbc.net*
  - Forest Hills Baptist Church - 201 Dixie Trail - (919) 828-6161 - *www.fhbc.info*
  - Tupper Memorial Baptist Church - 501 S Blount St - (919) 834-7249 - *www.tuppermbc.org*

- East Raleigh

PART V: THE NEWCOMER'S GUIDE TO THE RALEIGH AREA

- Beacon Baptist Church - 2110 Trawick Rd - (919) 876-6847 - www.ahomeforyourfamily.com
- Longview Baptist Church - 2308 N New Hope Rd - (919) 231-3147 - www.longviewbaptist.org
- Wake Chapel Baptist Church - 3805 Tarheel Club Rd - (919) 872-7776 - www.wakechapel.org
- Elevation Baptist Church - 4729 New Bern Ave - (919) 231-6418 - www.elevationbaptist.org
- Hillcrest Baptist Church - 3800 Hillcrest Dr - (919) 321-6278 - www.hillcrestraleigh.com

– South Raleigh
- Fellowship Baptist Church - 5029 Old Stage Rd - (919) 772-2423 - www.fellowshipbch.com
- Christian Faith Baptist Church - 509 Hilltop Dr - (919) 833-5834 - www.cfbc-ral.org
- First Cosmopolitan Baptist Church - 1515 Cross Link Rd - (919) 833-3283 - www.firstcosmopolitan.org
- Carolina Pines Baptist Church - 2655 S Saunders St - (919) 833-5170
- Progressive Missionary Baptist Church - 2504 Creech Rd - (919) 828-8373
- Greater Philadelphia Missionary Baptist Church - 1426 Carolina Pines Ave - (919) 829-7171
- Redeeming Love Missionary Baptist Church - 3425 Rock Quarry Rd - (919) 833-4815
- Inwood Baptist Church - 3700 Lake Wheeler Rd - (919) 828-2933 - www.inwoodbaptist.org

- Rolesville
  – Rolesville Baptist Church - 203 E Young St - (919) 556-3654 - www.rolesvillebaptist.org
  – New Bethel Baptist Church - 605 Rolesville Road - (919) 556-5395 - www.newbethelrolesville.com

- Wake Forest
    - Wake Forest Baptist Church - 118 E South Ave - (919) 556-5141 – www.wakeforestbaptistchurch.org
    - Friendship Chapel Baptist Church – 237 Friendship Chapel Rd. – (919) 556-1759 – www.friendship-chapel.org
    - Wakefield Baptist Church – 13029 Falls of Neuse Rd. – (919) 570-5777 – www.wakefieldbaptist.org
    - Olive Branch Baptist Church – 326 E. Juniper Ave. – (919) 556-7972 – www.olivebranch-baptist.org
    - Glen Royal Baptist Church – 731 Elizabeth Ave. – (919) 556-5463 – www.glenroyalbaptist.org
    - Woodland Baptist Church – 190 Woodland Church Rd. – (919) 556-5455 – www.wbchurch.com
    - Heritage Baptist Church of Wake Forest – 230 Capcom Ave # 102-103 – (919) 554-2320, (919) 554-8711 – www.hbcwf.org
    - Falls Baptist Church – 9700 Fonville Rd. (919) 847-0870 – www.fallsbaptist.com
    - Richland Creek Community Church – 3229 Burlington Mills Rd. – (919) 556-9292 – www.richlandcreek.com
    - Oak Grove Baptist Church – 2124 Oak Grove Church Rd. – (919) 556-2315 – www.oakgrovebaptistonline.com
    - Evans Grove Missionary Baptist Church – 12700 Creedmoor Rd. – (919) 870-8874 - www.evansgrove.org
    - Good Hope Baptist Church – 4038 Graham Sherron Rd. – (919) 556-5192 – www.goodhopebaptistnc.org
    - Sovereign Grace Baptist Church – 601 Woodland Church Rd. – (919) 570-3006 – www.sgbc-wakeforest.org
    - Stony Hill Baptist Church – 7521 Stony Hill Rd. – (919) 556-5708 – www.stonyhill.org
    - Wake Union Baptist Church – 13345 Wake Union Church Rd. – (919) 556-2010

PART V: THE NEWCOMER'S GUIDE TO THE RALEIGH AREA

- Wendell
  - Wendell Baptist Church - 3651 Wendell Blvd - (919) 366-1007 - *www.wendellbaptist.org*
  - Central Baptist Church - 11109 Poole Rd - (919) 365-6547 - *www.centralwendell.org*
  - Riley Hill Baptist Church - 6025 Riley Hill Rd - (919) 365-5277 - *www.rileyhillbaptistchurch.org*
  - Bethany Baptist Church - 3417 Rolesville Rd - (919) 266-3273 - *www.bethanybaptist-wendell.com*
  - Charity Freewill Baptist Church - 1850 Wendell Blvd - (919) 365-7326
  - Pleasant Grove Baptist Church - 952 Morphus Bridge Rd - (919) 365-7292
  - Wendell First Baptist Church - 119 Church St - (919) 365-3726
  - Clyde's Chapel Baptist Church - 16657 Buffalo Rd - (919) 365-6969
- Zebulon
  - Zebulon Baptist Church - 400 N. Arendell Ave - (919) 269-7329 - *www.zebulonbaptist.com*
  - Wakefield Central Baptist Church - 308 Proctor St - (919) 269-9512 - *www.wakefieldcentralbaptist.org*
  - Pine Ridge Baptist Church - 865 Pine Ridge Rd - (252) 478-5811 - *www.pine-ridge.org*
  - Tabernacle Independent Baptist Church - 5356 Pearces Rd - (919) 404-2001
  - Pearce Baptist Church - 4634 Pearces Rd - (919) 269-7510
  - Hales Chapel Baptist Church - 13396 Nc Highway 39 - (919) 269-0019
  - Springhill Baptist Church - 660 Antioch Church Rd - (919) 365-4557

- Zebulon First Baptist Church - 304 E Barbee St - (919) 269-7355

CATHOLIC

Area Catholics can find out more about the diocese of Raleigh by visiting the diocesan web site, *www.dioceseofraleigh.org*, calling the switchboard at (919) 821-9700, or visiting the Diocese House at 715 Nazareth St. in central Raleigh.

- Apex
  - St. Andrew - 3008 Old Raleigh Rd - (919)362-0414 - *www.saintandrew.org*
  - St. Mary Magdalene - 625 Magdala Pl - (919) 657-4800 - *www.stmm.net*
- Cary
  - St. Michael - 804 High House Rd - (919)468-6100 - *www.stmichaelcary.org*
  - Sts. Cyril and Methodius (Byzantine Rite) - 2510 Piney Plains Rd - (919)851-9266 - *www.saintscyrilandmethodius.org*
- Fuquay-Varina
  - St. Bernadette - 1005 Wilbon Rd - (919) 552-2922 - st-*www.bernadettechurch.org*
- Garner
  - St. Mary Mother of the Church - 1008 Vandora Springs Rd - (919) 772-5524 - *www.stmarygarner.org*
  - Sts. Voldymyr and Olha (Ukranian Rite) - 8312 White Oak Rd - (919) 376-8099 - *www.saintvando.org*
- Raleigh
  - North Raleigh
    - St. Francis of Assisi - 11401 Leesville Rd - (919) 847-8209 - *www.stfrancisraleigh.org*

- St. Luke the Evangelist - 12333 Bayleaf Chuch Rd - (919) 848-1533 - *www.stlukeonline.com*
- St. Raphael the Archangel - 5801 Falls of the Neuse - (919) 872-3723 - *www.saintraphael.org*
- Inside the Beltline
  - Our Lady of Lourdes - 2718 Overbrook Dr - (919) 861-4600 - *www.ourladyoflourdescc.org*
  - Sacred Heart Cathedral - 204 Hillsborough St - (919)832-4711 - *www.sacredheartcathedral.org*
- East Raleigh
  - St. Joseph - 2809 Poole Rd - (919) 231-6364 - *home.catholicweb.com/stjosephsraleigh*
- West Raleigh
  - St. Sharbel (Maronite Rite) - Cardinal Gibbons High School Chapel, 1401 Edwards Mill Rd - 919-234-9509 - *www.marsharbel.org*
- Wake Forest
  - St. Catherine of Siena - 520 W. Holding Ave - (919) 570-0070 - *www.saintcatherinesienawf.org*
- Wendell
  - St. Eugene - 608 Lions Club Rd - (919) 365-7114 - *www.steugeneparish.org*

EASTERN ORTHODOX

- Raleigh
  - West Raleigh
    - All Saints Antiochian Orthodox Christian Church - 520 Buck Jones Rd - (919) 859-1332 - *www.allsaintsnc.org*
  - North Raleigh

- Holy Trinity Greek Orthodox Church - 500 Lead Mine Rd - (919)781-4548 - *www.holytrinityraleigh.org*
- East Raleigh
  - St. Mary Coptic Orthodox Church - 3405 N New Hope Rd - (919)878-4477 - *www.coptic.org/stmaryra*
- Morrisville
  - Holy Transfiguration Orthodox Church - 3491 Pleasant Grove Church Rd - (919) 614-4902 - *www.holytransfiguration-oca.org*
- Wendell
  - St. Gregory Orthodox Church - 649 Wendell Rd - (919) 553-9707

EPISCOPALIAN

- Apex
  - Prince of Peace Episcopal - 1200 N. Salem St - (919) 367-7835 - *www.theprinceofpeace.org*
- Cary
  - St. Paul's Episcopal Church - 221 Union St - (919)467-3788 - *www.stpaulscary.org*
- Fuquay-Varina
  - Trinity Episcopal Church - 1128 S. Main St - (919) 552-1056 - *www.trinityfuquay.org*
- Garner
  - St. Christopher's Episcopal Church - 1101 Vandora Springs Rd - (919) 772-7125 - *www.stchristophers-garner.org*
- Raleigh
  - North Raleigh
    - Church of the Nativity - 8849 Ray Rd - (919) 846-8338 - *www.nativityonline.org*

- St. Timothy's Episcopal Church - 4523 Six Forks Rd - (919) 787-7590 - *www.sttimothyschurch.org*
  - East Raleigh
    - St. Mark's Episcopal Church - 1725 N. New Hope Rd - (919) 231-6767 - *www.stmarks-ral.org*
  - Inside the Beltline
    - St. Michael's Episcopal Church - 1520 Canterbury Rd - (919) 782-5085 - *www.stmichaels-raleigh.org*
    - Christ Episcopal Church - 120 E. Edeonton st - (919) 834-6259 - *www.christ-church-raleigh.org*
    - St. Ambrose Episcopal Church - 813 Darby St - (919) 833-8055 - *www.stambrose-church.org*
- Wake Forest
  - St. John's Episcopal Church - 830 Durham Rd - (919) 556-3656 - *www.stjohnswf.net*

HINDU AND BUDDHIST

- Cary
  - Sri Venkateswara Hindu Temple - 121 Balaji Place - (919)468-0040 - *www.svtemplenc.org/*
- Morrisville
  - The Hindu Society of North Carolina - 309 Aviation Parkway - (919)481-2574 - *www.hsncweb.org*
- Raleigh
  - Hindu Temple - 4608 Hiddenbrook Drive - (919)876-8566
  - Kadampa Center for the Practice of Tibetan Buddhism - 5412 Etta Burke Court - (919) 859-3433 - *www.kadampa-center.org*
  - Soka Gakkai International Buddhist Association Community Center - 6307-A Chapel Hill Rd. - (919)859-2112 - *www.sgi-usa.org/*

JEHOVAH'S WITNESS

- Angier
  - Kingdom Hall - 4200 Piney Grove Rd - (919) 639- 3132
- Cary
  - Kingdom Hall - 516 Reedy Creek Rd - (919) 481-4352
  - Kingdom Hall - 270 Towerview Ct - (919)463-8014
- Fuquay-Varina
  - Kindgom Hall - 6325 NC Hwy 55 - (919) 552 1054
- Raleigh
  - South Raleigh
    - Kingdom Hall - 801 Carolina Pines Ave - (919)821-5060
  - North Raleigh
    - Kingdom Hall - 8800 Honeycutt Rd - (919) 846-6647
  - East Raleigh
    - Kingdom Hall - 6320 Fox Rd - (919) 876-6129
    - Kingdom Hall - 3420 Barwell Rd - (919) 779 - 9718
- Zebulon
  - Kingdom Hall - 1216 E Gannon Ave - (919)269-5252

JEWISH

In addition to local synagogues, you can get more information about the local Jewish community from the Raleigh-Cary Jewish Federation (*www.rcjf.org*). Visit their web site for Jewish Community Center information, Jewish schools, campus resources, and events.

- Cary
  - Chabad Center of Cary (Orthodox/Lubavitch) - 115 W. Park St. - (919) 637-6950 - *www.chabadofcary.org*
- Raleigh
  - North Raleigh

PART V: THE NEWCOMER'S GUIDE TO THE RALEIGH AREA

- Chabad Center of Raleigh (Chabad) - 7400 Falls of The Neuse - (919)847-8986 - *www.jewishraleigh.org*
- Temple Beth Or (Reform) - 5315 Creedmoor Rd. - (919)781-4895 - *www.templebethor-raleigh.org*
- Beth Meyer (Conservative) - 504 Newton Rd. - (919)848-1420 - *www.bethmeyer.org*
- South Raleigh
    - Beth Shalom (Reform) - 5713 Yates Mill Pond - (919)858-7777 - *www.bethshalomnc.org*

LATTER DAY SAINTS

Wake County is home to three meetinghouses serving eight wards as well as a Mormon temple and a family history center. Members of the LDS Church can also consult the international LDS web site, *www.lds.org*, to find worship times and ward information.

- Raleigh
    - Meetinghouse - 5060 Six Forks Road - (919) 782-7367
    - Family History Center - 1953 Hilltop Rd - (919) 783-7752
- Garner
    - Meetinghouse -143 Aversboro Rd - (919) 779-7509
- Apex
    - Temple - 590 Bryan Dr - (919) 303-3347
- Cary
    - Meetinghouse - 1811 Seabrook Ave - (919) 481-1597
- Wake Forest
    - Meetinghouse - 1524 Jenkins Rd - (919)554-8801

LUTHERAN

Wake County has Lutheran churches representing the Missouri Synod, the Wisconsin Evangelical Lutheran Synod, and the Evangelical Lutheran Church in America. Many offer both traditional and contemporary worship services. Call your local church or visit their web site for more information about worship and affiliations.

- Apex
  - Jordan Lutheran Church - 1031 Pemberton Hill Rd - (919) 303-1613 - www.jordanchurchnc.org
- Cary
  - Resurrection Lutheran Church - 100 W. Lochmere Dr - (919) 851-7248 - www.rlcary.org
  - Tree of Life Lutheran Church - 114 MacKenan Dr - (919) 465-4400 - www.treeoflifenc.netfirms.com
  - Christ the King - 600 Walnut St - (919) 467-8989 - www.christthekingcary.org
- Fuquay-Varina
  - Abiding Presence Lutheran Church- 7300 Sunset Lake Rd - (919) 557-0060 -
- Garner
  - Lord of Life Lutheran Church - 2100 Buffaloe Rd - (919) 772-9044
- Knightdale
  - Living Spirit Lutheran Church - 7061 Knightdale Blvd - (919) 266-4113
- Raleigh
  - North Raleigh
    - Good Shepherd Lutheran Church - 7000 Creedmoor Rd - (919) 848-1573 - www.gslchurch.org
    - St. Philip Lutheran Church - 7304 Falls of the Neuse - (919) 846-2992 - www.stphilipnc.org

- Gethsemane Lutheran Church - 1100 Newton Rd - (919) 847-0579 - *www.themainthing.us*
- Grace Lutheran Church - 5010 Six Forks Rd - (919) 787-1815 - *www.gracelutheranraleigh.org*
  - Inside the Beltline
    - Holy Trinity Evangelical Lutheran Church - 2723 Clark Ave - (919) 828-1687 - *www.htelc.org*
    - Our Savior Lutheran Church - 1500 Glenwood Ave - (919) 832-8822 - *www.oslcraleigh.org*
- Wake Forest
  - Hope Lutheran Church - 3525 Rogers Rd - (919) 453-0388 - *www.hopelutheranwf.org*

MESSIANIC JEWISH

- Cary
  - Sha'arei Shalom - 700 Old Apex Rd. - (919)388-3678 - *www.shaareishalom.com*

METHODIST

- Apex
  - Apex UMC - 100 S. Hughes St - (919) 362-7807 - *www.apexumc.org*
  - Ebeneezer UMC - 724 Beaver Creek Rd - (919) 387-0944 - *ebenezerumc-apex.org*
- Angier
  - Angier Memorial UMC - 279 S. Wilma St - (919) 639-2176 - *www.angierumc.org*
- Cary
  - First United Methodist Church - 117 S. Academy St - (919) 467-1861 - *www.fumc-cary.org*

- Genesis UMC - 850 High House Rd - (919) 467-2128 - *genesis-umc.org*
    - White Plains UMC - 313 SE Maynard Rd - (919) 467-9394 - *www.wpumc.com*
    - St. Francis UMC - 2965 Kildaire Farm Rd - (919) 362-1666 - *www.saintfrancisumc.org*
    - Agape Korean UMC - 1427 Walnut St - (919) 496-1514 - *www.agapeumc.org*
- Fuquay-Varina
    - Fuquay Varina UMC - 100 S. Judd Pkwy - (919) 552-4331 - *www.fvumc.org*
    - First United Methodist Church - 402 N. Main St #N - (919) 567-8384 - *www.fumcfv.org*
    - Rogers Chapel CME Church - 210 Bridge St - (919) 552-3598
    - Bethlehem AME Zion Church - 461 Olive Branch Rd - (919) 552-1349 -
- Garner
    - Garner UMC - 201 Methodist Dr - (919) 772-2042 - *www.garnerumc.org*
    - Mt. Zion UMC - 15772 NC 50 N - (919) 772-8415 - *www.mountzion-umc.org*
- Holly Springs
    - Sunrise UMC - 5420 Sunset Lake Rd - (919) 303-3720 - *www.mysunrise.org*
    - Holly Springs UMC - 108 Avent Ferry Rd - (919) 557-3467 - *www.hsumc.net*
- Knightdale
    - Knightdale UMC - 621 N 1st Ave - (919) 266-2373 - *www.knightdaleumc.org*
- Raleigh
    - North Raleigh

PART V: THE NEWCOMER'S GUIDE TO THE RALEIGH AREA

- St. Mark's UMC - 4801 Six Forks Rd - (919)783-0640 - *www.stmarksraleigh.org*
- Asbury UMC - 6612 Creedmoor Rd - (919) 847-2818 - *www.asburyraleigh.org*
- Millbrook UMC - 1712 E. Millbrook Rd - (919)876-9767 - *www.millbrookumc.org*
- North Raleigh UMC - 8501 Honeycut Rd - (919) 847-1536 - *www.nrumc.org*

– South Raleigh
  - St. Andrews UMC - 1210 Maxwell Dr - (919) 772-4410 - *www.saintandrewsumc.org*
  - Hollands UMC - 9433 Ten Ten Rd - (919) 772-5294 - *www.hollandsumc.com*

– Inside the Beltline
  - Highland UMC - 1901 Ridge Rd - (919) 787-4240 - *www.highlandumc.org*
  - Hayes Barton UMC - 2209 Fairview Rd - (919) 832-6435 - *www.hbumc.org*
  - Fairmont UMC - 2501 Clark Ave - (919) 821-5484 - *www.fairmontumc.org*
  - Edenton Street UMC - 228 W. Edenton St - (919)832-7535 - *www.esumc.org*
  - Longview UMC - 2312 Milburnie Rd - (919)834-7554
  - Wilson Temple UMC - 1021 Oberlin Rd - (919) 828-9989

– East Raleigh
  - St. James UMC - 3808 St. James Church Rd - (919) 876-5796 - *www.stjamesraleigh.org*
  - Ebenezer UMC - 6020 Rock Quarry Rd - (919) 772-1664 - *www.umcebenezer.org*
  - Cokesbury UMC - 3315 Poole Rd - (919)231-6277

– West Raleigh

- Westover UMC - 300 Powell Dr - (919) 851-4431 - *www.gbgm-umc.org/Westover*
- Linconville AME Church - 6400 Chapel Hill Rd - (919)851-6085 - *www.lincolnvilleamechurch.org*
- Wake Forest
  - Wake Forest UMC - 905 S. Main St - (919) 556-2239 - *www.wakeforestumc.org*
- Wendell
  - Wendell UMC - 129 N. Main St - (919) 365-6266 - *www.wendellumc.org*
- Zebulon
  - Zebulon UMC - 118 W. Sycamore St - (919)269-9408 - *www.zumchurch.com/*

MORAVIAN

The Moravian church is one of the oldest denominations in the United States. Find out more about their historic connections to North Carolina at *www.moravian.org/history*.

- Holly Springs
  - Holly Springs Moravian Church - 110 Osterville Dr - (919)363-2138 - *www.moravianchurch.org*
- Raleigh
  - Raleigh Moravian Church - 1816 Ridge Rd - (919)787-4034 - *www.raleighmoravian.org*

MUSLIM

Wake County is home to a growing Muslim community and three private schools devoted to the teachings of Islam. You can find out more about Raleigh's Muslim community at the Muslim American Society of Raleigh (*www.masraleigh.org*).

PART V: THE NEWCOMER'S GUIDE TO THE RALEIGH AREA

- Cary
  - The Islamic association of Cary - 1076 W. Chatham St. - (919)460-6496 - *www.carymasjid.org*
- Raleigh
  - Inside the Beltline
    - The Islamic Center of Raleigh - 808 Atwater St. - (919)834-9572 - *www.islam1.org*
    - Shaw University - 122 Martin Luther King, Jr. Blvd - (919)522-9914 - *www.shawuniversitymosque.org*
    - Masjid Seifullah - 110 South Haywood St - (919)839-0710 -
  - East Raleigh
    - Masjid Seifuddin - 110 Lord Anson Dr - (919)212-0588 -

NON-DENOMINATIONAL / OTHER

- Apex
  - Sovereign Grace Church - 411 W. Williams St - (919)362-4220 - *www.sovgracenc.org*
  - Triangle Community Church - 4216 Kildaire Farm Rd - (919)362-9996 - *www.tcc.org*
  - Pleasant Grove Church - 1528 Davis Dr - (919)363-51198 - *www.pgccary.org*
- Angier
  - Solid Rock Ministries Church of the Living God - 340 E. Wimberly St - (919)639-2013 - *www.srmcotlg.org*
  - Grace Community Church - 2160 Harnett Central Rd - (919)639-3900 - *graceccnc.org*
- Cary
  - Grace Bible Fellowship - 9043 Chapel Hill Rd - (919)468-4590 - *www.gbf-nc.org*

- Crosspointe Chuch - 6911 Carpenter Fire Station Rd - (919)469-9111 - www.newlifenc.org
- Cary Christian Church - 1503 Walnut St - (919)467-9159 - www.carychristian.org
- Christ Our King Community Church - 1777 W. Chatham St - (919)233-4177 - www.cokcc.org

- Fuquay-Varina
  - Christian Light Church - 4351 Christian Light Rd - (919)552-1554 - christianlightchurch.org
  - Church Alive - 5309 Umstead Rd - (919)552-1554 - www.churchaliveag.org
  - Fuquay Varina Church of Christ - 6320 Whitted Rd - (919)552-3236 - www.fvchurch.org
  - Lifespring Community Church - 501 Wake Chapel Rd - (919)552-6411 - www.lifespringcommunitychurch.org
  - Wake Chapel Christian Church - 905 Wake Chapel Rd - (919)552-4147 - wakechapelchurch.org

- Garner
  - Victory Fellowship - 1250 Aversboro Rd, Garner, NC - (919)779-5180 - www.victory-fellowship.org
  - Garner Christian Fellowship - 1507 Hall Blvd, Garner, NC - (919)661-2300 - www.garnerchristianfellowship.org
  - Faith Zone Worship Center - 1540 Mechanical Blvd, Garner, NC - (919) 779-7984 - www.faithzone.us

- Holly Springs
  - Church of God of Prophecy - 623 Utle st - (919)577-6477 - www.cogop.org
  - New Life Community Church - 3515 Crittenden Ln - (919)362-9100

- Raleigh
  - West Raleigh

PART V: THE NEWCOMER'S GUIDE TO THE RALEIGH AREA

- - Connections Church - 1280 Buck Jones Rd - (919)233-1115 - *www.raleighchurch.org/*
  - East Raleigh
    - From the Heart Church Ministries - 2940 Trawick Rd - (919) 850-9602 - *www.fthcm.org*
    - Awesome Word Ministries - 3204 Flowery Branch Rd - (919) 662-2772 - *www.awesomewordministries.org*
    - Philippian Community Church - 6904 Poole Rd - (919) 217-0983 - *www.pccofnc.org*
    - Ark of Safety Christian Church - 5301 Old Poole Rd - (919) 250-0090 - *www.arkofsafety8.com*
  - Inside the Beltline
    - Wesleyan First Church of Deliverance - 1201 Boyer St - (919) 832-3473 - *www.wfcod.org*
    - Triangle Bible Church - 2309 Laurelbrook St - (919) 562-5053 - *www.trianglebiblechurch.org*
  - South Raleigh
    - Breath of Life International Church - 3763 Junction Boulevard - (919) 448-8198 - *www.breathoflifeintl.org*
  - North Raleigh
    - Covenant Church International - 12621 Strickland Rd - (919) 846-8742 - *www.ccifamily.org*
    - Evergreen Community Church   6904 Glenwood Ave - (919) 784-8088 - *www.evergreench.org*
    - River of Life Church - 5508 Munford Rd - (919) 781-8731 - *www.riverisflowing.com*
    - Higher Call Christian Church - 6638 Old Wake Forest Rd - (919) 850-9937 - *www.highercall.org*
    - Raleigh International Church - 4020 Capital Blvd # 152 - (919) 875-0950 - *www.richurch.org*
- Wake Forest

- Calvary Chapel - 927 Durham Rd # 105 - (919) 830-2907 - *calvarychapel.com*
- Triangle Bible Church - 1316 Highland Dr - (919) 562-5053
- Wendell
  - Community Tabernacle Apostolic Church - 3016 Rolesville Rd - (919) 217-4475
  - JMI Non Denominational Worship Center - 1100 Eagle Rock Road - (919) 366-1301 - *www.jministries.org*
- Zebulon
  - Living Water Fellowship - 815 N Arendell Ave - (919) 269-2244 - *livingwaterfellowship4u.org*
  - Harvest Word Ministries - 186 Westside Cir - (919) 404-0689

PRESBYTERIAN

- Apex
  - Ambassador Presbyterian Church - 616 W. Chatham St - (919) 387-1990 - *www.ambassadorpres.org*
- Angier
  - Providence Presbyterian Church - 14664 NC 210 Hwy - (919) 894-4063 - *www.providencepresb.org*
  - Plainview Presbyterian Church - 2712 Plain View Church Rd - (919) 639-3990
- Cary
  - Cary Presbyterian Church - 614 Griffis St - (919) 467-8700 - *www.carypresbyterian.org*
  - Fellowship of Christ - 1788 Kildaire Farm Rd - (919) 319-1000 - *www.fellowshipofchrist.org*
  - Kirk of Kildaire Presbyterian Church - 200 High Meadow Dr - (919)469-4895 - *www.kirkofkildaire.org*

PART V: THE NEWCOMER'S GUIDE TO THE RALEIGH AREA

- Peace Presbyterian Church - 2850 SW Cary Pkwy - (919) 467-5977 - www.peacepca.org
- Cornerstone Presbyterian Church - 2220 High House Rd - (919) 303-9200 - www.cspcusa.org
- Fuquay-Varina
  - Fuquay Varina Presbyterian Church 308 N. Ennis St - (919)552-0249 - www.fvpres.org
  - Grace Presbyterian Church - 119 E Vance St - (919) 557-5690 - www.gracefv.com
- Garner
  - First Presbyterian Church of Garner - 503 Lakeside Dr - (919) 772-0727 - www.firstpresgarner.org
- Raleigh
  - Inside the Beltline
    - White Memorial Presbyterian Church - 1704 Oberlin Rd - (919) 834-3424 - www.whitememorial.org
    - Westminster Presbyterian Church - 301 E. Whitaker Mill Rd - (919) 828-0507 - www.westminster-raleigh.org
    - Christ the King Presbyterian Church - 401 Oberlin Rd - (919) 546-0515 - www.ctkraleigh.org
    - Milner Memorial Presbyterian Church - 1950 New Bern Ave - (919) 231-7313 - www.milnermemorial.org
    - Davie Street Presbyterian Church - 300 E Davie St - (919) 834-8855
    - West Raleigh Presbyterian Church - 616 Tucker St - (919) 828-5468 - www.wrpc.org
    - Western Boulevard Presbyterian - 4900 Kaplan Dr - (919) 851-4713 - www.wbpresbyterian.org
  - North Raleigh
    - Hudson Memorial Presbyterian Church - 4921 Six Forks Rd - (919) 787-1086 - www.hmpc.org

- St Giles Presbyterian Church - 5101 Oak Park Rd - (919) 787-4790 - *www.saintgiles.org*
- Calvary Presbyterian Church - 6520 Ray Road - (919) 781-9015 - *www.calvarypca.org*
- Saint Andrews Presbyterian Church - 7506 Falls of the Neuse - (919) 847-1913 - *www.sapc.com*
- North Raleigh Presbyterian Church - 11905 Strickland Rd - (919) 848-9529 - *www.nraleighpc.org*
- East Raleigh
    - Trinity Presbyterian Church - 3120 N. New Hope Rd - (919) 872-1142 - *www.trinitypresbyterianchurch.net*
- South Raleigh
    - St Barnabas Presbyterian Church - 1420 Carolina Pines Ave - (919) 833-6043
- Wake Forest
    - Wake Forest Presbyterian Church - 12605 Capital Blvd - (919) 556-7777 - *www.wakeforestpres.org*
    - Christ our Hope Church - 203 Capcom Ave #107 - (919) 570-9717 - *www.christourhopechurch.com*
- Wendell
    - Covenant Presbyterian Church - 125 S. Selma Rd - (919) 365-7979 - *www.wendellpcusa.org*

QUAKER

- The Friends Meeting of Raleigh - 625 Tower St - (919) 821-4414 - *www.rtpnet.org/friends*

SEVENTH-DAY ADVENTIST

- Raleigh

PART V: THE NEWCOMER'S GUIDE TO THE RALEIGH AREA

- West Raleigh
    - Umoja Central SDA Chuch - 314 Bashford Rd - (919) 931-7877 - *umojacentral22.adventistchurchconnect.org*
    - Seventh-Day Adventist Church of Raleigh - 4805 Dillard Dr - (919) 851-1302 - *www.raleighadventist.org*
- North Raleigh
    - Raleigh North Seventh-Day Adventist Church - 11817 Falls of Neuse Rd - (919) 329-2511 - *www.rnsdac.org*
- South Raleigh
    - Raleigh Gethsemane Seventh-Day Adventist Church - 2521 Sanderford Rd - (919) 833-1844 - *raleighgethsemane22.adventistchurchconnect.org*

UNITARIAN UNIVERSALIST

- Unitarian Universalist Fellowship of Raleigh - 3313 Wade Ave - (919)781-7635 - *www.uufr.org*

CHAPTER 44

SHOPPING GUIDE

Like many quickly growing cities, Raleigh is chock full of shopping malls and shopping plazas, complete with nearly every national chain imaginable along with unique, local stores to boot. Whatever you're looking for – whether it's new furniture for your new home or groceries – there are numerous options available in Wake County. From traditional national chains to smaller mom-and-pop shops to flea markets and thrift shops, Raleigh is well equipped when it comes to shopping amenities.

SHOPPING MALLS

Most of Wake County's major shopping centers and malls are located in Cary and Raleigh. **Cary Towne Center**, **Crabtree Valley Mall**, and **Triangle Town Center** provide shoppers with the typical mall experiences. Cary Towne Center is home to 130 stores, while Crabtree Valley Mall – located several miles north of downtown Raleigh –boasts more than 200 stores and is home to the only Apple Store and Crate & Barrel locations in the Triangle. Triangle Town Center, which has more than 165 retail stores and kiosks, is located in North Raleigh.

On first glance, Wake County seems like an endless sea of national retail chains. However, if it's boutique shops you're looking for, **North**

PART V: THE NEWCOMER'S GUIDE TO THE RALEIGH AREA

Hills and **Cameron Village** will likely be more your style. North Hills and Cameron Village are both outdoor shopping centers and have more than 185 boutiques and stores between the two.

- **Arboretum at Weston**, 2058 Renaissance Park Place, Cary, 919-834-5900, *www.thearboretumatweston.com*;
- **Beaver Creek Commons**, 1581 Beaver Creek Commons Drive, Apex, 919-362-9385,
- **Brier Creek Commons**, 8000 Brier Creek Parkway, Raleigh, 919-821-2700, *www.shopbriercreekcommons.com*
- **Cameron Village**, 1900 Cameron Street, Raleigh, 919-821-1350, *www.shopsofcameronvillage.com*
- **Cary Crossroads**, 213 Crossroads Boulevard, Cary, 919-233-8087
- **Cary Towne Center**, 1105 Walnut Street, Cary, 919-460-1053, *www.shopcarytownecentermall.com*
- **City Market**, 220 Wolfe Street, Raleigh, 919-821-8023, *www.citymarketraleigh.com*
- **The Cotton Company**, 306 South White Street, Wake Forest, 919-570-0087, *www.thecottoncompany.net*
- **Crabtree Valley Mall**, 4325 Glenwood Avenue, Raleigh, 919-787-8993, *www.crabtree-valley-mall.com/*
- **The Factory**, 1839 South Main Street, Wake Forest, 919-453-1839, *www.eatshopplay.com*
- **North Hills**, 4261 Six Forks Road, Raleigh, 919-881-1146, *www.northhillsraleigh.com*
- **Seaboard Station**, 5 West Franklin Street, Raleigh, 919-832-5272, *www.seaboardstationshops.com*
- **The Shops of Baileywick**, 9650 Strickland Road, Raleigh, 919-845-5520, *www.theshopsofbaileywick.com*
- **Triangle Town Center**, 5959 Triangle Town Boulevard, Raleigh, 919-792-2222, *www.triangletowncenter.com*

OUTLET MALLS

- **Carolina Premium Outlets**, 1025 Industrial Park Drive, Smithfield, 919-989-8757, *www.premiumoutlets.com*, is only a 40-minute drive from Raleigh, just off I-95. It offers quite an expansive list of outlet shops for well-known brands in designer clothing, including Izod and Polo Ralph Lauren; shoes, such as Adidas and Rockport; and housewares, like Le Creuset and Le Gourmet Chef. It's an easy day trip for the bargain-hunting shopper.
- **Morrisville Outlet Mall**, 1001 Airport Boulevard, Morrisville, 919-380-9469; The Morrisville Outlet Mall features more than 40 outlet shops and is the only outlet mall in the Triangle. To get to the mall, take I-40 to exit 284.

DEPARTMENT STORES

- **Dillard's**, 800-345-5273, *www.dillards.com*; locations at Cary Towne Center and Triangle Town Center.
- **Hudson Belk**, 866-235-5443, *www.belk.com*; locations at Cary Towne Center, Crabtree Valley Mall, and Triangle Town Center. Hudson Belk is part of Belk Inc., the United States' largest privately owned department-store company. Hudson Belk department stores are found in 16 states in the South.
- **JCPenney**, *www.jcpenney.com*; locations in Cary Towne Center and the North Hills shopping center. JCPenney offers traditional department store fare, including men's and women's apparel, shoes, jewelry, and home goods.
- **Macy's**, *www.macys.com*; locations in Cary Towne Center, Crabtree Valley Mall, and Triangle Town Center. Macy's is a mid-range department store that offers a wide variety of women's, men's and children's clothing, home goods, perfume, and furniture.

PART V: THE NEWCOMER'S GUIDE TO THE RALEIGH AREA

- **Saks Fifth Avenue**, Triangle Town Center, 7700 Old Wake Forest Road, Raleigh, 919-792-9100, *www.saksfifthavenue.com*; This upscale department store is the destination for everything luxurious and chic. Saks Fifth Avenue is a must-stop for the high-end shopper looking to scoop up the latest Dolce & Gabbana sunglasses, Prada heels, and Gucci handbags.
- **Sears**, 800-349-4358, *www.sears.com*; locations in Triangle Town Center, Crabtree Valley Mall, and Cary Towne Center; Sears is one of the oldest names in the department store business and is likely most well known for its offerings outside the realm of apparel and home goods. Sears offers a wide variety of home appliances, lawn and garden equipment, and home electronics.

DISCOUNT RETAILERS

- **Kmart**, *www.kmart.com*; four locations in Raleigh and one location in Cary
- **Target**, *www.target.com*; 11 locations in and around Raleigh, three of which are Super Targets
- **Wal-Mart**, *www.walmart.com*; 12 locations throughout Wake County, eight of which are Wal-Mart Supercenters

HOUSEHOLD SHOPPING

With every new home comes the need – or maybe more accurately, the desire – for new appliances, furniture, lamps, rugs, and/or a new coat of paint. Below is a list of stores that can help you get your home improvement projects started and help you make your new house a home.

The list includes just a handful of the options available; don't forget **Target** and **Wal-Mart** (especially their "Super" locations) can also be great places to save a couple bucks on household basics. Though quick Google searches will definitely give you several names of stores to check out, the good 'ol Yellow Pages is the best resource to compile a comprehensive list of stores available in Wake County.

Appliances/electronics/cameras/computers

- **Appliance World**, 5910 Duraleigh Road, Suite 125, Raleigh, 919-571-1803, *www.applianceworldraleigh.com*
- **Best Buy**, 888-237-8289, *www.bestbuy.com*; six locations across Wake County, including locations in Brier Creek (Raleigh), Cary, Knightdale, and Garner
- **Garner TV & Appliances**, 875 Highway 70, Garner, 919-772-3757, *www.garnertv.com*
- **hhgregg**, 866-WSGREGG, *www.hhregg.com*; two locations in Raleigh and one location in Apex, specializes in appliances and home electronics
- **Lowe's**, 800-445-6937, *www.lowes.com*; nine locations in and around Raleigh
- **Office Max**, 800-283-7674, *www.officemax.com*; multiple locations in Wake County including locations in Raleigh, Knightdale, Garner, and Cary; offers home office electronics
- **Sears**, 800-349-4358, *www.sears.com*; locations in Raleigh, Cary, Knightdale, and Fuquay Varina
- **Staples**, 800-378-2753, *www.staples.com*; multiple locations in Wake County including locations in Raleigh, Garner, Cary, and Wake Forest; offers home office electronics

Beds, bedding, and bath

- **Baker Beds Inc.**, 1003 East Broad Street, Fuquay Varina, 919-567-2110

PART V: THE NEWCOMER'S GUIDE TO THE RALEIGH AREA

- **Bed Bath & Beyond**, 800-462-3966, *www.bedbathandbeyond.com*; one location in Cary, one location in Knightdale, and three locations in Raleigh
- **Fred's Beds**, 919-782-5827, *www.fredsbedsonline.com*; three locations in Raleigh
- **Home Comfort Furniture**, 919-781-3900, *www.homecomfortfurniture.com*; four locations in Wake County including one location in Cary and locations in Raleigh
- **The Original Mattress Factory**, 8917B Glenwood Avenue, Raleigh, 919-510-9977, *www.originalmattress.com*
- **Rooms to Go**, 5900 Glenwood Avenue, Raleigh, 919-785-2222, *www.roomstogo.com*

Carpets and rugs

- **Capel Rugs**, 8000 Winchester Dr, Raleigh (919) 881-0688, *www.capelnc.com*
- **Brentwood Carpets Inc.**, 4600 Paragon Park Road, Raleigh, 919-872-2775, *www.brentwoodcarpets.com*
- **Carpet Barn**, 1019 North Smithfield Road, Knightdale, 919-365-6506
- **Designer Flooring & Interiors Inc.**, 966 Trinity Road, Raleigh, 919-852-4426, *www.designerflooring.com*
- **DRS Carpet & Flooring**, 6241 Westgate Road, Raleigh, 919-789-8510
- **Fargo-Hanna Oriental Rug Gallery**, 816 Springfield Commons Drive, Raleigh, 919-790-8539, *www.fargohannarugs.com*
- **Just Rugs**, 8601 Glenwood Avenue, Raleigh, 919-863-0170, *www.justrugsstore.com*
- **USA Flooring**, 4011 Capital Boulevard, Raleigh, 919-878-0955, *www.usaflooringnc.com*

Furniture

North Carolina is often referred to as the furniture capital of the United States – or even the world – and the state has worked hard for the reputation. It's estimated that 35 percent of all the world's furniture is manufactured in North Carolina, and it's widely known that many furniture manufacturers have outlet or discount shops in North Carolina where furniture pieces are sold at deep discounts.

Yet, if you drive the streets of Raleigh and the surrounding area or even search for these discount centers, they're nowhere to be found in the Triangle. The reason for this is the epicenters of North Carolina's furniture manufacturing industries are located in High Point and Hickory. The drive to High Point (approximately one hour and 50 minutes) and Hickory (approximately three hours) can seem like quite the investment, but the savings that many furniture shoppers see make it worth the road time.

Travel journalist Ellen R. Shapiro published a book titled, "Shopping the North Carolina Furniture Outlets," which is a comprehensive guide to furniture shopping in High Point and Hickory. It includes an impressive list of manufacture's outlets and clearance centers in both cities and also includes valuable insiders tips on how to make the most of your time in the furniture capitals.

According to Shapiro, some of the not-to-miss locales include:

- **Rose Furniture Company**, 916 Finch Avenue, High Point, 336-886-6050
- **Utility Craft**, 2630 Eastchester Drive, High Point, 336-454-6153
- **Thomasville Outlet**, 401 East Main Street, Thomasville, 336-476-2211

PART V: THE NEWCOMER'S GUIDE TO THE RALEIGH AREA

If you're looking for more local options, you certainly have a long list from which to choose. Furniture retailers with showrooms located in and around Raleigh include:

- **Atlantic Bedding and Furniture**, 5720 Capital Boulevard, Raleigh, 919-747-9743
- **Badcock Home Furniture & More**, 38 South Park Drive, Garner, 919-661-9355, *www.badcock.com*
- **Basset Furniture Direct**, 8201 Glenwood Avenue, Raleigh, 919-781-5161, *www.bassettfurniture.com*
- **Cooper's Furniture Inc.**, 820 East Chatham Street, Cary, 919-467-2401, *www.copperfurniturenc.com*
- **Ecko Home Furnishings**, 6740 Fleetwood Drive, Raleigh, 919-781-0081, *www.eckointernational.com*
- **Havertys**, 919-792-0888 or 919-783-6115, two locations in Raleigh: 6140 Capital Boulevard and 6701 Glenwood Avenue Suite 121, *www.havertys.com*
- **Rooms to Go**, 5900 Glenwood Avenue, Raleigh, 919-785-2222, *www.roomstogo.com*

Houseware

- **Bed Bath & Beyond**, 800-462-3966, *www.bedbathandbeyond.com*; one location in Cary, one location in Knightdale, and three locations in Raleigh
- **Cost Plus World Market**, 877-WORLD MARKET, *www.worldmarket.com*; one location in Raleigh and one location in Cary
- **Crate & Barrel**, Crabtree Valley Mall, 4325 Glenwood Avenue, #1049 Raleigh, 919-881-9700, *www.crateandbarrel.com*
- **Pier 1 Imports**, 800-245-4595, *www.pier1.com*; multiple locations in Wake County including locations in Raleigh, Cary, and Garner

- **Pottery Barn**, Crabtree Valley Mall, 4325 Glenwood Avenue, Raleigh, 919-881-0188, *www.potterybarn.com*

Lamps and lighting

- **Accipiter**, 2046 Clary Avenue, Raleigh, 919-755-9309, *www.accipitergallery.com*
- **Carolina Tiffany**, 1505 Capital Boulevard, Raleigh 919-899-3880, *www.carolinatiffany.com*
- **Colonial Light & Design Center**, 910 Windy Road, Apex, 919-362-4577, *www.coloniallightingnc.net*
- **Lighting Inc.**, 500 West Peace Street, 919-828-0351
- **Wakefield Lighting**, 2004 South Main Street, Wake Forest, 919-562-7422, *www.wakefieldlightinginc.com*

Hardware/paint/home improvement

- **Ace Hardware**, 866-290-5334, *www.acehardware.com*; multiple locations throughout Wake County
- **B&W Hardware**, 232 South White Street, Wake Forest, 919-556-3562
- **Briggs Hardware**, 2533 Atlantic Avenue, Raleigh, 919-832-2025, *www.briggshardware.net*
- **Home Depot**, *www.homedepot.com*; multiple locations in Wake County including Wake Forest, Raleigh, Cary, Garner, Knightdale, Apex, and Fuquay Varina
- **Handy Man Hardware**, 1103 New Bern Avenue, Raleigh, 919-834-0341
- **Lowe's**, 800-445-6937, *www.lowes.com*; nine locations in and around Raleigh

PART V: THE NEWCOMER'S GUIDE TO THE RALEIGH AREA

ANTIQUE STORES

Greater Raleigh Convention and Visitors Bureau has put together a comprehensive list of antique stores in Wake County. For a complete list, visit the bureau's Website, *www.visitraleigh.com/visitors/things_to_do/antique*. A selection from the list has been reproduced below. In addition to antique stores, many vendors at the **Raleigh Flea Market** and other local flea markets specialize in selling antiques.

- **A.H. Danielson Antiques Ltd.**, 1010 Wake Forest Road, Raleigh, 919-828-7739
- **Aloma Crenshaw Antiques & Interiors**, 122 Glenwood Avenue, Raleigh, 919-821-0705
- **Antiques on Salem Street**, 114 North Salem Street, Apex, 919-362-1332
- **Antiques Emporium**, Cameron Village Shopping Center, 2060 Clark Avenue, Raleigh, 919-834-7250
- **Auburn House Antique Shop**, 400 East US 70 Highway, Garner, 919-772-6813
- **Carolina Antique Mall**, Cameron Village Shopping Center, 2050 Clark Avenue, Raleigh, 919-833-8227
- **Elisabeth's Antiques**, 13 North Main Street, Wendell, 919-365-6831
- **Gaston St. Antiques & Gifts**, 608 Gaston Street, Raleigh, 919-821-5169
- **Gresham Lake Antique Mall**, 6917 Capital Boulevard, Raleigh, 919-878-9381
- **Herb Highsmith Interiors**, 107 Glenwood Avenue, Raleigh, 919-832-6275
- **Ordinary & Extraordinary**, 115 West Chatham Street, Cary, 919-481-3955
- **Regan Lewis Antiques**, 5300 Atlantic Avenue, Raleigh, 919-872-8177

- **Thieves Market Mall**, 935 North Harrison Avenue, Cary, 919-466-7464
- **The William-Cozart Shop**, 320 South Harrington Street, Raleigh, 919-834-5708
- **Zebulon Antiques**, 124 North Arendell Avenue, Zebulon, 919-269-5925

FLEA MARKETS

Raleigh's flea market is one of the country's best. *Country Living* magazine has referred to the **Raleigh Flea Market**, 1025 Blue Ridge Road, 919-899-3532, *www.raleighfleamarket.net*, as a leading flea market in the southeast when it comes to home décor.

The Raleigh Flea Market is located on the North Carolina State Fairgrounds and is open every Saturday and Sunday from 9 a.m. to 6 p.m. Admission and parking is free. Visitors can browse merchandise – located both indoors and outdoors – from more than 600 vendors. A wide array of goods is on sale every weekend including antiques, jewelry, furniture, books, CDs, toys, memorabilia, and more.

In addition to the Raleigh Flea Market, there are also flea markets in nearby Fuquay Varina and Rolesville and smaller flea markets in Raleigh:

- **Fuquay Flea Market**, 6109 South North Carolina Highway 55, Fuquay Varina, *www.fuquayfleamarket.com*; 919-552-4143, hours of operation: Saturday and Sunday from 8 a.m. to 5 p.m.
- **Raleigh Flea Market Mall**, 1924 Capital Boulevard, 919-839-0038; hours of operation: Saturday and Sunday (inside) from 9 a.m. to 5 p.m., Friday through Sunday (outside) opens 8 a.m.
- **Rolesville Flea Market**, 105 East Young Street, Rolesville, 919-556-3226
- **Watson's Flea Market**, 1436 Rock Quarry Road, Raleigh, 919-832-6232; hours of operation: Saturday and Sunday (inside) from 8 a.m. to 5 p.m., Saturday and Sunday (outside) opens 6 a.m.

PART V: THE NEWCOMER'S GUIDE TO THE RALEIGH AREA

THRIFT AND VINTAGE SHOPS

Trying to find the diamond in the rough at thrift and vintage shops can be quite a task, but if you're up to the challenge, the payoff can be big.

Wake County has a number of thrift and vintage stores that can offer a lot of bang for the buck. To increase your chances of finding that "diamond," ask the stores' managers or sales associates when they typically put new items out. With a little bit of planning, you can take advantage of new stock before the crowds pick through them.

In addition, if you decide to do your thrift shopping at the **Salvation Army Thrift Store**, a **Goodwill** store, or even the **Cause for PAWS Thrift Store**, you're not only getting great deals but you're also helping great causes.

- **Abbeygail's Closet**, 5205 Hillsborough Street, Raleigh, 919-859-6337, *www.wcwc.org/closet.htm*; organized and operated by The Women's Center of Wake County
- **American Way Thrift Store**, 2409 Crabtree Boulevard, Raleigh, 919-832-3199, *www.americanwaythriftstores.com*; proceeds from the thrift store go to the N.C. Children's Hospital
- **Cause for PAWS Thrift Shop**, 2420 Crabtree Boulevard, Raleigh, 919-828-4864 *www.cfpaws.com*; proceeds are donated to Second Chance Pet Adoption in Cary
- **Goodwill**, 919-941-9600, *www.goodwillnc.org*; numerous locations throughout Wake County
- **Salvation Army Family Thrift Store**, 205 Tyron Road, Raleigh, 919-779-8867, *www.keepthebellringing.org*
- **Second Hand Rose Thrift Store**, 708 North Main Street, Wake Forest, 919-562-8687

FOOD

A number of national supermarket chains serve Raleigh and the surrounding areas. No matter where you live in Wake County, you'll more than likely only be a short drive away from at least one the Triangle's major grocery store chains: Food Lion, Harris Teeter, Kroger, or Lowes supermarkets.

For those looking to stretch their dollars a bit, there are a number of Super Targets and Wal-Mart Supercenters that offer formidable selections of produce, meat, bakery, and other grocery items that can help budget-conscious shoppers trim their grocery bills. For those looking to save by buying in bulk, there are also several wholesale warehouse retailers in Wake County.

In addition to the more traditional grocery stores, Raleigh residents also have access to a variety of stores and shops that can help them fill their kitchens and pantries with more than just the traditional fare. From the **Raleigh Farmers Market** to health food stores to seafood markets that offer the freshest fish, even the most discerning home cooks will find what they need in Wake County.

Supermarkets

Four main national supermarket chains serve Wake County:

- **Food Lion**, 800-210-9569, *www.foodlion.com*; has more than 40 locations across Wake County.
- **Harris Teeter**, 800-432-6111, *www.harristeeter.com*; has more than 20 locations in Wake County. Harris Teeter can be best described as a hybrid of the traditional supermarket and the natural foods supermarkets that have grown in popularity during the last decade. It offers organic produce and numerous other organic grocery items. Many of its locations include pharmacies and are open 24 hours.

- **Kroger**, 866-221-4141, *www.kroger.com*; 10 locations in and around Raleigh. At some of its locations, Kroger offers additional services including 24-hour service, film developing, pharmacy services. Moreover, at select locations, shoppers can even fill up their gas tanks at Kroger's gas stations.
- **Lowes Foods**, 888-537-8646, *www.lowesfoods.com*; more than 15 locations throughout Wake County. Lowes Foods offers shoppers a slew of extra services including film developing, pharmacy services, in-store bank branches, and even gas station services. For those looking to purchase concert and event tickets through Ticketmaster, Ticketmaster retail kiosks are located in Lowes Foods locations.

Natural food grocers and specialty market chains

As the market for organic food and other "green" products grows, the number of national chains specializing in organic produce and health-food products continues to increase. In addition, a number of specialty market chains have popped up, providing not only premium produce but also a wide variety of gourmet foodstuffs. These stores make up a small segment of the food-shopping market in Raleigh, but they're nonetheless worth a mention, especially for shoppers with an eye for organic or the home cook in search of some not-so-common ingredients.

- **The Fresh Market**, 866-532-5989, *www.thefreshmarket.com*; With two locations in Raleigh and one in Cary, The Fresh Market provides shoppers with a boutique market experience. Fresh Market shoppers can take advantage of The Fresh Market's top-notch produce department, deli, expansive specialty cheese selection, and coffee selection.
- **Trader Joe's**, 1393 Kildaire Farm Road, Cary; and 3080 Wake Forest Road, Raleigh; *www.traderjoes.com*; Trader Joe's offers much of the traditional grocery fare but with the added bonus of

a wide selection of organic produce, health foods, specialty cheeses, and affordable wine. For those looking for quality organic foods and products at reasonable prices, Trader Joe's is a good option.
- **Whole Foods**, *www.wholefoods.com*; one location in Raleigh and one location in Cary. Whole Foods is the mega store of natural and organic products and produce. If you're looking for a one-stop shop for organic produce, organic meats, and health food supplements and products, Whole Foods will likely meet your shopping needs.

Warehouse shopping

Buying in bulk can be one of the most effective ways to trim a grocery budget, especially if you're feeding a crowd. There are three chain stores that serve Wake County – **BJ's Wholesale Club, Costco Wholesale**, and **Sam's Club** – but don't forget: These stores don't just open their doors to anyone. Each chain requires customers to have memberships in order to shop in their warehouses. Check each chain's Website for details on the cost and terms of their memberships.
- **BJ's Wholesale Club**, *www.bjs.com*; two locations in Raleigh and one location in Cary
- **Costco Wholesale**, 2838 Wake Forest Road, Raleigh, 919-755-2801, *www.costco.com*
- **Sam's Club**, *www.samsclub.com*; two location in Raleigh and one in Morrisville

Seafood markets

Raleigh may not be coastal town, but its proximity to the coast ensures Wake County residents have access to top notch, fresh seafood. The city's supermarkets often run specials on fish and seafood, but nothing beats what you can find in Raleigh's seafood markets. The markets below offer better, fresher seafood than traditional supermarkets and at much lower prices. They may be out of the way, but the drive is certainly worth it.

- **Capital Seafood Market**, 676 Maywood Ave, Raleigh, 919-838-1300; located across the street from the Raleigh Farmers Market
- **Earp's Seafood Market**, 1414 South Saunders Street, Raleigh, 919-833-3158, *www.consultwebs.com/clients/raleigh_seafood_market_earps.html*

Farmer's markets

The State of North Carolina owns five farmers markets, which are operated by the North Carolina Department of Agriculture and Consumer Services. Luckily for those in Wake County, one of farmers market is located just outside downtown Raleigh.

The **Raleigh Farmers Market**, 1201 Agriculture Street, Raleigh, 919-73-7417, *www.ncfarmfresh.com*, has more than 35,000 spaces that are rented to local farmers. The Raleigh Farmers Market is open year round (Sundays 8 a.m. to 6 p.m., Mondays through Saturdays 5 a.m. to 6 p.m.), and both large and small farmers sell locally grown fruit and vegetables.

The Raleigh Farmers Market is open to the public, but don't expect to use your credit card to buy up the week's best produce. Like most farmers markets, vendors only accept cash. There is an ATM on the premises, but it's best to get cash before you get there especially during high-traffic times such as Saturday mornings.

In addition to the state's farmers market, many of Raleigh's neighborhoods and nearby municipalities have smaller, weekly farmers market. For details and directions, visit *www.ncfarmfresh.com/farmmarkets.asp*.

- **Apex Farmers Market**, 220 North Salem Street, Apex, 919-772-5472; every Saturday, 9 a.m. to 2 p.m., April through first weekend in November

- **Cary Downtown Farmers Market**, Harrison Ave and Academy, Cary, 919-772-4906; every Tuesday, 3 p.m. to 6 p.m. and Saturday 8 a.m. to 12:30 p.m., April through late November
- **Holly Springs Farmers Market**, 128 South Main Street, Holly Springs, 919-567-4010; every Saturday, 8 a.m. to noon, May through October
- **North Hills Farmers Market**, 4321 Lassiter at North Hills Avenue, Raleigh, 919-719-5471; every Saturday, 8 a.m. to noon, April 11 through November 28
- **North Raleigh Farmers Market**, Falls River Town Center at Falls River Avenue, Raleigh, 919-349-7918; every Wednesday, 4 p.m. to 7 p.m., and Saturday, 8 a.m. to noon, May 2 through October 28
- **Wake Forest Farmers Market**, 110 South White Street, Wake Forest, 919-556-1579; every Saturday 8 a.m. to noon, April through November and once a month during the winter
- **Western Wake Farmers Market**, 1226 Morrisville Carpenter Road, Cary, 919-460-1469; every Saturday, 8 a.m. to noon, May 2 through November

Ethnic districts

Raleigh's stable job market and attractive real estate market is attracting professionals, couples, and families from all across the country. With this slow but steady migration has come an influx of people from all backgrounds, making Raleigh a melting pot of different cultures.

However, unlike many of the larger metropolitan areas of the South such as Atlanta, true ethnic districts have yet to pop up in Raleigh. While it may take a little time before Raleigh has its own true China Town (or ethnic districts for other cultures), there are a number of businesses in the Triangle that cater to different ethnicities and cultures.

PART V: THE NEWCOMER'S GUIDE TO THE RALEIGH AREA

- **A&C Supermarket**, 3210-131 South Wilmington Street, Raleigh, 919-232-2288; specializes in Asian grocery items, produce, and meat
- **Afrika Exotic Africa Groceries**, 2245 New Hope Church Road, Raleigh, 919-873-0079
- **Around the World Market**, 6715-100 Hillsborough Street, Raleigh, 919-859-5403; specializes in Indian grocery items and products.
- **Caspian International Food Mart**, 2909 Brentwood Road, Raleigh, 919-954-0029; specializes in Iranian, Turkish, Greek and other Middle Eastern foods and also offers Russian, Polish, and other Eastern European products
- **Compare Foods**, 2215 New Hope Church Road, Raleigh, 919-850-2400; specializes in Mexican and Latin American grocery items, produce, and household goods
- **El Mandado**, 4020 Capital Boulevard, Raleigh, 919-878-1800; specializes in produce from El Salvador but also carrier other Latin American grocery items
- **Grand Asia Market**, 1253 Buck Jones Road, Cary, 919-468-2988, *www.grandasiamarket.com*; specializes in Asian grocery items, produce, and meat
- **Jerusalem Bakery & Grocery,** 2233 Avent Ferry Road, Suite 105 Raleigh, 919-833-7008; specializes in Middle Eastern bakery goods and products
- **Nur Grocery and Deli**, 2233-108 Avent Ferry Road, Raleigh, 919828-1523; specializes in Middle Eastern grocery items
- **Triangle Indian Market**, 740-A E. Chatham Street, Cary, 919-380-0350; specializes in Indian and Pakistani products
- **Triangle Oriental Market**, 5003-G Falls of the Neuse Road, Raleigh, 919-790-7044; specializes in Chinese and Japanese grocery items and products

CHAPTER 45

CULTURAL LIFE

Raleigh brings together the best of small-town charm and many of the best aspects of big-city living. In fact, more often than not, you'll hear the many Raleigh transplants point to that very aspect of their adopted hometown as one of its best attributes.

Nowhere is Raleigh's ideal balance between metropolitan amenities and quaint Southern living more evident than in the cultural life Raleigh offers. There's certainly something for everyone: professional Broadway productions, community theatre, museums, art galleries, lecture series, and the list goes on and on. So, if you're just moving to Raleigh, welcome! We can guarantee there is a lot for you (and your family) to experience.

The centerpiece of Raleigh's performing arts culture is the **Progress Energy Center for the Performing Arts**, 1 East South Street, Raleigh, 919-834-4000, *www.progressenergycenter.com*. It is home to the A.J. Fletcher Opera Theater, Kennedy Theatre, Memorial Auditorium, and Meymandi Concert Hall, all of which play host to various national, regional, and local theatre companies and performing arts organizations throughout the year.

Raleigh can be viewed as a convergence of a number of cultural forces. Drawing influence from its Southern roots, influence from

PART V: THE NEWCOMER'S GUIDE TO THE RALEIGH AREA

scholars and professionals studying the arts, and even influence from those who consider the arts simply a hobby, Raleigh has established itself as a hub of cultural life in its own right. While it would be unfair to compare our growing city to major cultural centers such as San Francisco, Chicago, or New York, Raleigh certainly provides an oasis for the young and the old looking to soak up the fine arts.

With the abundance of concerts, events, lecturers, and performances hosted throughout Wake County, it's hard to know where exactly to start. **Raleigh Metro Magazine**, *www.metronc.com*, has a great events calendar on its Website. The calendar includes a rundown of the month's art exhibitions, concerts, festivals, and other cultural events.

Another helpful resources for tips and tools to explore Wake County's cultural scene is the Greater Raleigh Convention and Visitors Bureau, 421 Fayetteville Street, Suite 1505, Raleigh, 919-834-5900, *www.visitraleigh.com*. Though the Greater Raleigh Convention and Visitors Bureau does cater, of course, to tourists, it's a great place to start if you're a new Raleigh resident.

Like Raleigh Metro Magazine, the Bureau maintains a comprehensive events calendar on its Website. If you drop by the Visitor's Center in downtown Raleigh, you can also grab the Raleigh Wide Discovery Guide, a small, handy foldable map (of both downtown Raleigh and Wake County) and pamphlet that details cultural events going on in and around Raleigh. The Convention and Visitors Bureau publishes the guide three times a year so it's by no means a complete guide, but it highlights the areas "best of the best" cultural attractions and events.

TICKETS

Tickets for most major concerts, theatre productions, and other cultural events are available through the venues' box offices. If you're keen on avoiding service charges, purchasing tickets directly from the venue's box office will be your best option.

Most event tickets are also available through **Ticketmaster**. You can purchase tickets through Ticketmaster over the phone by calling 800-745-3000 or by visiting *www.ticketmaster.com*. If you prefer to buy the tickets in person, Ticketmaster has a number of retail locations throughout Wake County. Visit *www.ticketmaster.com* to find the most convenient location.

Concerts and performances can sell out quickly, and if you find yourself looking for tickets to a sold-out show, **StubHub** may be a good solution. Fans and concerts goers often use StubHub to sell their extra or unneeded tickets. To search for available tickets for events in and around Raleigh, visit *www.stubhub.com*.

But buyers beware: Purchasing tickets through Ticketmaster and StubHub often come with significant service changes and processing fees. Ticketmaster's fees can vary from state to state and event to event; make sure to check what (and how much) these fees will be to avoid unexpected costs. StubHub charges a service fee equal to 10% of the full ticket price in addition to a delivery fee.

CONCERT HALLS, STADIUMS, AND ARENAS

Wake County has a number of performance venues, ranging from the 7,000-person Koka Booth Amphitheatre to the 19,000-plus-person RBC Center. From rock concerts to Broadway shows to live operas, Wake County offers performance facilities that rival many larger metropolitan areas. These venues play host to some of biggest names in the performing arts. For the most up-to-date information about upcoming shows, available tickets, ticket prices, and seating, contact each venue or visit the venue's Website.

- **Carter-Finley Stadium**, 4600 Trinity Road, Raleigh, 919-865-1510, *www.gopack.com*

PART V: THE NEWCOMER'S GUIDE TO THE RALEIGH AREA

- **Five County Stadium**, 1501 N.C. Highway 39, Zebulon, 919-269-2287, www.gomudcats.com
- **Joseph M. Ryan Jr. Theatre in the Museum Park**, North Carolina Museum of Art, 2110 Blue Ridge Road, Raleigh, 919-715-5923, www.ncartmuseum.com
- **Koka Booth Amphitheatre at Regency Park**, 8003 Regency Parkway, Cary, 919-462-2025, www.boothamphitheatre.com
- **North Carolina State Fairgrounds**, 1025 Blue Ridge Road, Raleigh, 919-821-7400, www.ncstatefair.org
- **Progress Energy Center for the Performing Arts**, 1 East South Street, Raleigh, 919-834-4000, www.progressenergycenter.com; home to A.J. Fletcher Opera Theater, Kennedy Theatre, Memorial Auditorium, Meymandi Concert Hall.
- **RBC Center**, 1400 Edwards Mill Road, Raleigh, 919-861-2300, www.rbccenter.com
- **Time Warner Cable Music Pavilion at Walnut Creek**, 3801 Rock Quarry Road, Raleigh, 919-831-6400, www.livenation.com

PERFORMING ARTS

Music – Symphonic, Horal, Opera, Chamber

Raleigh brings together the best in both professional and community music. From symphony orchestras to choral performances to even handbell choirs, the organizations listed below provide extensive programs through which musicians and vocal performers share their talents with Greater Raleigh:

- **North Carolina Master Choral**, 919-856-9700, www.ncmasterchorale.org, has provided the Triangle with masterful choral music performances since 1942. Currently under the direction of Dr. Alfred E. Sturgis, the North Carolina Master Choral consists of a 170-person symphonic chorus and a 22-

person professional chamber choir. The primary mission of its choral program is to perform fine choral music, promote the art of choral performance, and help enhance the cultural life of North Carolina.

- **North Carolina Symphony**, Suite 105, 4361 Lassiter at North Hills Avenue, Raleigh, 919-733-2750, *www.ncsymphony.org*, has deep roots in North Carolina's cultural landscape. Since its founding in 1932, the North Carolina Symphony has played a key role in the development of Raleigh's musical history. The orchestra performs 175 time per year (40 of these performances are performed for free as part of student music education programs across North Carolina). Though the orchestra performs in venues across the state, the orchestra is based at Meymandi Concert Hall at the Progress Energy Center for the Performing Arts and performs regularly during the summer at Rengency Park in Cary.

- **The Opera Company of North Carolina**, 414 Fayetteville Street, Suite 100, Raleigh, 919-792-3850, *www.operanc.com*, presents full-scale opera productions and has done so for the past 12 years. The company was established in 1996 by Robert and Margaret Galbraith and merged with Durham's Triangle Opera in 2002. Today, the company's performances are held at the Fletcher Opera House in downtown Raleigh. For performance schedules and information, visit *www.operanc.com*. Tickets can be purchased through Ticketmaster, *www.ticketmaster.com*, or directly from the Progress Energy Center Box Office, 2 East South Street, Raleigh, 919-834-4000.

- **The Raleigh Boychoir**, 919-881-9259, *www.raleighboychoir.org*; Since its founding in 1968, the Raleigh Boychoir has aimed to educate and train boys in the art of signing while also adding to the musical culture of Raleigh. The organization offers choral group for boys 8 to 15 years old. The choir performs at numerous

venues in and around the Triangle. For concert information, visit *www.raleighboychoir.org*.
- **The Raleigh Chamber Music Guild,** 919-821-2030, *www.rcmg.org*, offers two concert series: the Masters Series and Sights & Sounds. The Masters Series is held at the **Progress Energy Center for the Performing Arts**, 1 East South Street, Raleigh, 919-834-4000, *www.progressenergycenter.com*. The Guild's second series—Signs & Sounds—is a collaboration between the Guild and **North Carolina Museum of Art**, 2110 Blue Ridge Road, Raleigh, 919-839-6262, *www.ncartmuseum.org*; performances are held on the museum's campus. Established in 1941, The Raleigh Chamber Music Guild's primarily objective is to promote and present chamber music to the Greater Raleigh area.
- **Raleigh Civic Symphony and Chamber Orchestra**, Price Music Center, 2620 Cate Avenue, Raleigh, 919-515-8279, *www.ncsu.edu/rcs*, provides community and student musicians with the opportunity to work along side professional leaders. The orchestras are based at North Carolina State University and are under the direction of Music Director Dr. Randolph Foy. The orchestras put on several concerts every year. For information on concert dates and ticket information, visit *www.ncsu.edu/arts/ticketcentral/*.
- **The Raleigh Ringers**, 8516 Sleepy Creek Drive, Raleigh, 919-847-7574, *www.rr.org*, is a handbell choir based in Raleigh whose goals include providing audiences with advanced sacred and secular handbell music and promoting the art of handbell ringing. The choir performs in concerts and festivals around the country. For more information on concert schedules, visit *www.rr.org*.
- **Raleigh Symphony Orchestra**, 919-546-9755, *www.raleighsymphony.com*, is a professional orchestra that has

provided Greater Raleigh with symphonic music performances for 27 years.

Dance – Ballet and Modern

- **Carolina Ballet**, 3401-131 Atlantic Avenue, Raleigh, 919-719-0800, *www.carolinaballet.com*; Carolina Ballet's roots go back to the Raleigh Dance Theatre, which was founded in 1984 by Ann Vorus. Established originally to provide opportunities for its students, the Raleigh Dance Theatre was very successful, and in the early 1990s began efforts to launch a professional dance company. The company achieved its goal in the late 1990s. The professional Carolina Ballet was established in 1997, under the direction of artistic director Robert Weiss. Since then, the company has received acclaim from critics representing international, national, and local publications including the Frankfurter Allgemeine Zeitung, the Washington Post, and the News & Observer.
- **Even Exchange Dance Theater**, 114 St. Mary's Street, Raleigh, 919.828.2377, *www.evenexchange.com*; specializes in modern dance. The company was founded in 1997 as an adult ensemble spin-off of The Rainbow Dance Company.
- **The Rainbow Dance Company**, 114 St. Mary Street, 919-828-1713, *www.artstogether.org/rainbowdancecompany.htm*; a multi-age dance company specializing in modern dance and sponsored by Arts Together, a community arts school.

Theatre – Professional and Community

If you're looking for high-caliber Broadway performances, **Broadway Series South**, *www.broadwayseriessouth.com*, at the Progress Energy Center for the Performing Arts should be at the top of your list. Broadway Series South brings some of the biggest and most well-known stage productions to Raleigh, though show runs are typically short (about five to seven days). All performances take place at Raleigh Memorial Auditorium, 2 East South Street, 919-831-6011, *www.progressenergycenter.com*. You can order tickets to individual shows or purchase season tickets at the Memorial Auditorium box office or online at *www.broadwayseriessouth.com*.

If your wallet is tight or if local, smaller productions are more up your alley; Raleigh has a number of well-established professional and community theatre groups:

- **Burning Coal Theatre Company**, 919-834-4001, *www.burningcoal.org*, holds its performances at two locations in Raleigh: **Meymandi Theatre**, Murphey School, 224 Polk Street, Raleigh; and **the Rehearsal Warehouse**, Kennedy Space Center, 3056 Barrow Drive, Raleigh. Burning Coal specializes in often-overlooked classics and modern plays that address issues still relevant in today's communities.
- **North Carolina Theatre**, 1 East South Street, Raleigh, 919-831-6941, *www.nctheatre.com*, is a regional professional, not-for-profit regional theatre company that produces a number of Broadway musicals each year. North Carolina Theatre is a permanent resident of the Raleigh Memorial Auditorium and put on at least four major productions each season.
- **Raleigh Ensemble Players Theatre Company**, ARTSPACE, 201 East Davie Street, Raleigh, 919-832-9607, *www.realtheatre.org*; established 27 years ago, making it the oldest professional theatre company in the Triangle.
- **Raleigh Little Theatre**, 301 Pogue Street, 919-821-4579, *www.raleighlittletheatre.org*, was established in 1936 and is now one of the oldest continuously operating community theatres in the country. The theatre company produces 11 shows every season, which reach 40,000 people each year.

- **Theatre in the Park**, 107 Pullen Road, Raleigh, 919-831-6058, *www.theatreinthepark.com*, offers an array of productions including comedy, contemporary drama, musicals, and Shakespeare plays. Theatre In The Park is located in the northern end of Raleigh's Pullen Park.

FILM

Raleigh may not be the mecca for small, independent films, but that's not to say there aren't theatres in and around Raleigh featuring not-so-mainstream flicks. You may be far from the Hollywood glitz and glamour in Wake County, but there are certainly theaters and local film festivals that can win over even the most discerning cinephile. Below are some great theatres and local film festivals for catching some of the latest "indy" and foreign films.

If you're in the mood for a Hollywood blockbuster, there are a number of national theatre chains in Wake County including Regal Entertainment Group theaters and Carmike Cinemas. For theatre location and ticket information, visit the movie-ticket Website Fandango at *www.fandango.com*.

- **The Rialto Theatre**, 1620 Glenwood Avenue, Raleigh, 919-856-8683, *www.therialto.com*; features foreign and independent films and has a weekly showing of The Rocky Horror Picture Show every Friday at midnight.
- **Colony Theatre**, 5438 Six Forks Road, Raleigh, 919.847.5677, *www.therialto.com*; features foreign and independent films and has a "Cool Classics" showing on the third Wednesday of every month.
- **The Campus Cinema,** Witherspoon Student Center, 2810 Cates Avenue, Raleigh, 919-515-5161, *www.ncsu.edu/cinema/*

PART V: THE NEWCOMER'S GUIDE TO THE RALEIGH AREA

Just Around The Triangle...

If you're craving a top-notch foreign or independent film, Chapel Hill's Chelsea Theatre, Weave Dairy Road, Chapel Hill, 919-968-3005, *www.chelseavarsity.com*; and Varsity Theater, 123 East Franklin Street, Chapel Hill, 919-967-8665, *www.chelseavarsity.com*, are also great options.

Film Festivals

- **Full Frame Documentary Film Festival**, various locations throughout Durham, 919-687-4100, *www.fullframefest.org*; features non-fiction cinema from the around the world. During the festival's four-day run, more than 100 films are shown.
- **Pinwheel Film Festival**, Witherspoon Student Center, 2810 Cates Avenue, Raleigh, 919-515-5161, *www.ncsu.edu/cinema/pinwheel/*; features local and independent short films at NC State University's Campus Cinema.
- **Riverkeeper Film Festival**, various locations throughout the Triangle, 919-856-1180, *www.neuseriver.org/filmfestival.html*; is organized by the Neuse Riverkeeper Foundation and is part of the foundation's goal of protecting and restoring the Neuse River basin through education, advocacy, and enforcement.

MUSIC (CONTEMPORARY) AND NIGHT LIFE

When most people think of "cultural life," they associate the phrase with Broadway theatre or symphony orchestras. Yet for many, live contemporary music is just as much a part of their cultural life as art museums or literature. Below is a list of clubs and bars that offer nightly or weekly live music. Also included are several music festivals that bring even more musical talent to the Triangle.

Alternative, Rock and Hip Hop

- **The Pour House**, 224 South Blount Street, Raleigh, 919-821-1120, *www.the-pour-house.com*
- **Downtown Live,** Moore Square Park, intersection of Blount & Martin Streets, Raleigh, 919-844-1515, *www.raleighdowntownlive.com*; free outdoor summer concert series.

Blues

- **Berkeley Café**, 217 W Martin Street, Raleigh, 919-821-0777, *www.berkeleycafe.net*
- **Raleigh Blues Festival**; held annually. For more information, visit *www.rbccenter.com*.

Country

- **City Limits Saloon**, 901 Tryon Hill Drive, Raleigh, 919-829-3939, *www.hellyeahraleigh.com*
- **Long Branch Saloon**, 600 Creekside Drive, Raleigh, 919-829-1125, *www.longbranchsaloon.com*

Jazz

- **Amra's**, 106 Glenwood Avenue, Raleigh, 919-828-8488, *www.amrasraleigh.com*
- **Irregardless Café**, 901 West Morgan Street, Raleigh, 919-833-8898, *www.irregardless.com*
- **Zydeco Downtown,** 208 Wolfe Street, Raleigh, 919-834-7987, *www.zydecodowntown.com*

Irish

- **Hibernian Restaurant & Pub**, 311 Glenwood Avenue, Raleigh, 919-833-2258, *www.hibernianpub.com*
- **Napper Tandy's Irish Pub**, 126 North West Street, Raleigh, 919-833-5535, *www.nappertandysirishpub.com/raleigh*
- **Tir Na Nog Irish Pub**, 218 South Blount Street, Raleigh, 919-833-7795, *www.tnnirishpub.com*

Nightclubs

- **Ess Lounge and Nightclub**, 327 West Davie Street, 919-829-5482, *www.esslounge.com*
- **The Office**, 310 S West St, Raleigh, 919-828-9994, *www.theofficenightclub.com*
- **White Collar Crime**, 319 W Davie Street, Raleigh, 919-828-0055, *www.dosometime.com*

Reggae

- **Club Ital Lion**, 110 Hargett Street, Raleigh, 866-704-ITAL, *www.club-ital-lion.com*

ART MUSEUMS

- **Gregg Museum of Art & Design**, Talley Student Center, 2610 Cates Avenue, 919.515.3188, *www.ncsu.edu/gregg*; one of the six visual and performing art programs that comprise the North Carolina State University's ARTS NC STATE program. The museum hosts a number of traveling exhibits as well as its own permanent collections of work from local, national, and international artists. All exhibits and programs are free.
- **North Carolina Museum of Art**, 2110 Blue Ridge Road, Raleigh, 919-839-6262, *www.ncartmuseum.org*; the permanent

collections housed at the museum include pieces of art from ancient Egypt through the present day. Permanent exhibits include important works from artists such as Giotto, Claude Monet, Georgia O'Keeffe, and Anselm Kiefer. Admission is free to the museum and to the museum's permanent collection; however, there are admission fees for special exhibitions and some programs, such as concerts, films, classes, and performances. For more information on ticket pricing, call the museum's box office at 919-715-5923.

ART GALLERIES

On the first Friday of every month, the Downtown Raleigh Alliance hosts **First Friday**, *www.godowntownraleigh.com/firstfirday,* 919-832-1231. During First Friday, galleries, art studios, museums, and alternative art venues throughout downtown Raleigh are open late and open to the public.

Some of the galleries you can visit during First Friday include:

- **311 West Martin St Galleries & Studios**, 311 West Martin Street, 919-821-2262, *www.311galleriesandstudios.org*; comprised of three galleries, which are filled by work from 12 different artists.
- **Artspace**, 201 East Davie Street, 919-821-2787, *www.artspacenc.org*, is a non-profit visual art center, which includes artist studios, educational programs, and exhibitions.
- **Morning Times**, 10 East Hargett Street, 919-838-1204, *www.morningtimes-raleigh.com*; a combo coffee shop and art gallery.
- **Points of View Photography Gallery**, 20 Glenwood Avenue, 919-829-1000, *www.povgallery.com*; features local and regional fine art photographers.

PART V: THE NEWCOMER'S GUIDE TO THE RALEIGH AREA

HISTORICAL AND CULTURAL MUSEUMS

- **African America Cultural Complex**, 119 Sunnybrook Road, Raleigh, 919-250-9336, *www.aaccmuseum.org*, first opened its doors in 1989, then named the Black Heritage Park. The museum blossomed from a hobby of Dr. and Mrs. E.B. Palmer, the founders of the museum, into a facility that includes three exhibit houses, a mini amphitheatre, bird sanctuary, nature preserve, picnic area, and botanical gardens. The exhibits feature artifacts, documents, and displays of outstanding contributions made by African Americans.
- **North Carolina Railroad Museum & New Hope Valley Railway**, 5121 Daisey Street, New Hill, 919-362-5416, *www.nhvry.org*; The North Carolina Railroad Museum provides visitors with an in-depth look into the history and heritage of the railroad. Visitors can also take a one-hour ride on the New Hope Valley Railway. Before visiting, make sure you are prepared for the weather. The museum is a primarily outdoor exhibit, and New Hope Valley Railway trips operate in all weather conditions.
- **North Carolina Sports Hall of Fame**, 5 East Edenton Street, Raleigh, 919-845-3455, *www.ncshof.org*, is a North Carolina sports fan's dream. The North Carolina Sports Hall of Fame features a collection of memorabilia from some of the state's most famous sports names. The first class of Hall of Famers was inducted into the Hall of Fame in December 1963, and each donated a memento of their careers. Since then, new inductees have followed suit, and those mementoes comprise the museum's current collection.
- **Raleigh City Museum**, Briggs Building, 220 Fayetteville Street, Raleigh, 919- 832-3775, *www.raleighcitymuseum.org*, is a private, non-profit organization whose goal is to collect and preserve the history of Raleigh. The museum features two permanent exhibits,

one chronicling the beginnings of Raleigh and the other detailing the changes that swept over Raleigh during the mid-1950 through the mid-1970s. Visitors can also view the museum's temporary exhibits. Admission to the museum is free.

- **Wake Forest Birthplace Museum**, 450 North Main Street, Wake Forest, 919-556-2911, *www.wakeforestbirthplace.org*, is dedicated to preserving the history of the town of Wake Forest and Wake Forest College (now known as Wake Forest University) before it was relocated to Winston-Salem in the 1950s. Its collection includes 15,000 pages of original documents, 2,000 photographs, more than 600 books, and more than 1,000 college publications. Visitors are welcome to view the museums exhibits and tour the historic Calvin Jones home at no charge.

SCIENCE MUSEUMS

- **North Carolina Museum of Natural Sciences**, 11 West Jones Street, Raleigh, 919-733-7450, *www.naturalsciences.org*, offers visitors nine exhibit halls spread throughout the museum's four floors. The museum features an *Acrocanthosaurus* dinosaur skeleton, which is the most complete specimen of its kind on display in the world. The museum also provides families and school groups a number of guided learning facilities. One such facility is The Discovery Room, where visitors are given a more hands-on experience, such as touching fossils, feeling bird wings, smelling tropical scents, and watching the beehives.

Just around the Triangle ...

- The **Museum of Life + Sciences**, 433 Murray Avenue, Durham, 919-220-5429, *www.ncmls.org*, is only a short drive from Raleigh and offers another great collection of exhibits and programs. The museum has both indoor and outdoor exhibits; its indoor collections are showcased throughout a 65,000-sq.ft. facility, while the outdoor exhibits are sprawled out over 13 acres! Visitors can sit inside a real Apollo space capsule, touch a 13-foot tornado, and see the East Coast's largest butterfly conservatories.

CULTURE FOR KIDS

The days when your children say, "I'm bored!" are now a thing of the past – at least for the time being! Raleigh has a broad range of attractions and programs specifically designed with kids in mind. Below are some of the top picks for indoor and outdoor kid fun, learning, and entertainment.

Most of the museums and many of the area's annual festivals and events offer children's programs and/or family friendly activities. For more information, check venue or event Website.

Museums

- **Marbles Kids Museum**, 201 East Hargett Street, Raleigh, 919-834-4040, *www.marbleskidsmuseum.org*, is a museum designed specifically to help kids learn through play and discovery. Hands-on learning is not only the norm at this museum but is encouraged. Kids and their families work their way through four permanent exhibits in addition to special temporary exhibits, when the kids (or the parents) need a short sit-down break, the museum campus includes the **Wachovia IMAX Theatre at Marbles Kids Museum**.
- **Museum of Life + Sciences**, 433 Murray Avenue, Durham, 919-220-5429, *www.ncmls.org*, offers Classes for Young Children program, which combines hands-on activities, role play, and self-guided investigations to help kids learn about the museum's exhibits. Programs are available for children 2½ to 3 years old

and children 4 to 6 years old. The museum also offers day camps during summer and spring breaks.
- **Raleigh City Museum**, Briggs Building, 220 Fayetteville Street, Raleigh, 919- 832-3775, *www.raleighcitymuseum.org*, offers a self-guided mystery tour designed for kids. Stop by the Raleigh City Museum to pick up an "investigation notebook" for the **Fayetteville Street Mystery Tour for Kids**. Using clues in the notebook, kids take a walking tour to collect important information to solve mysteries. The tour is appropriate for children 6 years and older. The tour takes about one hour to complete.

Arts and Theatre

- **Artspace**, 201 East Davie Street, 919-821-2787, *www.artspacenc.org*, offers a variety of intensive youth art programs. Classes are designed for kids as young as those in the third grade.
- **KidzArt**, various locations, 919-264-8234, *www.kidzartraleigh.com*; If your kids are aspiring artists or if you're looking to provide them with a creative outlet, KidzArt could be your answer. KidzArt hosts art classes throughout Wake Forest and North Raleigh. All classes are taught by certified instructors.
- **Kazoom Children's Theater and The Carolina Puppet Theater**, 431 West Peace St, Raleigh, 919-365-0555, *www.carolinapuppets.com*, performs weekly shows during which puppets act out children's tales or holiday stories. Performers regularly use audience participation to make the shows funs and exciting. Kids in the audience also have the opportunity to be puppeteers or "child stars" during the performance.

PART V: THE NEWCOMER'S GUIDE TO THE RALEIGH AREA

OUTDOOR

- **Durant Nature Park**, 8305 Camp Durant Road, 919-870-2871, Raleigh, *www.raleigh-nc.org/parks&rec*; includes five miles of walking trails and a playground. The City of Raleigh offers a number of children's nature programs. Visit *www.raleigh-nc.org/parks&rec* for more information.
- **North Carolina Botanical Garden**, 100 Old Mason Farm Road, Chapel Hill, 919-962-0522, *www.ncbg.unc.edu*, is part of the University of North Carolina at Chapel Hill. The Botanical Gardens offer a number of family- and children-focused programs every month. Some of these programs include "Nature Tales: Storytime at the Garden" and "Nature Explorers," a summer day camp.
- **Stevens Nature Center**, 2616 Kildaire Farm Road, 919-387-5980, *www.townofcary.org*; built to complement the Hemlock Bluffs Nature Preserve. The center has a hands-on educational exhibit and provides information about the area's natural history and the native plants and animals in the Nature Preserve.

LITERARY LIFE AND HIGHER EDUCATION

Bookstores

Wake County has quite a lot to offer when it comes to satisfying your inner bookworm. From the familiar national book retailers to independent booksellers to the not-so-familiar (and often eccentric) used bookstores, the wide array of booksellers in Wake County are sure to offer something for everyone's literary tastes.

Chain Book Retailers

- **Barnes & Noble**, 800-843-2665, *www.barnesandnoble.com*, multiple locations throughout Wake County
- **Book Warehouse**, Morrisville Outlet Center, 1001 Airport Boulevard, Suite 255, Morrisville, 919-481-9253, *www.book-warehouse.com*; national discount bookseller
- **Books-A-Million**, 800-201-3550, *www.booksamillion.com*, multiple locations throughout Wake County
- **Borders**, 800-770-7811, *www.borders.com*, multiple location throughout Wake County
- **Cary LifeWay Christian Store**, 2450 Walnut Street, Cary, 919-859-7379, *www.lifewaystores.com*; Christian book and gift retailer
- **Family Christian Store**, *www.familychristian.com*, two locations: 6210 Plantation Center Drive #101, Raleigh, 919-501-5055; and 301 Crossroads Boulevard, Cary, 919-851-2244; Christian book and gift retailer

Independent And Used Booksellers

- **2nd Chance Books**, Harrison Square Shopping Center, 1821 North Harrison Avenue, Cary, 919-677-0070, *www.2ndchancebooks.com*; specializes in gently used books and audio books
- **ABDebs Books & Gifts**, 4001 Widewaters Parkway, Suite B, Knightdale, 919-217-6976, *www.abdebs.com*; general independent bookseller
- **Books at Stonehenge**, 7414 Creedmoor Road, Raleigh, 919-846-1404
- **Dancing Moon Books and Gifts**, 1840 Wake Forest Road, Raleigh, 919-833-8081, *www.dancingmoonraleigh.com*; one of the largest independent, New Age retailers in the Southeast

PART V: THE NEWCOMER'S GUIDE TO THE RALEIGH AREA

- **Falls River Books**, 1141 Falls River Avenue, Raleigh, 919-870-9800, *www.fallsriverbooks.com*; deals in fine and used books
- **Foundations Edge**, 2526 Hillsborough Street, Raleigh, 919-832-0044, *foundationsedge.ypguides.net*; specializes in comics and also maintains a large selection of science fiction, fantasy, and horror books
- **Nice Price Books**, 3106 Hillsborough Street, Raleigh, 919-829-0230
- **Quail Ridge Books & Music**, 3522 Wade Ave, Raleigh, 919-828-1588, *quailridgebooks.booksense.com*; specializes in fine literature for adults and children, with a special focus on the South
- **Reader's Corner, Inc.**, 3201 Hillsborough Street, Raleigh, 919-828-7024
- **White Rabbit Books & Things**, 309 West Martin Street, Raleigh, 919-856-1429, *www.whiterabbitbooks.com*.

Literary Workshops And Groups

Whether you're an aspiring writer looking for constructive criticism or a book lover hoping to share your literary passion with others, there are likely a number of literary groups and book clubs that can match your needs and interests.

Libraries and many national book retailers as well as independent booksellers host book clubs or other literary groups. Check with your local library branch and booksellers for more information.

Another great resource to find local writers' workshops or book clubs is a Website called Meetup, *www.meetup.com*. The Website provides a great directory of local social groups, and groups use the site to keep their members up-to-date on information about upcoming events. Literary groups in Raleigh are plentiful on Meetup. Some examples include Raleigh Write 2 Publish, *writers.meetup.com/500/about/*, for writers focused on getting their work published and The Cary Book Club, *bookclub.meetup.com/cities/us/nc/raleigh/*.

Other literary groups and book clubs include:
- **Quail Ridge Books & Music**, 3522 Wade Ave, Raleigh, 919-828-1588, *quailridgebooks.booksense.com*; this independent book stores hosts a number of different book clubs. For more information and meeting schedules, visit the store's Website.
- **Raleigh Writer's Forum Workshop**, Borders, 1751 Walnut Street, Cary, 919-469-1930, is for writers of all levels and meets every first and third Tuesday at 6:30 pm.

Libraries

Nineteen public libraries and branches make up the Wake County Public Library system. Wake County library cardholders are welcome to use computers and to check out books and materials from any of the Wake County libraries.

Each library hosts a variety of literary events, book clubs for various age groups, and family-friendly activities. For more information on events, contact each branch directly or visit the Wake County Public Libraries Website at *www.wakegov.com/libraries/*.

Two of the libraries in the Wake County Public Library system maintain historical collections, which include books, documents, and other artifacts relating to the local, family, and cultural history of Raleigh and the surrounding areas.

Raleigh's colleges and universities also offer additional resources, including extensive collections of academic texts and journals. While college and university libraries are generally open to the public, their hours and services for non-students and non-faculty patrons may vary. Check directly with each library for more details on services available to the public.

PART V: THE NEWCOMER'S GUIDE TO THE RALEIGH AREA

Public

- **Athens Drive Community Library**, 1420 Athens Drive, Raleigh, 919-233-4000
- **Cameron Village Regional Library**, 1930 Clark Avenue, Raleigh, 919-856-6710
- **Cary Public Library**, 310 South Academy Street, Cary, 919-460-3350
- **Duraleigh Road Library**, 5800 Duraleigh Road, Raleigh, 919-881-1344
- **East Regional Library**, 946 Steeple Square Court, Knightdale, 919-217-5301
- **Electronic Information Center**, 336 Fayetteville Street, Raleigh, 919-856-6868
- **Eva H. Perry Regional Library**, 2100 Shepherd's Vineyard Drive, Apex, 919-387-2100
- **Fuquay-Varina Library**, 133 South Fuquay Avenue, Fuquay-Varina, 919-557-2788
- **Green Road Library**, 4101 Green Road, Raleigh, 919-790-3200
- **Holly Springs Library**, 300 West Ballentine Street, Holly Springs, 919-577-1660
- **Leesville Library**, 5105 Country Trail, Raleigh, 919-571-6661
- **North Regional Library**, 7009 Harps Mill Road, Raleigh, 919-870-4000
- **Olivia Raney Local History Library**, 4016 Carya Drive, Raleigh, 919-250-1196
- **Richard B. Harrison**, 1313 New Bern Avenue, Raleigh, 919-856-5720
- **Southeast Regional**, 908 Seventh Avenue, Garner, 919-662-2250
- **Southgate Branch Library**, 1601-14 Cross Link Road, Raleigh, 919-856-6598

- **Wake Forest Branch**, 400 East Holding Avenue, Wake Forest, 919-554-8498
- **Wendell Branch Library**, 207 South Hollybrook Road, Wendell, 919-365-2600
- **West Regional Library**, 4000 Louis Stephens Drive, Cary, 919-463-8500
- **Zebulon Branch Library**, 1000 Dogwood Drive, Zebulon, 919-404-3610

Historical Libraries

- **Olivia Raney Local History Library**, 4016 Carya Drive, Raleigh, 919-250-1196, *www.wakegov.com/libraries/*; originally used as a branch library, the Olivia Raney Local History Library was created in response to a group of Wake County's residents push for a local history library in the Wake County Library System. The library maintains a collection of 18,178 items documenting primarily local and family history.
- **Richard B. Harrison Library**, 1313 New Bern Avenue, Raleigh, 919-856-5720, *www.wakegov.com/libraries/*; founded by the first African American librarian in Wake County, the library houses a collection of non-fiction and fiction texts, pamphlets, and other media chronicling the local and national experience of African Americans.
- **State Library of North Carolina**, 109 East Jones Street, Raleigh, 919-807-7430, *statelibrary.ncdcr.gov*; part of the North Carolina Department of Cultural Resources and helps develop and support historical collections including genealogy and North Caroliniana.

PART V: THE NEWCOMER'S GUIDE TO THE RALEIGH AREA

College And University Libraries

- **Meredith College, Carlyle Campbell Library**, 3800 Hillsborough Street, Raleigh, 919-760-8531, *www.meredith.edu/library/*
- **North Carolina State University Libraries**, 2 West Broughton Drive, Raleigh, 919-515-3364, *www.lib.ncsu.edu*
- **Peace College, Lucy Cooper Finch Library**, 15 East Peace Street, Raleigh, 919-508-2302, *library.peace.edu/*
- **Saint Augustine's College, Prezell R. Robinson Library**, 1315 Oakwood Avenue, Raleigh, 919-516-4000, *www.st-aug.edu/library/library.htm*
- **Shaw University Libraries**, 118 East South Street, Raleigh, 919-546-8200, *www.shawuniversity.edu/libraries.htm*
- **Southern Baptist Theological Seminary, The Library**, 114 North Wingate Street, Wake Forest, 919-761-2251, *www.sebts.edu/library*

Lectures

Regular lecture series are abundant in Raleigh and the surrounding areas. A number of organizations in the area including colleges, universities, museums, Wake County's public libraries, and local churches sponsor and organize regular lecture series.

On one hand, lecture series can be great resources for those doing professional research or considering the next step in their career paths. On the other hand, lecture series can simply provide a fun outlet for intellectual curiosity. Lecture series in the Raleigh area have focused on everything from leadership development (the Wachovia Executive Lecture Series at **North Carolina State University**) to the history and uses of chocolate (The Chocolate Lecture Series at the **North Carolina Museum of Natural Sciences**).

Organizations and institutions that regularly host lecture series include:

- **City of Raleigh**, 919-807-8480, various locations, *www.raleighnc.gov/lectureseries*, hosts the Designing a 21st Century City Lecture Series, which was established to encourage open conversation regarding Raleigh's current and future challenges and opportunities as they relate to urban design.
- **Gregg Museum of Art & Design**, Talley Student Center, 2610 Cates Avenue, 919.515.3188, *www.ncsu.edu/gregg*, invites artists of all mediums to share their work.
- **Meredith College**, 3800 Hillsborough Street, Raleigh, 919-760-8600, *www.meredith.edu/owor/lecture-series.htm*, hosts The Blue Cross and Blue Shield of North Carolina Presidential Lecture Series. Speakers invited to participate in this lecture series are national and internationally recognized speakers.
- **North Carolina Museum of Art**, 2110 Blue Ridge Road, Raleigh, 919-839-6262, *www.ncartmuseum.org*, regularly invites scholars and experts for lectures on various aspects of art history and research.
- **North Carolina Museum of Nature Sciences**, 11 West Jones Street, Raleigh, 919-733-7450, *www.naturalsciences.org*; for information on upcoming lectures, visit the museum's "Programs and Events" Webpage and click on "Science Talks."
- Various departments of **North Carolina State University**, 919-513-1200, *www.ncsu.edu*, offer regular lecture series. For information, visit the homepages of individual schools and/or department within NC State, such as the NC State School of Management or NC State College of Design.

PART V: THE NEWCOMER'S GUIDE TO THE RALEIGH AREA

Higher Education

Raleigh is consistently recognized as one of the most educated cities in the nation (according to the U.S. Census Bureau, nearly 50% of Raleigh residents 25 years and older have at least a bachelor's degree), and those looking for intellectual stimulation will find plenty of options in Raleigh.

Raleigh and its surrounding areas are home to some of the country's top universities and leading research institutions. Seven universities and colleges have made their home in Raleigh, but if they don't fit the bill, Chapel Hill and Durham will certainly provide additional alternatives.

- **Meredith College**, 3800 Hillsborough Street, Raleigh, 919-760-8600, *www.meredith.edu*, was charted in 1891 and is one of the United States' largest private women's colleges. Its 225-acre campus is home to more than 2,000 undergraduate students and approximately 250 graduate students. In keeping with the Triangle's tradition of leading-edge technology development and adoption, Meredith provides each of its full-time students with a laptop as part of the Meredith Technology Initiative. Meredith began the program in 2001 and was the first women's college to launch such a program.
- **North Carolina State University**, 1210 Varsity Drive, E. Carroll Joyner Visitor Center, 919-513-1200, *www.ncsu.edu*, is known as a leader in science, engineering, and technology research. Its facilities include the Centennial Campus, which the university describes as a "technopolis" comprised of multi-disciplinary "R&D neighborhoods" where members of the corporate, government, and university community can closely collaborate. In fact, it has been said NC State graduates are recruited by more corporate and government entities than any other university in the state.

- **Peace College**, 15 East Peace Street, Raleigh, 919-508-2044, www.peace.edu, is an all-women's liberal arts and science college and has close ties with North Carolina's Civil War-era history: The Confederate Army used Peace College's Main Building as a military hospital. Founded in 1857 by Raleigh's First Presbyterian Church, Peace is named after William Peace, a church elder who donated $10,000 and the first eight acres of land on which the first Peace facilities were built. Today the Peace is independent and enrolls roughly 700 women each year.
- **Saint Augustine's College**, 1315 Oakwood Avenue, Raleigh, 919-516-4000, www.st-aug.edu, has more than 10,000 living alumni. Some of its most famous alums include Ruby Butler DeMesme, who served as the Assistant Secretary of the Air Force for manpower, installations, and environment; and Hannah Diggs Atkins, who served in the Oklahoma House of Representatives from 1968-1980 and who was the first African American women to be elected to that office. Its campus consists of 37 facilities, three of which are registered historic landmarks: the Chapel, Saint Agnes Hall, and Taylor Hall.
- **Shaw University**, 118 East South Street, Raleigh, 919-546-8200, www.shawuniversity.edu, was the first historically black college established in the South. Founded in 1865, Shaw is a private liberal arts university affiliated with the Baptist Church and is part of the Southern Association of Colleges and Schools. It offers 30 undergraduate majors and awards associate, bachelor, and Master degrees. The university's Shaw Divinity School is one a very few divinity schools in North Carolina that are fully accredited by the Association of Theological Schools.
- **Southeastern Baptist Theological Seminary**, 120 S. Wingate Street, Wake Forest, 919-761-2100, www.sebts.edu, offers associate's, bachelor's, master's, and doctoral degrees. SEBTS is dedicated to integrating faith and learning and maintains the

motto: "Every classroom, a Great Commission classroom." The seminary has been educating aspiring ministers since it was established in 1950 by the Southern Baptist Convention.
- **Wake Technical Community College**, 9101 Fayetteville Road, Raleigh, 919-866-3500, *www.waketech.edu*, has facilities throughout Wake County. Wake Technical Community College consists of four area campuses, the Adult Education Center, the Public Safety Training Center, and the Eastern North Carolina Plastics Technology Center. It provides courses and programs in more than 150 academic, vocational, and technical specialties.

Just around the Triangle...

Durham and Chapel Hill complete the area known as "the Triangle," and only add to the quality of higher-education programs available to those in Raleigh and the surrounding areas.

- **Duke University**, 2138 Campus Drive, Durham, 919-684-8111, *www.duke.edu*, was founded in Durham in 1924 by James Buchanan Duke. James Buchanan Duke was a decedent of The Dukes, a Durham family that built its fortune in the tobacco and energy production business. Today, Duke is known as one of the leading and most selective universities in the country.
- The **University of North Carolina at Chapel Hill**, CB 9100,103 South Building, Chapel Hill, 919-962-2211, *www.unc.edu*, is consistently ranked among the best public universities in the United States. It is well known for its top-notch masters and doctoral programs in medicine, public health, nursing, and business administration.

CHAPTER 46

CLIMATE AND ENVIRONMENT

How hot, and cold, will it get in North Carolina? How often will a hurricane hit and how should I prepare? When will you pick your first home-grown tomato, and what else will be trying to eat it? Why is the City of Oaks full of pine trees? The climate, flora and fauna of your new home will impact your life in a number of ways, so read on to learn more about them.

WEATHER IN THE TRIANGLE

Centrally located between the Blue Ridge Mountains to the west and the Atlantic Coast to the east, Triangle temperatures are mild most of the year while still allowing residents to experience all four seasons. The average temperature is 60 degrees. And as so many transplants from further north have found, sunshine abounds. There are typically about 220 days with sunshine a year, and rainfall is well distributed throughout the year.

PART V: THE NEWCOMER'S GUIDE TO THE RALEIGH AREA

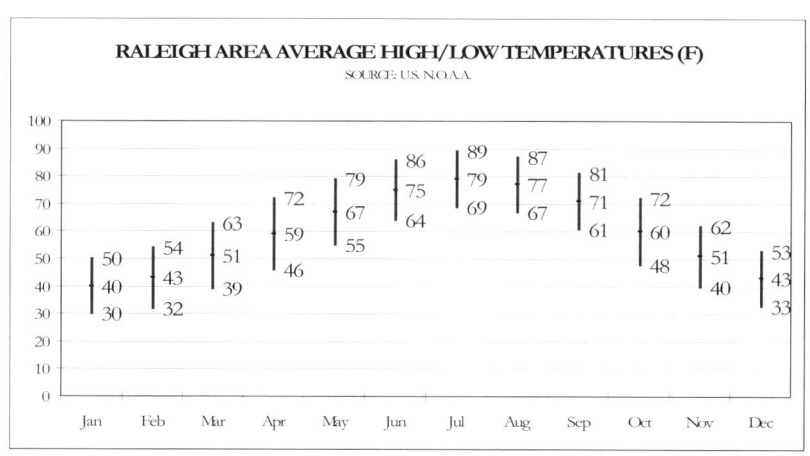

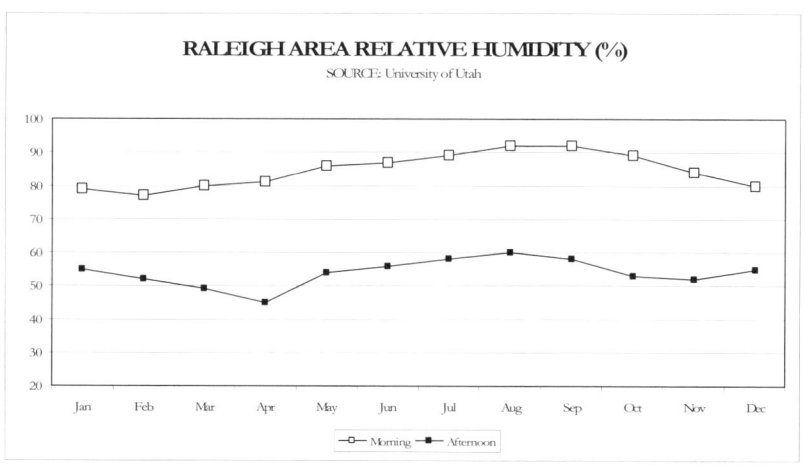

WHAT ARE WINTERS LIKE?

Since many newcomers come to the Triangle from colder climates further north, a good number of those moving here will find mild winters to be the most notable feature of the local climate. Winter temperatures generally range from highs in the low 50s to lows in the 30s, though 60-degree weather is not uncommon. An average year will see a handful of snowy days -- though some years pass with no snow at all -- and the small amounts often do not even accumulate on the ground. The average snowfall is about 7 inches per year, although we rarely experience more than 3 inches at a time.

Freezing rain and sleet occur most winters, but major, damaging ice storms are rare. Our last major ice storm was in December 2002. The most common damage from ice storms is when trees fall across power lines causing power outages. For more on these and other types of storms, see the "Severe Weather" section below.

The infrequency of harsh winter weather does have a downside. Local governments, not to mention residents, are not always as prepared to deal with these events as their northern counterparts. Salt is not always applied to roads in advance of snow, and when it is, many smaller roads will not be treated. Local drivers are generally wary of hitting the road in snowy weather. As a result, be prepared for "snow days" off of school or work even when only small amounts of snow fall. Monitor local news on television and online for information on closings. See more on closings under "Ice Storms" in the "Severe Weather" section below.

WHAT ABOUT THE OTHER SEASONS? CAN I SURVIVE THE SUMMER?

Some who come here to escape cold winters discover an unpleasant flipside to their new climate: steamy hot summers. No doubt about it, the summers are hot in the Carolinas. The good news, however, is that the most extreme heat, when temperatures exceed 90 degrees, is short-lived – on average restricted to a few scattered weeks in July and August. Most natives and longtime residents plan trips to the mountains or the coast – or back to their former homes out of state – during the hottest months. It's also a great time to splash around in a pool or lake. Try doing arduous outdoor activities, such as moving the lawn or jogging, in the morning or late evening during the hot summer months. And monitor local news outlets for advisories when ozone levels get high on hot days. Authorities will often recommend that vulnerable people –

children and those with respiratory problems, for instance – stay inside on these days.

When rainfall is below average, the Triangle area sometimes suffers from drops in the water levels of our lakes, prompting water restrictions imposed by local governments. This happens most often in the summer, when the hot air evaporates more moisture. Later summer also marks the start of hurricane season. For more tips on dealing with hurricanes and drought, see the "Severe Weather" section below.

Though warm summers and mild winters are largely pleasant, the real treat of living here might be spring and fall, when most days are neither too hot nor too cold for comfort. Try turning off the heat and air conditioner and opening the windows on a cool spring morning, or strolling through one of many gardens in the area as hundreds of flowering plants come into bloom.

In the fall, head out for a stroll through woods colored yellow, orange and red, either nearby or amidst the more spectacular views in the North Carolina mountains. Each year millions of residents and tourists drive along the famous Blue Ridge Parkway, taking in breathtaking views of the kaleidoscope of color as the leaves change. For more on viewing the leaves, visit *www.chiff.com/travel/north-carolina-foliage.htm*. To make sure you head out when the leaves are at the peak of color, check out the updated fall color report kept by the U.S. Forest Service, 800-354-4595, *www.cs.unca.edu/nfsnc/press/fall.htm*.

SEVERE WEATHER

The beauty of the North Carolina weather is that you get the variety of seasons without the extreme winters you see up north or the scorching heat you might see down in Florida. This same position in the middle of the East Coast, however, makes the Piedmont a target for all kinds of severe weather. Hurricanes roll in from the Atlantic to the east or dump heavy rains as they slog northward from the Gulf of Mexico. Warm and cold air often clash in North Carolina, spawning thunderstorms and tornadoes. All told, North Carolina ranks fourth in the nation for the number of storms producing, strong winds or tornadoes. While few of these events cause widespread damage, it's good to be prepared for all types of severe weather.

To keep tabs on the weather on your own or contact local officials during a storm, try these Web sites and contacts:

Forecasts

- Forecasts from the Raleigh office of NOAA, *www.erh.noaa.gov/rah*
- Online weather at Weather Underground, *www.wunderground.com/US/NC/Raleigh.htm*
- Local TV news station WRAL offers a comprehensive online weather report, *www.wral.com/weather*.

Severe Weather

- The Federal Emergency Management Agency, *www.fema.gov/hazard*, offers advice for dealing with different types of hazards and links to weather maps.
- The Centers for Disease Control and Prevention, *www.bt.cdc.gov/disasters*, offers tips for dealing with all types of severe weather.
- Wake County Emergency Management, 919-856-6480, *www.wakegov.com/em*. You can even sign up to get emergency notifications from the county through Twitter and other social networking sites at *www.wakegov.com/connect*.
- N.C. Department of Crime Control and Public Safety, 919-733-3867, *www.nccrimecontrol.org* (choose "Emergency Info" tab), maintains a comprehensive Web site, *readync.org*, with

information on how to prepare for different disasters common to North Carolina.

WHAT SHOULD I KNOW ABOUT HURRICANES?

While Piedmont residents watch warily as many a hurricane heads their way, most of these storms have dissolved into large swirls of thunderstorms by the time they reach the Triangle, which lies more than 150 miles from the coast. As a result, most of the damage from these storms is actually due to flooding caused by excessive rains brought by tropical fronts and the downed trees that result from the combination of heavy rains and wind.

On rare occasions, however, actual hurricanes do strike inland in North Carolina. One such hurricane, Fran, shocked residents when it hit the coast and then kept coming inland to ravage the Triangle in September 1996 -- the first major hurricane to hit inland since Hazel in 1954. Nearly a half-million tourists and residents were evacuated from the coasts of North and South Carolina. The storm caused about $900 million worth of damage in Wake County alone, making it the worst recorded economic disaster ever to occur in North Carolina. (It is interesting to note that during that time, Raleigh acquired its National Hockey League team. Many loyal fans wonder what our champion Carolina Hurricanes would have been named had Fran not hit Raleigh as the NHL franchise was being formed.)

More often, the Triangle will see tropical storms or heavy thunderstorms caused by tropical fronts. In any case, residents should prepare for heavy winds, lots of rain and the possibility of storm damage and electrical outages.

To be prepared for a hurricane or tropical storm, make sure you have the items listed in the 'Storm Preparation" section above. In addition, consider taking these steps suggested by FEMA:

- Secure your property. Permanent storm shutters offer the best protection for windows. A second option is to board up windows with 5/8" marine plywood, cut to fit and ready to install. Tape does not prevent windows from breaking.
- Install straps or additional clips to securely fasten your roof to the frame structure. This will reduce roof damage.
- Clear loose and clogged rain gutters and downspouts.
- Determine how and where to secure your boat.
- Consider building a safe room.

During a hurricane or tropical storm warning, stay indoors and monitor the weather on TV, radio or online. If a serious storm is approaching, some areas may be evacuated. Follow the directions of local authorities and stay inside, even if the weather seems to clear. An abrupt clearing of storm conditions may signify that the eye of the storm is passing, which means the storm will return just as abruptly as it stopped. Also, take the advice below on tornadoes, which often come along with hurricanes or other tropical weather.

Here are some other helpful Web sites for hurricane season:

- National Hurricane Center, *www.nhc.noaa.gov*, offers up-to-the-minute information on storms.
- The News & Observer Hurricane Center, *www.wunderground.com/auto/newsobserver/tropical*, gives more localized information about storms.
- Accuweather Hurricane Center, *hurricane.accuweather.com/hurricane*, has tracking maps and satellite images
- N.C. Automated Flood Warning System, *www.afws.net/states/nc/nc.htm*, updates rainfall amounts every 15 minutes.

PART V: THE NEWCOMER'S GUIDE TO THE RALEIGH AREA

- The FEMA, CDC and ReadyNC.org sites, listed above under "Storm Preparation" offer comprehensive information on preparing for a hurricane.
- UNC-TV, *www.unctv.org/hurricane*, has information on previous hurricanes, advice for upcoming ones, and a site for children on hurricanes.

WHAT SHOULD I KNOW ABOUT ICE STORMS?

The term "Ice Storm" encompasses the worst of adverse winter weather in a region where blizzards and other frequent storms are rare. The phenomenon is most clear when a hard freeze descends on the area in wet conditions, causing clumps of ice to freeze onto trees and power lines. The predictable result is electricity outages caused by falling limbs and trees. During the ice storm of 2002, some Triangle residents were without power for a week or more during some of the coldest weather of the year. A number of trees, even the region's largest oaks, toppled over under the weight of heavy ice coupled with soil softened by rain.

To prepare for an ice storm, make sure that you are equipped with the supplies listed above under "Storm Preparation." In addition, prepare for the possibility of a power outage during extremely cold weather. Make sure you have plenty of warm blankets and clothing on hand. Stock up on wood for fireplaces or woodstoves, or equip your home with an alternate heating source or generator in case the electricity goes out. Or make plans to stay at a hotel or other location with electricity once the storm itself has ended if you are without power, particularly if you have small children or other vulnerable people in your home.

Once the storm hits, stay indoors in a safe location and monitor weather reports. Even if you lose electricity, do not evacuate your home until the storm has ended. Do not use a gas oven to heat your home. This can lead to carbon monoxide poisoning.

ARE TORNADOES COMMON IN THE TRIANGLE?

The answer is yes and no. North Carolina is not known for prevalent tornadoes like Kansas and other states to the west. But serious tornadoes pass through the Piedmont every few years, causing widespread damage, injuries, and at times fatalities. The peak months for tornadoes in North Carolina are March, May and November, when collisions of warm and cold fronts produce heavy rains and wind, along with tornadoes. Hurricanes can also spawn tornadoes.

To be prepared for a tornado, plan in advance where you will go in the event of a tornado warning. The best location is generally on the lowest level of your house and away from windows. If you live in a mobile home, you should plan to evacuate to a safer structure. (Often local schools or churches will serve as shelters. Check with local authorities to see where you can go during severe weather.) Pay close attention to weather reports during hurricanes and thunderstorms.

The most deadly tornadoes are the 30 percent statewide that touch down after dark, when sleeping residents have little or no time to prepare or evacuate. A recent NOAA report found that the state ranks first in the nation for the percentage of fatalities from nighttime tornadoes, with 80 percent of deaths from tornadoes occurring at night. To be prepared for this possibility, man your house with a NOAA-approved weather radio, preferably one that can be programmed for your specific county. These radios will send off an alarm that will wake you up if a tornado is spotted in your area, giving you time to seek out a safe place. Keep your weather radio on while you sleep if tornadoes are forecast. (See the "Storm Preparation" section above for more on weather radios.)

Also, be familiar with your tornado terms. A tornado watch simply means that weather conditions are ripe for tornadoes to form. A tornado warning means that at least one has been spotted, and residents in the area should take cover. People who have lived through tornadoes say they are extremely loud as they approach, making a sound often compared to a train approaching. If you suspect a tornado is approaching, take precautions even if you are not sure.

When tornadoes have been spotted in your area, state authorities suggest a three step plan: get in, get down and cover up. Stay inside in a safe place, and don't drive. If you suspect a tornado will hit your house or shelter, crouch down in the lowest part of the structure possible, cover yourself with pillows and try to move under a desk or other heavy furniture.

Here are some Web sites with information on tornadoes:
- NOAA's Tornado Guide, *www.nssl.noaa.gov/edu/safety/tornadoguide.html*, has information on how tornadoes form, the types and frequency of tornadoes, and tips for preparing for them.
- NOAA also has information on the F-scaled used to rate tornado intensity at *www.spc.noaa.gov/efscale*.
- The FEMA, CDC and ReadyNC.org sites, listed above under "Storm Preparation" offer comprehensive information on tornadoes.

WHY DO THUNDERSTORMS MATTER?

By far the most common severe weather event in the Triangle would be the lowly thunderstorm. But don't count them out just because they don't sound as dramatic as hurricanes or tornadoes. Thunderstorms bring deadly lightning, hail, and falling branches or trees loosened by wind in rain that can knock out electricity, and cause injury or damage.

Most thunderstorms happen, between 2 p.m. and 9 p.m., and they are most common in the late spring and early summer. A report generated by the Raleigh office of NOAA found that more than 60 percent of thunderstorms in the Piedmont region occurred during May, June and July over the 55-year period from 1950 to 2005. About 34 percent of these storms included hail.

During thunderstorms, stay indoors and monitor weather reports. Stay in the lowest floor of your house, particularly if nearby trees or limbs could hit your house. Be prepared for losing electricity.

WHAT ABOUT DROUGHT?

Every few years, it seems, the Triangle experiences a dry spell. Some are minor, but others turn into full-scale droughts that threaten to deplete the water supply and force local governments to impose restrictions on the use of water. Water restrictions are usually voluntary and apply to the use of water outside on lawns and gardens. In more extreme cases, such as the severe drought of 2007, we have had mandatory water restrictions in which residents are required to only water on even or odd days. Those who fail to comply face fines or loss of water service.

Falls Lake is the source of most of Wake County's water. At print time, most of Wake County, including the City of Raleigh, remained under mandatory conservation measures adopted in 2008. Raleigh's water restrictions apply to a number of Wake County towns that the city provides with water, including Garner, Knightdale, Wendell, Zebulon, Wake Forest and Rolesville.

To prepare, the best way to ease the pinch of water restrictions during drought is to landscape using drought-tolerant plants. Planting plants and laying sod during the rainy spring months will also help you avoid the pain of dry summers. Inside, make sure your toilets and other appliances use as little water as possible.

When dry weather hits, use a rain barrel to capture water for outside use. Reuse water from inside on your plants outside. Put off planting sensitive plants or sodding a new lawn.

Here are some useful Web sites about dry weather and droughts, including the rules for most Wake County towns:

- Wake County, *www.wakegov.com/water/restrictions.htm*, tracks water restrictions in its municipalities and offers links to other information on conservation.
- Town of Apex Current Water Restriction, 919-249-3427 *www.apexnc.org/depts/pw/water_restrictions.cfm*.
- City of Raleigh Water Conservation, 919-857-4540, *www.slowtheflowwake.com*
- Town of Cary Water Conservation, 919-469-4387 *www.townofcary.org/depts/pwdept/water/waterconservation/overview.htm* (Cary conservation rules also apply to Morrisville.)
- Town of Fuquay-Varina Public Utilities, 919-753-1024, *www.fuquay-varina.org/utilities*
- Town of Holly Springs Water Conservation, 919-577-1090 *www.hollyspringsnc.us/service/watercon.htm*
- The N.C. Division of Water Resources, *www.ncwater.org/Drought_Monitoring*, offers updated statewide drought information.
- The N.C. Drought Management Advisory Council, *www.ncdrought.org*, offers information on current conditions in addition to a wealth of general information about drought conditions in North Carolina.
- The National Integrated Drought Information System, *www.drought.gov*, is a nationwide resource for information on drought.

PLANTS AND ANIMALS

What kinds of plants and animals live in the Triangle?

Raleigh is known as the "City of Oaks" for its many oak trees, though a keen observer might notice that pine trees are the dominant species.

More importantly, visitors often note that the area has a lot of trees – including more than 120 species, more than can be found from Scandinavia to the Mediterranean – that make important shade in the winter, keep the air clean, and make the area beautiful.

Hiding beneath those trees are thousands of flowering plants and animals of all types – both friendly and not so friendly. Hundreds of types of birds such as woodpeckers and blue birds make their way to the area in the spring, and many stay all winter long. Deer are common, as are foxes, coyotes, and black bear in the mountains.

Among the least desirable of our animal neighbors are a wide variety of biting insects, such as the mosquitoes that make their presence known on warm summer evenings. In all, however, the state has relatively few dangerous animals to worry about, including only six venomous snakes out of the dozens of species native to North Carolina.

Here are some resources on the Web to help you enjoy the area's plants and animals:

- Trees: This guide from Duke University, *www.duke.edu/~cwcook/trees*, will help you identify trees in the Piedmont.
- Birds: Amateur and experienced birders should consult the Triangle Birder's Guide, *tbg.carolinanature.com*, for information on good birding spots and a list of local species.
- Mammals: The American Society of Mammologists, *www.mammalsociety.org/statelists/ncmammals.html*, offers a list of mammals native to the state.
- Reptiles: This guide from Davidson College, *www.bio.davidson.edu/projects/herpcons/herpcons.html*, helps you identify snakes and has other reptile information.
- Insects: The Department of Entymology at N.C. State University, *www.ces.ncsu.edu/depts/ent/notes/Urban/index.htm*, offers a listing of local pests, including those that bite, damage property and harm crops.

PART V: THE NEWCOMER'S GUIDE TO THE RALEIGH AREA

Gardening in the Triangle

The Triangle presents a world of opportunity for people who love to garden. With a long growing season and ample sunshine, plants that may not be supported by other climates flourish here. With careful planning, a dedicated gardener could fill their yard with flowers or vegetables all year long. Nonetheless, the clay soil in the Piedmont will present difficulties for some plants. Before planting, consult your garden center about what type of amendments you should make to the soil for the plants you are using, or contact an extension agent to test your soil and get advice on preparing it for planting.

Wake County falls in the climate zone 7 for plant hardiness of the 11 zones designated U.S. Department of Agriculture, with 11 being the warmest. The beginning vegetable gardener might start with summer crops of tomatoes, squash, and cucumbers, which can be planted after the last freeze in the spring. Cabbage, carrots and collard greens are planted in the fall. On average, the first freeze comes in Wake County between October 21 and October 31. The last freeze of the year comes, on average, between April 1 and April 11.

To learn more about gardening, try these resources:

- N.C. Cooperative Extension, *www.ces.ncsu.edu/depts/hort/consumer*. based at N.C. State University, offers a wealth of information on maintaining lawns and gardens, including fact sheets on different plants that include information on soil and pests.
- The extension also runs the master gardener program, which allows you to call an expert for gardening advice: 919-250-1116 for Wake County, *wake.ces.ncsu.edu*.
- The UNC-Chapel Hill Botanical Garden, *ncbg.unc.edu/pages/44*, offers advice on using plants native to the area in your garden, along with information on gardening in a drought.

- For lawn care information, see the extension's comprehensive guide to types of grass and lawn maintenance, *www.turfgrass.ncsu.edu/guides/CarolinaLawns2008.pdf*

To see firsthand what type of shrubs and plants grow well locally, visit one of the area's public gardens:
- J.C. Raulston Arboretum at N.C. State University, 919-515-3132, *www.ncsu.edu/jcraulstonarboretum*
- N.C. Botanical Garden at UNC-Chapel Hill, 919-962-2211, *www.ncbg.unc.edu*
- Sarah P. Duke Gardens at Duke University, 919-684-3698, *www.hr.duke.edu/dukegardens*
- For a list of more public gardens, visit *www.ces.ncsu.edu/depts/hort/consumer/pgpages.html*.

CHAPTER 47

TRANSPORTATION IN THE TRIANGLE

The Triangle benefits from a network of interstates and major state roads that make getting from Raleigh to Durham to Chapel Hill to the airport and other points of interest a fast trip. Of course, this convenient network of roads has helped fuel the area's growth, which in turn has helped crowd those roads with traffic. A continuing regimen of highway expansions and improvements is in place to accommodate the influx of drivers, though at a pace that can seem slow when you're parked on Interstate 40. To put some numbers behind that feeling, the Triangle region ranked 37th of 90 major metropolitan areas in 2007 in hours of traffic delays, according to a national study by the Texas Transportation Institute.

For going longer distances, planes, and increasingly trains, are convenient options. Within the Triangle, bus remains the primary mode of public transportation, though other options, such as light rail, are on the drawing board. Old-fashioned ways to get around – walking and biking – are also gaining fans in the Triangle. On the coast, a network of ferries is a popular way to get to and from the beaches of the Outer Banks.

For more information on getting around, try the N.C. Department of Transportation, 877-DOT-4YOU, *www.ncdot.org*. DOT works in concert with federal agencies to oversee transportation infrastructure in the state, including highways, railways and ferries, as well as public transportation and facilities for walking and biking.

ON THE ROAD

Despite a growing number of public transportation options, driving is still the number one way to get from place to place in the Triangle, and dealing with traffic is a way of life. A few major highways form the region's major corridors. Interstate 40 connects Raleigh to the rest of the Triangle, along with the coast. Two other major interstates near Wake County are Interstate 85, a major north-south corridor that hits I-40 near Durham, and I-95, which hits I-40 just a ways east in Johnston County.

Interstate 440, known as the Beltline, makes a tight circle around the core of the city of Raleigh. (In real estate, it also marks the dividing line between ITB, inside the Beltline, and the more recently built areas outside.) Interstate 540, know as the "Outer Loop," is slated to eventually make a larger loop around Raleigh. For now, it runs north of the city from I-40 near the Wake-Durham county line east to U.S. 64 near Knightdale.

To date, all of the roads in the Triangle, and statewide for that matter, are free. But that will soon change. In August 2009, the state broke ground on its first toll road, the Triangle Expressway. The 19-mile-long highway will connect the Durham Freeway (N.C. 147) to I-540, and is expected to be completed in 2011.

To learn more about roads in the state, try these resources:
- DOT publishes an annual updated state travel map. You can order a free printed map by calling 877-DOT-4YOU or visiting *www.ncdot.org/maps*, which also has a map of the state's scenic byways and rest areas. Or you can download specific parts

PART V: THE NEWCOMER'S GUIDE TO THE RALEIGH AREA

of the state travel map at *www.ncdot.org/it/img/DataDistribution/StateTravelMap*.
- DOT offers information about regional construction projects and plans by choosing the Triangle from the drop-down menu at *www.ncdot.org/construction/projectsstudies*.
- American Automobile Association (AAA), 919-832-0543, *www.aaacarolinas.com*, has an office in Raleigh that offers extensive travel information to members.

WHAT IS TRAFFIC LIKE IN THE TRIANGLE?

Traffic is a top concern for Triangle residents. But let's put this in perspective. We are not talking New York City traffic, nor are we talking Washington, D.C. or Atlanta traffic. A Texas Transportation Institute comparison found that in 2007, the average time commuters in the Raleigh-Durham area spent stuck in traffic was 34 hours per year, just under the average for similarly sized metropolitan areas. Even during rush hour, traffic generally keeps flowing, albeit at a slower rate than usual. The real enemy of the daily commuter is traffic accidents, which can snarl traffic for hours or even bring it to a dead halt. Highway construction – a fact of life in this growing area -- is another culprit, though most projects are planned for non-peak driving hours.

Of particular concern for commuters is traffic on I-40 near Research Triangle Park, which lies roughly between Cary and Durham. (Note to air travelers: the airport is very close to RTP, which could make you late if you're heading there at rush hour.) Eastbound traffic, heading from Raleigh and RTP to Johnston County, can also back up considerably. The heaviest traffic will be from about 7 a.m. to 9 a.m. and again from 4:30 p.m. to about 6:30 p.m.

The best way to avoid traffic is to try to travel at non-peak times if at all possible. To save hassles and gas, consider carpooling or using public transportation, including one of the Triangle Transit Authority's Park-

and-Ride lots or carpooling vans (see "Public Transportation" below.) Many employers, including some of the large ones at RTP, allow employees to set flexible schedules that let them avoid traffic. And working from home, at least part of the time, is becoming more and more common in the Triangle and beyond.

Try these ways to keep tabs on real-time traffic and construction:
- DOT's Traveler Information Management System, known as TIMS: Call 511 or search for specific regions and roads at *www.ncdot.org/traffictravel*
- TV station WRAL's traffic center, *www.wral.com/traffic*

IS RALEIGH FRIENDLY TO PEDESTRIAN AND BIKE TRAFFIC?

The answer to the question is, well, sorta. Wake County residents are big exercisers who can be seen biking and walking at any hour of the day and night throughout Raleigh and beyond. Local officials tend to tout their efforts to make the area friendly to pedestrians and cyclists, particularly by creating greenways just for them. But some would argue that much progress still needs to be made when it comes to making roads safer for those who share them with automobiles.

WALKING

Walkers along the roads in Raleigh will find ample sidewalks, except on some major roads that were not designed for walking due to safety concerns. In addition, rural roads in the outer parts of the city and beyond will have less traffic, but very few sidewalks and shoulders to seek refuge from cars.

Downtown is by far the most walkable part of the city, with established neighborhoods such as Oakwood and Mordecai within walking or biking distance of downtown amenities. Further from the city center, fewer options will be within walking distance and sidewalks may not always have been built. In recent years, as the trend toward walkable

PART V: THE NEWCOMER'S GUIDE TO THE RALEIGH AREA

communities has taken root, a number of newer subdivisions further out have also been built with amenities such as shopping and schools within walking or biking distance from homes.

BICYCLING

Avid bicyclists will find that using two wheels for transportation is feasible, but can be a bit hairy on Raleigh's bustling roads, few of which offer bicycle lanes or wide shoulders. At the same time, cyclists used to pedaling along two-lane rural roads outside the city that once saw little traffic are finding themselves crowded out by cars. Many biking enthusiasts suggest biking in groups as a safer way to enjoy these rural roads. (For information on meeting up with other cyclists and finding places to bike, visit the "Sports and Recreation" and "Outdoor Fun" chapters.)

On the up side, a push is on to make Triangle roads more bike-friendly. Cary (along with Carrboro to the west) has been named a bike-friendly community by the League of American Bicyclists, thanks both to its efforts to create better infrastructure for bicycles and for encouraging cycling. The town has adopted a plan to add more bike lanes and marked bike routes, and to create a map for bicyclists. Most bus systems throughout the region have bike racks, and bikes can be brought onto trains.

In addition, off-road cyclists will find that the area's network of greenways offers a wealth of pleasant, tree-lined routes for biking and walking, some paved and some more primitive. A few of them can also be used to get from place to place, and many more plans for connecting greenways are in the planning stages or under way. To learn more about greenways, see the "Outdoor Fun" chapter.

For more information on bicycle routs throughout the state, download DOT's state bicycle map at *www.ncdot.org/maps*, or order one by calling the DOT at the number above. DOT also offers a safety guide on sharing the road with cars and other information for cyclists at *www.ncdot.org/transit/bicycle*.

WHAT ABOUT TAXIS?

Taxis are widely available throughout Wake County, though they are a more logical option if you are traveling relatively short distances due to their higher rates. Most charge $1.95 just to get in and $2.50 per mile. Fees for extra passengers or bags may apply. Here is how to contact a few of the area's main taxi companies:

- Yellow Cab, Inc., 919-832-5811
- Cardinal Cab, 919-828-322
- Raleigh Taxi Cab, 919-414-6865, *www.raleightaxicab.com*

AREN'T THERE SOME FUN WAYS TO RIDE AROUND DOWNTOWN RALEIGH?

There are a few options if you want to see downtown from outside your car without relying on your two feet:

- Horse-drawn carriages congregate at a few places downtown mostly on weekends, including the Capitol, Moore Square and the entrance to the N.C. Museum of Natural Sciences.
- The Historic Raleigh Trolley runs an hour-long tour around downtown from 11 a.m. to 3 p.m. every Saturday from March to December. It leaves from Mordecai Historic Park, but riders can hop on at other locations. Call the park, 919-857-4364, for more information.
- Or for something truly unusual, hop on a rickshaw, or pedicab, which is pulled by a bicyclist. Raleigh Rickshaw, 919-623-5555, *www.raleighrickshaw.com*, offers these unusual rides seven days a week and for special events such as weddings.

PART V: THE NEWCOMER'S GUIDE TO THE RALEIGH AREA

TRAVELING BY AIR

How do most people fly in and out of Raleigh?

The Raleigh-Durham International Airport, 919-840-2123, *www.rdu.com*, is centrally located just north of Cary near the 540/40 intersection, and is widely known by its Federal Aviation Administration call letters, "RDU." RDU serves North Carolina's central and eastern regions as well as parts of southern Virginia. The airport served more than 10 million people in 2007, and continues to grow, according to data from the airport authority. That said, it still has for many years maintained the feeling of a small-town airport, with two terminals, relatively few amenities and little of the glitzy architecture common in newer airports.

That provincial look is changing, however, as the airport undertakes a major upgrade. Terminal 2 has been renovated, complete with glass walls and ceilings, fancy shops and several public art projects. Another wing of that terminal is being built from the ground up. Terminal 1, for now still a low-slung, dingy blue cluster of buildings, will be fully refurbished, too, eventually. (Another recent improvement: changing to 1 and 2 what were until recently perplexingly named terminals A and C – with no corresponding terminal B.)

Airlines

RDU's terminals each serve different airlines, so it is vital to note which airline you are traveling on. Here's where each airline is and how to contact them:

Terminal 1
- Air Tran, 800-247-8726, *www.airtran.com*

- Continental and Continental Express, 800-525-0280, *www.flycontinental.com*
- Jet Blue, 800-538-2583, *www.jetblue.com*
- Southwest, 800-435-9792, *www.southwest.com*
- US Airways and US Airways Express, 800-428-4322, *www.usairways.com*

Terminal 2
- Delta and Delta Connection, 800-221-1212, *www.delta.com*
- Northwest, 800-225-2525, *www.nwa.com*
- Air Canada and Air Canada Jazz, 888-247-2262, *www.aircanada.ca*
- American and American Eagle, 800-433-7300, *www.aa.com*
- United and United Express, 800-864-8331, *www.united.com*

Security

Security rules used nationally are in place at RDU, though most travelers will find that security lines tend to move pretty quickly. Only passengers will be allowed to the gates, and they will have to take off their shoes and jackets and pass through scanners before getting there. Liquids and gels are not allowed on planes, except for toiletry items of three ounces or less, which must be enclosed in a quart-size zip-lock bag. Laptop computers must be taken out of carry-on bags as you go through security.

Parking

RDU has ample parking available with different rates for different periods of time. The lot closest to the terminals, most of which is covered, offers hourly parking for $1 an hour or $24 a day and daily parking for $2 an hour or $10 a day. These lots (and General Aviation lots) use the ExitExpress automated payment option, with payment kiosks located in the garage between terminals. To pay by this method, be sure to bring your ticket with you into the airport and keep it with you until you're ready to leave. Pay at the machine on the way to your car.

Further out, several Park-and-Ride lots charge $6 a day. Free shuttles pick up passengers from these lots at least every 20 minutes from 4 a.m. until 1 a.m. or after the last flight of the evening lands. Payments stalls allow you to pay as you leave the Park-and-Ride lots.

Getting to and from the airport

Most taxi services in the area will take you to the airport. The RDU Airport Taxi Service, *www.rdu.com/groundtrans/taxis.htm*, 919-840-7277, may not always be the cheapest, but they are reliable and have consistent rates that add up to about $30 for the 14-mile trip to Raleigh or Durham. Handicap vans are also available. This service also has a line of taxis waiting to bring passengers home from the airport as they leave the terminals: near the Southwest airlines at Terminal 1 and on the lower level of Terminal 2.

The airport is also home to eight rental car agencies: Alamo, Avis, Budget, Dollar, Enterprise, Hertz, National and Thrifty. A shuttle bus will take you from either terminal to the rental car provider of your choice.

See the RDU Ground Transportation page, *www.rdu.com/groundtrans/bustrain.htm*, for more options on getting to and from the airport. They include the Triangle Transit Airport Shuttle, which will take you from the airport to central stops in Raleigh, Cary, Research Triangle Park and other locations for $2 one way or $4 for an all-day pass. Greyhound, 800-231-2222, *www.greyhound.com*, will also go to Raleigh and Durham by bus. Amtrak, 800-872-7245, *www.amtrak.com*, offers train service to Raleigh. A popular private option is the Morrisville-based SuperShuttle, 919-840-5170, *www.supershuttle.com*, which provides shared door-to-door rides to and from the airport.

What about general aviation at RDU? Are there other GA airports nearby?

RDU also houses a vibrant General Aviation terminal, one of several sites in the area surrounding the Triangle where owners of smaller planes can land and keep them – or where travelers can catch a chartered flight. At RDU, the GA terminal encompasses 22,000-square feet with 30 acres of aircraft parking space for a variety of aircraft sizes. The terminal has its own parking lot, a café and a Hertz car rental station on site.

The GA terminal also houses two fixed-base operators:

- Landmark Aviation, 840-2200, *www.landmarkaviation.com*, provides business charter and other services.
- TAC (Truman Arnold Companies) Air, 919-840-4400, *www.tacair.com*, offers heated hangars, taxi services, fuel, wireless Internet access and other services for pilots and their guests.

Several smaller public use airports dot the Piedmont near Wake County. They include:

- Triple W Airport (FAA ID:5W5), 919-782-1855, is located about 11 miles southwest of Raleigh in Wake County.
- Triangle North Executive Airport in Franklin County (FAA ID: LHZ), 919-496-1234, *www.flytrianglenorth.com*, is in Louisburg, northeast of Wake County. (It is often simply called the "Franklin County Airport, its former name.)
- Johnston County Airport (FAA ID: JNX), 919-934-0992, *www.johnstonnc.com* (choose "airport" from the drop-down menu), is about 30 miles southeast of Raleigh.
- For more detailed information on the facilities at each airport, look them up by FAA code at *www.ncdot.org/transit/aviation/ncairports* or *www.airnav.com*.

PART V: THE NEWCOMER'S GUIDE TO THE RALEIGH AREA

- To get oriented in North Carolina skies, pilots can download an aeronautical chart at *www.ncdot.org/maps* or get a printed version by calling DOT or the Department of Aviation, 919-840-0112.

CAN I TAKE A TRAIN INSTEAD?

With concerns about traffic delays and the environmental damage done by cars and trucks, rail travel has become an ever more popular option. Railways are also seeing a bump in funding in recent years, which is helping North Carolina and other states to update aging infrastructure that for decades was used nearly exclusively for freight, not people.

Rail tickets are generally cheaper than airlines, and sometimes comparable to driving, especially since you can use your time aboard for work or pleasure. A one-way ticket from Raleigh to Charlotte starts at $25, and a trip from Raleigh to Washington, D.C. starts at $45. Unfortunately, train travel remains slow, and improvements are slow in coming thanks to the steep cost of railway upgrades. Currently, the trip to Charlotte takes nearly 4 hours, almost twice what it takes by car.

DOT's Rail Division, 919-733-7245, *www.bytrain.org*, oversees the state's railroad system and maintains a wealth of information on North Carolina routes and plans for future service (though most routes are run by private companies). Options for short day-trips from Raleigh to nearby towns such as Burlington, Selma and Wilson are also available.

Amtrak, 800-USA-RAIL, *www.amtrak.com*, has twelve passenger trains serving 16 North Carolina cities daily, including stations in Raleigh, 320 W. Cabarrus St., 919-833-7594, and Cary, 211 N. Academy St. Find routes and schedules at *www.bytrain.org/passenger/groupinfo/trips.html*.

Among the routes passing through Raleigh are the Piedmont, which makes daily trips between Charlotte and Raleigh, and the Carolinian, which passes through on a daily route between Charlotte and New York. The Silver Service and Palmetto routes link New York to Florida. The

Crescent comes through Raleigh on its route from New Orleans to New York.

WHAT ABOUT BUSES?

For local or regional travel, your best bet will be the publicly run bus lines below. To go longer distances, try Greyhound, 919-834-8275, www.greyhound.com, which has a station at 314 W. Jones St. in Raleigh. Prices generally beat trains and planes, but service will be considerably slower, too.

Public Transportation

Want to leave your car in the garage and let someone else drive for a change? You have several options in Raleigh and the surrounding areas, though it may take a few steps to get exactly where you want to go.

How do the buses work in the Triangle?

Bus ridership has been increasing every year in the Triangle, perhaps in part thanks to the efforts of local transit agencies to expand routes and develop options that suit the needs of commuters. Still, most public officials still would like to see more bus riders – and the saved traffic congestion they bring with them. While each Triangle city -- and some towns – have their own bus systems, regional options are growing, too.

If you're traveling within Wake County, you'll probably turn to one of these systems run by Raleigh, Cary and N.C. State University:

- Capital Area Transit, known as CAT, 919-890-3030, www.raleighnc.gov/transit, provides service throughout the city of Raleigh. Fares are $1 per trip, $2 for a day pass, $11 for a week pass and $36 for a 31-day pass. The CAT R-line in downtown Raleigh is free. Riders who are disabled or over 65 receive discounts after showing a Medicare card or CAT ID.

PART V: THE NEWCOMER'S GUIDE TO THE RALEIGH AREA

- C-Tran, Cary's transit system, 919-469-4086, *www.townofcary.org/ctran/ctranoverview.htm*, offers six fixed routes around town from Monday to Saturday for $1 a trip. Door-to-door service is available for the disabled and people at least 60 years old by calling 919-481-2020.
- The N.C. State Wolfline, 919-515-WOLF, *www.ncsu.edu/wolfline* offers free service every day that class is in session between all three campuses, two park-and-ride lots and all official N.C. State housing. Anyone – not just students – can ride. You can also track Wolfline buses in real time and get other updated information at *ncsu.transloc.com*.

For more regional travel, the Triangle Transit Authority, 919-485-RIDE, *www.triangletransit.org*, runs buses and vans on routes throughout the Triangle, working in cooperation with local transit agencies. Here are some of the regional services they offer, along with prices:

- Weekday routes run between Raleigh, Durham, Chapel Hill, RTP, RDU, N.C. State, and the Wake County towns of Wake Forest, Cary, Garner, Apex, including five express routes.
- Weekend service is restricted to five routes that run between Raleigh, Chapel Hill, Durham, RTP and RDU.
- The regular cost of a TTA trip is $2, and $2.50 for express routes. A regional day pass costs $4, and 30-day regional day pass costs $64. A bundle of six regional day passes costs $20; other sizes of bundles are also available. Disabled riders and those over 65 pay half price for single trips, day passes and 30-day passes, with varying discounts for other services.
- Shuttles run to the airport and Research Triangle Park – with several hitting the major employers at rush hour: *triangletransit.org/bus/shuttles*.

- Park-and-Ride lots, where commuters can drop off their cars and catch a bus to their destination rather than walk to a bus stop. For a list of lots – including four in Cary, six in Raleigh, two in Apex, and one each in Garner and Wake Forest – visit *triangletransit.org/bus/park-and-ride*.
- TTA also operates passenger vans for commuters who live and work near one another and have similar work hours. Riders must live 20 miles or more from where they work and pay a monthly fee. For more about vanpooling, call 919-485-7462 or visit *triangletransit.org/vanpool*.

Options for the disabled:

- Both CAT in Raleigh and the regional TTA system offer discounts for disabled riders. C-Tran in Cary offers door-to-door service. (See listings above.)
- Physically or mentally disabled residents who are unable to ride the CAT system in Raleigh can use the Accessible Raleigh Transit (ART) program, 919-890-3030, *www.raleighnc.gov/transit*. Funded and administered by the City of Raleigh, ART provides curb-to-curb transportation within the city of Raleigh via participating taxi services. Some riders may need to schedule their trips in advance. The hearing and speech impaired can call 800-735-2962 to connect to the ART number.
- A regional option for the disabled is T-linx Services, *triangletransit.org/bus/accessibility*, a curb-to-curb van system run by TTA.

Is there any other kind of public transportation in the Triangle?

For the most part, not yet. While leaders have been hashing out plans for a regional light rail system and other options for years, funding

problems and sometimes tepid public support have made progress slow. Here's where to find more information on some of those efforts:
- The Southeast High Speed Rail Corridor, *www.sehsr.org*, would run trains at speeds of up to 110 miles per hour from Richmond, VA through Raleigh to Charlotte. First proposed in 1992, the project is still in the planning stages but has not been fully funded.
- Locally, plans for an extensive commuter rail system using existing tracks and starting with a route from Raleigh through Cary to RTP recently fizzled amidst funding concerns. A regional Special Transit Advisory Commission, *www.transitblueprint.org*, is charged with devising a new plan.

WHY DOES NORTH CAROLINA HAVE A PUBLIC FERRY SYSTEM? HOW DOES IT WORK?

The North Carolina ferry system started out back in the 1920s, supplying a few coastal villages with a link to the rest of the state and country. Now the DOT Ferry Division, 800-BY-FERRY, *www.ncferry.org*, runs 21 ferries over seven routes. The ferries bring people and their cars across the sounds and rivers that lie between much of the coastal areas along the Atlantic and the mainland. These routes cross five bodies of water: the Currituck and Pamlico sounds and the Cape Fear, Neuse and Pamlico rivers.
- Several routes are free, including Currituck to Knotts Island, Bayview to Aurora, Hatteras to Ocracoke, and Cherry Branch to Minnesott Beach.
- The Cedar Island to Ocracoke to Swan Quarter route charges one way fees of $1 per person, $3 per bicycle, $10 per motorcycle, $15 for vehicles under 20 feet and up to $45 for larger vehicles.

- The Southport to Fort Fisher route charges one-way fares of $1 per person, $2 per bicycle, $3 per motorcycle, $5 for vehicles under 20 feet and up to $15 for larger vehicles.
- Only the Cedar Island-Ocracoke and Swan Quarter-Ocracoke routes accept reservations. All others work on a first-come, first-serve basis. Be sure to check for changes in schedules (which can be downloaded from the *www.ncferry.org* Web site) due to weather or seasonal fluctuations.

CHAPTER 48

SPORTS & RECREATION

If you've only recently moved to North Carolina, you will soon notice that sports talk revolves around college basketball. With four powerhouse teams in the Triangle alone, that's no wonder. But Raleigh and the surrounding areas offer a wealth of sports for spectators and players to enjoy, from professional hockey to local tennis leagues, minor league baseball to pedal boat rentals.

PROFESSIONAL SPORTS

Hockey

Yes, it's no joke. Hockey is rising in popularity throughout the steamy Southeast, and the Raleigh-based Carolina Hurricanes put an exclamation point on that fact when they brought home the National Hockey League's Stanley Cup in 2006. The team also made the playoffs in 1999, 2001, 2002 and 2009. They have a large and loyal following, though tickets are still available at the gate for most games.

The Hurricanes, 1-866-NHL-CANES, *hurricanes.nhl.com*, have played at the RBC Center (formerly the Raleigh Entertainment & Sports Arena) in West Raleigh since 1999. The team came to North Carolina from Hartford, Connecticut in 1997, and played in Greensboro for several years until the Raleigh arena was built.

Hockey season runs from October to April, and can extend into May depending how far into the playoffs the team advances. Tickets to games cost between $25 and $200 at the gate. Season tickets run from $950 to more than $5,000 depending on the seats you purchase. You can also buy 12-game packages for $250 to $800 and 26-game packages from $800 to $2,000. Groups of 20 or more can buy discounted single-game tickets. Parking is ample at the RBC Center. Expect to pay about $10 and walk a bit to the arena.

Baseball

Perhaps the most famous Triangle-based sports team is the Durham Bulls, the minor league baseball team made famous in the 1988 movie of the same name starring Kevin Costner. The Bulls, 919-956-BULL, *durhambulls.com*, have played in a state-of-the-art facility adjacent to the historic American Tobacco Campus since 1995, though they brought some accents from the historic ballpark where the film was made, most notably a huge bull head with smoking nostrils. With a history stretching back to 1902, the Bulls are now the Triple-A affiliate of the Tampa Bay Devil Rays.

On the other side of the Triangle is the lesser known but increasingly popular Carolina Mudcats. They play at Five-County Stadium, which is near the Eastern Wake County town of Zebulon. The Mudcats, 919-269-2287, *carolina.mudcats.milb.com*, are the Double-A affiliate of the Cincinnati Reds. Formerly the Columbus Mudcats, the team moved to North Carolina from Georgia in 1991.

The minor league baseball season runs from April to September. With tickets starting at only $7, these games make for a fun and inexpensive family outing. The league has focused on making its games family events, and both Triangle teams offer a variety of child-focused attractions, from on-field games with Bulls mascot "Wool E. Bull" between innings to a youth clinic with the coaches at Five County Stadium. Contact each team for more details. Full- and half-season tickets, as well as discounted tickets for groups over 25 and bundles of four or five games, are also available for both teams. Most games start at 5 p.m. or 7 p.m., though a few are scheduled for 1 p.m.

Football

Though some Carolina Panthers fans will beg to differ, the Charlotte-based National Football League team does not enjoy the massive fan following in the Triangle that you might expect for an NFL team that's less than a three hour drive from Raleigh. In part, the lukewarm reception here speaks to the rivalry between the state's two largest cities. But the flow of newcomers to the Triangle with allegiances to their hometown teams hasn't helped. When the Panthers, 704-358-7000, *www.panthers.com*, were founded in 1993, they were the NFL's first expansion team in nearly 20 years. Single tickets start at $76. The number to buy tickets is 704-358-7800.

Soccer

While still a fairly minor presence in the Triangle, professional soccer is getting more and more attention. That's due in part to an influx of soccer-crazed Latino immigrants, as well as the increasing popularity of youth leagues.. The Carolina RailHawks, 919-859-5425, *www.carolinarailhawks.com*, is an expansion team in the United Soccer League's First Division. Their season runs from March to September, and tickets start at $10 for adults and $5 for children. The RailHawks play their home games at WakeMed Soccer Park in Cary.

Auto Racing

Auto racing was born in the North Carolina Piedmont, at least according to local lore, and it's still huge in North Carolina despite the closing of several major speedways in recent years. Major NASCAR stars such as Dale Earnheart and Richard Petty were born here. Much to the chagrin of many local racing fans, however, the state's only NASCAR venue is now several hours away at Lowe's Motor Speedway, 704-455-3200, *www.lowesmotorspeedway.com*, in Concord (near Charlotte). But there are still some local venues for stock car racing that might be worth a trip for fans.

- Rockingham Speedway, 910-205-8800, *www.rockinghamracewaypark.com*, has recently opened under new ownership. It was formerly the historic North Carolina Speedway, which was home to dozens of NASCAR's Cup Series races from 1965 to 2004.
- Wake County Speedway, 919-779-2171. *www.wakecountyspeedway.com*, holds races on Friday nights from May to August at its site just south of Raleigh at 2109 Simpkins Road.
- Orange County Speedway, 336-364-1222, *www.ocstrack.com*, holds weekly races on Saturdays and other events from April to October at its Rougemont site.

COLLEGE SPORTS

Led by the intense basketball rivalry between Duke and UNC-Chapel Hill, college athletics rule the Triangle sports universe. N.C. State in Raleigh chimes in with winning football and basketball teams, while nearby Wake Forest is another basketball powerhouse. Here's a rundown of area college athletics and contacts at those schools in case you want to chase down tickets.

- **N.C. State University:** The Raleigh-based Wolfpack, *www.gopack.com*, is a member of the Atlantic Coast Conference and fields men's and women's teams in 14 sports. Its football team plays at Carter-Finley Stadium, near the State Fairgrounds

PART V: THE NEWCOMER'S GUIDE TO THE RALEIGH AREA

in West Raleigh. Though most of its national championships date back decades, the Pack still regularly gives its rival Tar Heels and other ACC competititors run for their money in football and basketball.

- **University of North Carolina at Chapel Hill:** The Tar Heels, *tarheelblue.com*, also an ACC member, fields men's and women's teams in 16 sports, though men's basketball gets most of the attention. The Heels brought home national championships in 2005 and 2008. Michael Jordan is the most famous alumnus of Tar Heel basketball.
- **Duke University:** The Durham-based Blue Devils, *www.goduke.com*, belong to the ACC also. Their basketball team, led by Coach Mike Krzyzewski since 1980, has brought home three championships since 1991.
- **Wake Forest University:** The Winston-Salem-based Deamon Deacons, *wakeforestsports.com*, another ACC member, is best known for its basketball program, which has produced some top-ranked NBA players and taken several ACC championships.
- **Elon University:** The Elon Pheonix teams, *www.elonpheonix.com*, are part of the Southern Conference. The university is in Elon, west of Burlington.
- **St. Augustine College:** The Raleigh-based Falcons, *www.st-aug.edu/sports-page*, field 10 men's and women's athletic teams. They compete in the NCAA Division II Central Intercollegiate Athletic Division, which is made up primarily of historically black colleges and universities.
- **Shaw University:** The Raleigh-based Bears, *www.shawbears.com*, also compete in the CIAA conference.
- **Meredith College:** The Avenging Angels, *www.meredith.edu/athletics*, is the mascot of this Raleigh-based

all-female school, which competes at the NCAA Division III level in six sports.
- **Peace College:** The Pacers, *www.gopeacepacers.org*, competes in the NCAA Division III USA South Athletic Conference in six sports. The Raleigh-based college is also an all-women's institution.

PARTICIPANT SPORTS AND ACTIVITIES

Parks and Recreation Departments

Whether you're looking for a place to play tennis or a youth soccer league, a good place to start your search is your nearest park and recreation departments. Most offer youth and adult leagues in tennis, basketball and other sports as well as facilities for those who just need a place to play. Many also offer fitness classes, activities for kids and more.

- Apex, 919-249-3419, *www.apexnc.org/depts/parks*
- Cary, 919-469-4062, *www.townofcary.org/tupage/recreation.htm*
- Fuquay-Varina, 919-552-1430, *www.fuquay-varina.org/parks*
- Garner, 919-662-5051, *www.ci.garner.nc.us/prdept.htm*
- Holly Springs, 919-557-9601, *www.hollyspringsnc.us/dept/park/index.htm*
- Knightdale, 919-217-2230, *www.ci.knightdale.nc.us/parksandrecreation.html*
- Morrisville, 919-463-7114, *www.ci.morrisville.nc.us* (Choose "community services" under the "town departments menu," then "parks, recreation and cultural resources.)
- Raleigh, 919-831-6836, *www.raleigh-nc.org* (Choose "leisure.")
- Rolesville, 919-554-6582, *www.ci.rolesville.nc.us/recreation/default.htm*
- Wake County, 919-460-2723, *www.wakegov.com/parks/default.htm*

PART V: THE NEWCOMER'S GUIDE TO THE RALEIGH AREA

- Wake Forest, 919-554-6180, *www.wakeforestnc.gov/parksrecreation.aspx*
- Wendell, 919-366-2266, *www.townofwendell.com/Wendell/ParksandRec/tabid/60/Default.aspx*
- Zebulon, 919-269-8265, *www.ci.zebulon.nc.us/P&R.htm*

Multi-Sport Groups

Some area employers may offer a chance to play sports through corporate teams, so be sure to ask your employer if there are existing teams – or if you might start one. These independent groups also offer several sports each.

- Apex Sports Authority, 919-961-2785, *www.apexsportsauthority.com*, offers youth football, cheerleading, lacrosse, and wrestling.
- Fuquay-Varina Athletic Association, 919 -552-5465, *www.fvaa.org*, offers youth soccer, baseball, softball, football, cheerleading, basketball, and volleyball.
- Wilders Grove Youth Center in Raleigh, 919-231-4070, *www.wildersgrove.com*, offers youth baseball, cheerleading, dance, softball and football.
- Upward, 800-585-4721, *www.upward.org*, provides youth basketball, soccer, flag football and cheerleading at some area churches.
- The Salvation Army of Wake County Community Center, 832.6918 ext. 114, *www.keepthebellringing.org/page/community-center*, offers youth basketball, baseball, soccer and flag football.
- NC USSSA, *www.northcarolinausssa.com*, offers baseball, basketball, fastpitch, flag football, golf, karate, lacrosse, soccer, taekwondo and volleyball.

Adventure Racing

The up-and-coming adult sport of adventure racing combines cycling, running, hiking, paddling, climbing and orienteering in team races. Contact these local groups for more information:
- Triangle Adventure Racing Team, *www.triangle-ar-team.com*
- The Triangle Chapter of the national TrailBlazers Adventure Racing Club, *www.trailblazerar.com/hq_rd*

Indoor Facilities

If you want to head inside during those super-hot summer months, these commercial groups offer youth sports at indoor facilities. Some have outdoor places to play, too.
- Carolina Sportsplex, Morrisville, 919-319-9910, *www.rinksmart.com/asp/Locations/fs_location.asp?Location=Carolina*, offers indoor hockey and soccer.
- Dream Sports Center, Apex, 919-387-2955, *www.dreamsportscenter.com*, offers hockey, soccer and lacrosse.
- Grand Slam USA, Raleigh, 919-233-7522, *www.grandslamusa.biz*, offers baseball and basketball.

Baseball

In addition to lessons and leagues at most parks and recreation departments, these independent leagues offer baseball for children:
- Babe Ruth League, 1-800-552-1350, *www.baberuthleague.org*
- Little League Baseball, 727-344-2661, *www.littleleague.org*
- Baseball Players Association, 704-596-2270, *www.playbpa.com*

For adults, try the Central North Carolina Senior Baseball League at *www.scorebook.com/cncmsbl*.

PART V: THE NEWCOMER'S GUIDE TO THE RALEIGH AREA

Basketball

- N.C. Amateur Athletic Union has teams for boys, 704-517-7111, *www.ncaauboysbasketball.com* and girls, 336-288-2803, *www.ncaaugirlsbasketball.org*
- Youth Basketball of America, 407-363-9262, *www.yboa.org*
- U.S. Basketball Association, 704-649-6812 , *www.usbahoops.com*

Bicycling

The Triangle offers many places to ride a bike for fun and exercise -- whether on paved or more rustic trails, alone or with a group -- including the area's various greenways (For more on greenways and trails, see the "Outdoor Fun" chapter.) Here are some groups that can help you get started.

- Triangle Cycling, *www.trianglecycling.com*, online forum is a place for cyclists to meet up and share information.
- The North Carolina Bicycle Club, *www.ncbikeclub.org*, organizes group rides at varying levels and speeds.
- The Carolina Tarwheels, *www.tarwheels.org*, organizes rides across the Triangle, including an annual Bikefest event.
- Triangle Mountain Biking, *www.trianglemtb.com*, connects mountain biking enthusiasts and advocates for access to bike trails. The site offers lists and reviews of trails throughout the region.
- Cycle North Carolina, *www.ncsports.org/nccyclemain.php*, promotes cycling and holds annual rides across the state.

BMX Bicycle Racing

The nonprofit Capital City BMX, 919-834-4BMX, *www.ccbmx.com*, promotes BMX racing among children and adults in the Triangle. They are based at Lion's Park in Raleigh.

Boating/Sailing/Windsurfing

The Piedmont's many lakes and rivers offer a variety of spots for boating, whether in a canoe, sailboat or motor boat. (For a complete listing of area lakes and rivers, see the "Outdoor Fun" chapter. For more information on licenses and rules for boating, see the "Hunting, Fishing and Boating" section of that chapter.)

Paddling

- Carolina Canoe Club, *www.carolinacanoeclub*, schedules river trips and other events, and puts out a bi-monthly newsletter on canoeing.
- Paddling Eastern North Carolina, 919-781-3080, *www.pocosinpress.com*, is a comprehensive guide book to canoeing in this part of the state.
- Triangle Kayak Club, 919-368-2151, *www.trianglekayak.com*, offers information on local kayaking and a meeting place for enthusiasts.
- Raleigh offers kayaking lessons at local pools and on the Neuse River. For more information, follow the "Leisure" link on *www.raleigh-nc.org*.

Sailing

- Carolina Sailing Club, *www.carolinasailingclub.org*, promotes sailing and organizes races in the Piedmont, including several events at Jordan Lake.
- Carolina Sailing Foundation, 919-522-4531, *www.carolinasailingfoundation.org*, offers sailing classes for children and adults.

PART V: THE NEWCOMER'S GUIDE TO THE RALEIGH AREA

Rowing (Crew)

- The Raleigh Rowing Center, *rrcx.wordpress.com*, at Lake Wheeler, promotes recreational and competitive rowing.
- Wake Rowing, *www.newwakerowing.com*, is a competitive team of students in 8th grade and up that practices at Lake Wheeler.
- To find other rowing groups throughout, the Triangle, browse the "Rowing Clubs by State" list compiled by U.S. Rowing, *www.usrowing.org/NewToRowing*.

Other

Raleigh offers **rental boats** such as pedal boats, sailboats and Jon boats at several locations including Lake Johnson. For those who want to use their own **motor boats**, Lake Wheeler has a boat launch and Lake Crabtree allows electric motors only. For more information on these, follow the "Leisure" link at *www.raleigh-nc.org*.

Falls Lake and Jordan Lake both offer boat launches. For more information on these, visit *www.ncparks.gov* or call 919-733-4181.

Bowling

Several bowling alleys in the area offer both a place for the casual bowler and a place to join a club for camaraderie and league play.

- Capital Lanes, Raleigh, *www.amf.com/capitallanesnc*, 919-832-3747
- Pleasant Valley Lanes, Raleigh, *www.amf.com/pleasantvalleylanes*, 919-783-0080
- South Hills Lanes, Cary, *www.amf.com/southhillslanes*, 919-467-2411
- Buffaloe Lanes, *www.buffaloelanes.com*, has three Wake County locations: South Raleigh, 919-779-1888; North Raleigh, 919-876-5681; and Cary, 919-468-8684.

- Western Lanes (near N.C. State University), 919-832-3533

Gymnastics/Cheerleading

Gymnastics is as popular as ever, and many of these gyms are now also offering cheer classes. Not just for the sidelines anymore, cheerleading is a serious competitive youth sport. In addition to school teams, these facilities offer classes and independent teams.

- Apex Gymnastics, 919-303-7976, *www.apexgymnastics.com*
- Artistic Gymnastics School, Inc., Raleigh, 919-772-9463
- C&C Cheer Company, *www.candccheer.com*, 919-522-7267, is a Cary-based company that offers classes at several locations.
- Carolina All Stars, Raleigh, 919-954-0909, *www.carolinaallstars.com*
- Carolina Legacy, Cary, 919-380-2152, *www.carolinacheerdance.com*
- Cheer Extreme Raleigh, 919-987-8325, *www.cheerextremeraleigh.com*
- The DanZe Zone, Garner, 919-772-7755, *www.thedanzezone.com*
- Elite Cheer and Dance, 919-255-6524, *www.elite-cheer.com*
- Gymcarolina Gymnastics Academy, 919-848-7988, *www.gymcarolina.com*
- Impact Gym Cheerleading and Gymnastics Training Center, Apex, 919-363-1770 *www.impactgym.com*
- Kenney's Gymnastics Academy, 919-851-1188, *www.kenneysgymnastics.com*
- Knightdale Academy of Gymnastics, 919-266-4005, *www.geocities.com/knightdalegym*
- The Little Gym of Holly Springs, 919-567-2018, *www.tlghollyspringsnc.com*

PART V: THE NEWCOMER'S GUIDE TO THE RALEIGH AREA

- Impact Athletics, Cary, 919-467-2281, *www.impactathleticsnc.com*
- North Raleigh Gymnastics, 919-790-9400, *www.tumblewithus.com*
- Raleigh-Cary School of Gymnastics, 919-878-8249, *www.raleighgymnastics.com*
- Raleigh Rage Cheer Gym, 919-233-0611
- Southern Spirit Unlimited, Cary, 919-463-5534, *www.southernspiritallstars.com*
- Superior Gymnastics, Morrisville, 919-388-1632, *www.asuperiorgym.com*
- Team Esteem LTD, Cary, 252-562-1228, *www.teamesteemltd.com*
- Wake Forest Allstars, 919-554-0606, *www.wakeforestallstars.com*
- Wake Forest Gymnastics, 919-556-5445
- Youngs Gymnastics and Cheerleading, 919-554-0606, *www.youngsgym.com*

Dance

Triangle Chapter of USA Dance, *triangleusadance.org*, offers a listing of ballroom dance lessons and special events

- The Triangle Swing Dance Society, *www.triangleswingdance.org*, organizes lessons and events
- Triangle Vintage Dance, 919-9-DANCE-2, *www.trianglevintagedance.com*, focuses on the Waltz, Polka and other vintage dances
- Triangle Country Dancers, *www.tcdancers.org*, based in Chapel Hill
- To find more dance groups in North Carolina, visit *www.musicanddance.com*

Equestrian

For competitive equestrian sports, enthusiasts gather at the Gov. James B. Hunt Horse Complex at the State Fairgrounds. For a listing of events, check *www.ncstatefair.org/events/HorseComplex.htm*. Wake County is also dotted with trails for those who already own a horse and farms offering lessons for those seeking a chance to ride. To find them, try the N.C. Horse Council, 919-854-1990, *www.nchorsecouncil.com*, or search for the Raleigh area at *www.equinenow.com*.

Fishing

- (See "Outdoor Fun" chapter for information on hunting, fishing and boating.)

Frisbee

Ultimate Frisbee, or Frisbee golf, has a loyal following locally that enjoys a host of local places to play both competitively and just for fun. The Triangle Flying Disc Association, *www.tfda.org*, offers a listing of places to play and contact information for youth and adult leagues. The site also lets you hook up with other enthusiasts for pick-up games.

Golf

While the pros might drop in most often a few hours away at Pinehurst, there are plenty of places for other golfers to play at whatever level they choose. Here are some places to get started:

- The N.C. Department of Commerce keeps a listing of golf courses statewide at *www.visitnc.com/journeys/highlights/golf-in-nc*
- The Carolinas Golf Association, 910-673-1000, *www.carolinasgolf.org*, holds tournaments for amateur golfers, including separate ones for seniors, women and juniors.

- The Raleigh chapter of the American Singles Golf Association, 888-GOLFMATE, *www.singlesgolf.com* (search for Raleigh), can help you meet up with local golfers
- The Executive Women's Golf Association's Raleigh-Triangle Chapter, 919.831.5026, *www.ewga-raleigh.net*, has resources for women golfers
- The First Tee of Wake County, *www.thefirstteetriangle.org*, offers free golf lessons for youth who are new to the game
- The Tar Heels Seniors Golf Association, 919-215-7676, *www.tarheelseniors.com*, has an annual competition for men and women golfers over 50.

Hockey/Ice Skating

Most of these "ice houses" offer paid skating hours, as well as lessons and leagues for children in hockey and figure skating.
- Polar Ice House has locations in Cary, 919-460-2756, *cary.pucksystems.com*, Wake Forest, 919-453-1500, *wakeforest.pucksystems.com*, and Garner, 919-460-2756, *garner.pucksystems.com*
- RecZone, Raleigh, 919-754-0441, *www.reczone.net*
- Raleigh IcePlex, 919-878-9002, *www.iceplex.com*

Hunting

- (See "Outdoor Fun" chapter for information on hunting, fishing and boating.)

Ice Skating

- (See "Hockey/Ice Skating/Figure Skating" above.)

In-line/Roller Skating/Skateboarding

- Jellybeans, *www.skatejellybeans.com*, has facilities in Raleigh, 919-467-5283, and Cary, 919-562-2326, for in-line and roller skating. They offer paid skating hours, summer camps and lessons for children, as well as in-line hockey classes and supplies.
- Skate Ranch of Raleigh, 919-790-3808, *www.skateranchofraleigh.com*, offers paid skating hours, summer camps and after-school programs in in-line and roller skating.

Lacrosse

This sport is up and coming in area schools, and now also has some independent teams, too. Try the nonprofit North Carolina Lacrosse Academy, 919-303-6068 *www.nclaxacademy.com*, in Apex to get started with this fast-paced sport.

Martial Arts

Adult or child, amateur or pro, you can find a place to learn and practice judo, karate and other martial arts in the Triangle. A good place to start is the Durham-based American Martial Arts Alliance, 919-489-6100, *www.martialarts-alliance.com*, a national group with members from different martial arts disciplines. These groups can also help you find local schools:

- North Carolina Judo, *www.ncjudo.com*
- USA National Karate-Do Federation, *www.usankf.org*
- USA Taekwando, *www.usa-taekwondo.us*
- Aikido Web, *www.aikiweb.com*

Running

While Driving through Raleigh on spring and fall Saturday mornings, you're likely to see hoards of runners participating in one of the many local marathons put on for sport or for charity. These events are indicator of how big running is in the Triangle.

To further illustrate the point, there are at least a dozen running clubs in Raleigh alone. To find them, search by zip code at *www.usatf.org*. One of the largest local groups is the North Carolina Roadrunners, *www.ncroadrunners.org*, which has group runs, trainings and social events for runners of all levels.

Soccer

A number of youth and adult soccer leagues pepper the area, in addition to privately run soccer facilities.

- The N.C. Youth Soccer Association, 336-856-PLAY, *www.ncsoccer.org*, oversees youth leagues and recreational programs throughout the state
- The N.C. Adult Soccer Association, *www.ncsoccer.org/ncasa*, organizes adult leagues
- Capital Area Soccer League, 919-834-3951, *www.caslnc.com*, is one of the longest running leagues in the area
- XL Soccer World, Raleigh, 919-859 2997, *www.xlsoccerworld.com*, offers indoor soccer leagues and lessons for adults and youth.

Swimming

For recreational swimming, head to one of Raleigh's city pools, 919-831-6852, *www.raleigh-nc.org* ("Leisure"), which offer swim classes and open swimming for competitive prices. (For more on local pools, see the "Outdoor Fun" chapter.) Outside of Raleigh, you will find a network of private and community pools. Most competition occurs on school swim teams, though there are also private leagues.

- N.C. Swimming, *www.ncswim.org*, keeps a list of private swim clubs and teams.

- The Tarheel Swimming Association, *www.tsanc.org*, runs summer leagues for swim clubs.

Tennis

The area's largest tennis center is at Millbrook Road Park in North Raleigh, though public and private courts abound throughout the region. Check your local parks and recreation department and these local groups:
- The U.S. Tennis Association's North Carolina Chapter, 336-852-8577, *www.nctennis.com*
- Tennis-Raleigh-Durham, *www.tennis-raleigh-durham.com*, allows you to find partners or sign up for league play
- The Raleigh-Durham Tennis Meetup, *www.rdutennis.com*, is another place to meet up with other players

Volleyball

Carolina Regional Volleyball Association, *www.carolinaregionvb.org*, organizes teams for youth and adults
- *www.vh1vball.com* organizes grass and sand tournaments for all age levels and a listing of places and times to play

Yoga

Check your local recreation department for yoga classes, as well as the listing of gyms and fitness centers below.

HEALTH CLUBS AND GYMS

- Peak Fitness, 888 - 833 – PEAK, *www.peakfitnessclubs.com*, is a Carolinas-based gym with locations in North Raleigh, Downtown Raleigh, Cary, Fuquay-Varina, Knightdale and Garner

PART V: THE NEWCOMER'S GUIDE TO THE RALEIGH AREA

- O2 Fitness, *o2fitnessclubs.come*, has two locations in Raleigh and one in Cary
- Snap Fitness has locations in Raleigh, 919-847-1441, *www.snapfitness.com/nraleigh*, and Cary, 919-233-3444
- Impact Athletics, Cary, 919-IMPACT-1, *www.impactathleticsnc.com*, also offers competitive jump rope and gymnastics
- Butterfly Life, *www.butterflylife.com*, a national women's fitness center with a location in Cary, 919-367-7905
- National chain Gold's Gym, *www.goldsgym.com*, has one location in Cary, 919-462-9065, and three in Raleigh: North Hills, 919-787-1665; Pleasant Valley, 919-781-6755; and Six Forks, 919-847-8189

TRIANGLE YMCAS

Wake County has six locations offering sports, fitness activities and more. Most locations have pools and programs such as summer camps for children, as well as daycare. For more information on programs, rates and membership, go to *www. ymcatriangle.org* or call 919-719-9622.

- A.E. Finley YMCA, 9216 Baileywick Rd., Raleigh, 919)-848-9622
- Banks D. Kerr Family YMCA, 2500 Wakefield Pines Dr., Raleigh, 919-562-9622
- Cary Family YMCA, 101 YMCA Dr., Cary, 919-469-9622
- YMCA of Garner, 1701 Aversboro Rd., 919-773-3621
- John M. Alexander Family YMCA, 1603 Hillsborough St., 919-832-6601
- Southwest Wake YMCA, 1610 Center Street, Suite 110, Apex, 919-657-9622

CHAPTER 49

OUTDOOR FUN (GREEN SPACE)

Ah, the great outdoors. One of the reasons the Raleigh area earns top spots on so many lists of great places to live is the greenways and parks that are always close by despite the area's rapid growth – everything from neighborhood play spaces for kids to thousands of acres of state parkland. While newcomers will find a wealth of places to hike, bike, or picnic near their new homes, even longtime residents are continually finding unknown spots. Best of all, the mild Triangle weather allows for outdoor fun nearly all year long. Here are some of the more and lesser known green spaces in Wake County, and some ideas of how to enjoy them.

CITY PARKS IN RALEIGH

The City of Raleigh operates dozens of parks through its parks and recreation department, 919-831-6640, *www.parks.raleighnc.gov*. These include unstaffed playgrounds, lakes, pools and more. The list below includes some of the larger categories of city parks.

To find other parks and to keep up with the many activities offered at these centers, consider subscribing to the "Leisure Ledger," a quarterly listing of everything from T-ball to swimming lessons to yoga. These activities are open to residents and non-residents, who pay a slightly higher fee. The magazine also has maps of the city's parks and greenways.

LAKES

Hanging out at the city lakes is free, as is dipping your bait in the water. Other activities, such as boating and nature walks, will cost a small fee.

- Lake Benson, Buffaloe Road, Garner, 919-662-5703, offers boat rentals and fishing.
- Lake Johnson, 4601 Avent Ferry Rd, 919-233-2121, offers boat rentals, fishing, picnic facilities, a concession stand, and a hiking trail around the lake.
- Lake Wheeler, 6404 Lake Wheeler Rd., 919-662-5704, has boats for rent, fishing, a children's playground, hiking and exercise trails, and picnic tables.
- Shelley Lake, 1400 W. Millbrook Road, 919-420-2331, a children's playground, an exercise trail, and a hiking path around the lake.

POOLS

The city pools are generally open from June through August, though a few will open in late May every year and three indoor pools are open year-round. Most have Olympic-sized pools offering lap and free swimming as well as shallow pools for children. A few pools also offer popular splash playgrounds for children.

They charge $1 per visit for children from 1-12, $3 for adults and $2 for senior citizens. Non-residents pay twice the regular fee. Punch-cards for 15 visits will bring the per-visit price down, as will monthly or annual passes for frequent visitors. Reasonably priced swim classes are available throughout the summer. The city's two indoor pools offer year-round swim lessons and fitness classes for adults.

- Biltmore Pool, 701 Crown Crossing Lane, 831-6736,
- Chavis Pool, 501 MLK Jr. Blvd., 831-6565
- Lake Johnson Pool, 1416 Athens Drive, 233-2111
- Longview Pool, 321 Bertie Dr., 831-6343
- Millbrook Pool (year-round, indoor), 1905 Spring Forest Rd., 872-4130
- Optimist Pool, (year-round, indoor/outdoor) 5902 Whittier Dr., 870-2882
- Pullen Aquatic Center (year-round, indoor), 410 Ashe Ave., 831-6197
- Ridge Road Pool, 1709 Ridge Rd., 420-2322

PARKS

Raleigh runs more parks than we can list here, including some that are little more than just a small space with a few benches or a short walking trail. Explore these in the Leisure Ledger, online or by calling the parks department. Below are some of the city's more notable parks.

- Pullen Park, 520 Ashe Ave., 831-6468, is a historic park offering a wide variety of amusements, including a children's train that circles the park, a carousel, several playgrounds and rental boats on its small pond. Ample picnic facilities and a concession stand are also available. The train, carousel, and boats cost a small fee. Park hours change seasonally.
- Laurel Hills Park and Community Center, 3808 Edwards Mill Rd., 420-2383, offers outdoor baseball and basketball, an indoor gymnasium, a large children's playground, hiking trails and indoor activities such as fitness classes and children's playtimes.
- Millbrook Exchange Community Center, 1905 Spring Forest Rd., 872-4156, is situated on a massive campus that includes

children's playgrounds, a year-round pool, an off-leash dog park and the city's largest tennis center.
- Durant Nature Park, 8305 Camp Durant Rd., 870-2871, houses many of the city's nature study programs, as well as a children's playground, fishing in the park's lake and picnic facilities.
- Chavis Community Center, 505 MLK Jr. Blvd., 831-6989, boasts a gymnasium, tennis courts, lighted ballfields, outdoor basketball, a pool and children's play equipment.

COUNTY, TOWN AND STATE PARKS

County Parks

Wake County runs several parks that highlight the area's history in addition to offering places to hike and bike. The Web sites for these parks can be found by going to *www.wakegov.com/parks* and clicking on the park of your choice. Most county parks are free and open to the public from 8 a.m. to dusk year-round, though staffed centers will have more limited hours. Contact each facility for more information on tours.

- Blue Jay Point, 3200 Pleasant Union Church Rd., Raleigh, 870-4330, is a county-run park on the shores of Falls Lake in northern Wake County offering environmental education facilities as well as hiking trails, a picnic area, playgrounds and an overnight lodge.
- Lake Crabtree, 1400 Aviation Parkway, Morrisville, 460-3390, is a 215-acre site adjacent to a 520-acre flood control lake where visitors can enjoy boating, fishing, hiking, mountain biking, picnicking and nature programs.
- Historic Oak View, 4028 Carya Drive, Raleigh, 250-1013, is a 19th-century historic farmstead offering free educational tours and programs on the agricultural heritage and rural history of the state for students of all ages.

- Historic Yates Mill, 4620 Lake Wheeler Road, Raleigh, 856-6675, *www.wakegov.com/yatesmill*, is a fully restored gristmill – the only one of what used to be many, remains in Wake County. Visitors can tour the mill and take a stroll around the lake or take part in a free, organized tour.
- Crowder District Park, 4709 Ten Ten Road, Apex, 662-2850, offers 33 acres of landscaped grounds for hiking, picnicking, and nature programs. The site also has a sand volleyball court, an outdoor amphitheater, three playgrounds and a point with a boardwalk and observation deck.
- Harris Lake, 2112 County Park Drive, New Hill, 387-4342, located on a peninsula in the Shearon Harris Reservoir, offers a playground, primitive camp sites, picnic facilities, a disc golf course and a pond for fishing and boating.

Town Parks

Most of Wake County's towns have at least one park of their own. To see a full list, contact the parks and recreation department in your town (See Chapter 2, Sports and Recreation for a full list of them.) Here are some of the highlights among town parks.
- Apex Community Park, 2200 Laura Duncan Rd., 249-3402, *www.apexnc.org/depts/parks/facilities/commPark.cfm*, the largest and most elaborate of that town's parks, offers a 30-acre lake with a fishing dock and boat launch, picnic areas with grills, hiking and exercise trails, playgrounds and facilities for soccer, baseball, basketball, volleyball and tennis.
- Fred G. Bond Metro Park, 801 High House Rd., Cary, 469-4100, is one of the largest of dozens of parks run by Cary's parks and recreation department, *townofcary.org/depts/prdept/parkhome.htm#parks*. Bond Park features a lake with boathouse,

playgrounds, ball fields, hiking trails, an amphitheater, picnic facilities and a challenge rope course.
- Another popular spot for children in Cary is Kids Together Playground, *www.kidstogethercary.org*, located at Marla Dorrel Park, 111 Thurston Dr., 481-3180. The site offers picnic facilities and a series of playgrounds for children of all ages, including a large climbable dragon. A greenway trail connects this park to MacDonald Woods Park, where there is a smaller playground.
- Garner's soon-to-be-completed White Deer Park, *www.garnerparks.org*, will feature a nature center, wildflower meadows, arboretum, hiking trails, playgrounds and picnic shelters. It will also house the stuffed white deer that is central to the town's local lore.

State Parks

Three state parks await visitors just a short drive from Raleigh and other Wake County locations. To find other parks throughout the state, contact the N.C. Division of Parks and Recreation, 733-4181, *www.ncparks.gov*. (Each of the parks below can also be found through this site. Other sites listed below were included because they list more information on each park than the official state site.)
- Falls Lake State Park, 13304 Creedmoor Rd., Wake Forest, 676-1027, *www.ncparks.gov/Visit/parks/fala/main.php*, offers boating, fishing and swimming at seven access points around the 12,000-acre lake. Hiking, mountain biking and camping are also frequent activities in the surrounding 26,000 acres of woodland, part of which is a section of the Mountains-to-Sea Trail.
- William B. Umstead State Park, 8801 Glenwood Avenue, Raleigh, 571-4170, *www.stateparks.com/william_b_umstead.html*, boasts 5,579 acres of parkland wedged between Raleigh, Cary,

Durham and Research Triangle Park. The park's two main sections, Crabtree Creek and Reedy Creek, are easily accessible from Interstate 40 and U.S. 70. Visitors will find facilities for camping and picnicking and miles of hiking trails, as well as nature programs and options for fishing and hunting.
- Jordan Lake State Park, 280 State Park Road, Apex, 362-0586, *www.ncparks.gov/Visit/parks/jord/main.php*, offers nine recreation areas for boating, swimming, camping and picnicking.

DOG PARKS

- For a listing of off-leash dog parks, see the "Pets" section of the "Getting Settled" chapter.

TRAILS AND GREENWAYS

One of the best-known features of Raleigh's outdoor scene are the greenways, a network of public hiking and biking trails maintained by various towns, counties and cities across the Triangle. Some are freestanding, while the hope of greenway planners is to connect existing trails. In addition to these, most towns, cities and counties have their own trails run through their parks and recreation department. To find these, check with your town or city. Below are some highlights of the region's trails, focusing on trail-building efforts that span individual towns and cities.

Greenways

The Triangle boasts more than 150 miles of mostly paved trails called greenways that are great for walking and biking. Some intersect with other trails, and others allow you to walk along lakes or rivers. Check out *www.wakegov.com/parks/trailsgreenways.htm* for a town-by-town breakdown of local greenways, or you can download a map of greenways throughout the county. Here are some of the largest or most popular in Wake County:

- Apex: Beaver Creek greenway, which is now 2.5 paved miles, will eventually connect downtown Apex with the American Tobacco Trail, which runs all the way to Durham.
- Cary: Black Creek greenway has more than five paved miles from Lake Crabtree County Park north to Chapel Hill Road. White Oak Creek greenway goes from Bond Park to McArthur Drive. Eventually, these two paths will span 15 miles, linking Umstead Park to the American Tobacco Trail.
- Raleigh: The Reedy Creek Trail offers a popular, paved 2.5-mile hike from the N.C. Museum of Art (and its impressive collection of outdoor sculptures), across Interstate 440 on a pedestrian bridge to Meredith College on Hillsborough Street.

Other Regional Trails

- American Tobacco Trail: This 22-mile trail follows the path of a historic railway through Durham and Chatham counties. Extensions of it are planned in Apex, Cary and near Falls Lake.
- Mountains-to-Sea Trail, *www.ncmst.org*, is a statewide initiative that would create a continuous walking path form the mountains to the coast. Currently, includes nearly 1,000 miles of paths, roads and bike routes stretching from Clingmans Dome in the Great Smoky Mountains to Jockey's Ridge on the Outer Banks. The web site offers maps of various trails.

Trail Information

- Triangle Rails to Trails Conservancy, *www.triangletrails.org*, offers lists of the region's trails, directions to trailheads and updates on trail construction.

- The Carolina Outdoors Guide can help you track down places to hike and camp statewide (*www.carolinaoutdoorsguide.com*).
- A good resource for the sports of hiking, cycling, paddling and climbing is *www.takeitoutsidenc.com*.
- For more information on mountain biking and running, including local groups, see the "Sports and Recreation" chapter.

HUNTING, FISHING AND BOATING

Native North Carolinians are serious about hunting, fishing and boating, and many of the area's newcomers have enjoyed joining them as avid outdoors men and women. The N.C. Wildlife Resources Commission, *www.ncwildlife.org*, creates policies regarding where and when you can hunt, trap and fish, and issues permits for these activities. It also enforces safety rules for operating personal watercraft.

To obtain hunting or fishing permit, go to the website or call 888-2HUNTFISH. A basic annual hunting fishing permit costs $20. For more information on fishing and boating, look for these topics in the "Sports and Recreation" chapter.

Hunting

North Carolina outdoorsmen hunt everything from bear to opossum, but by far the most popular pastime is deer hunting. The deer season generally runs from October to January, though bow hunters get an early start. Bag limits apply, and vary by year depending on the prevalence of game animals. The state has traditionally banned hunting on Sundays, but recently started allowing bow hunting on private lands every day of the week.

The state maintains about 2 million acres of public game lands for hunting. Hunting regulations can also vary based on whether an area is public or private. To use the public lands a game land license is required on

PART V: THE NEWCOMER'S GUIDE TO THE RALEIGH AREA

top of the hunting or trapping license. The game land permits costs $15 a year. In addition, special permits may be required to hunt certain species.

Locally, the Butner-Falls of Neuse Game Land encompasses 41,115 acres in Durham, Granville and Wake counties. Also, the Jordan Game Land includes 40,595 in Durham, Chatham, Orange and Wake counties. Harris Game Land comprises 14,090 acres in Chatham, Harnett and Wake counties.

The commission also offers safety courses for hunters and trappers. Call 919-707-0031 for more details.

Fishing

This old-time pastime is still huge in the Triangle, from the smallest creeks to the largest lakes in the area. Raleigh, Wake County and North Carolina allow fishing at most government owned lakes and rivers. In addition, Raleigh offers fishing classes for youth and adults. For more information, follow the "Leisure" link at *www.raleigh-nc.org*. To find more information and to connect with other anglers, try *www.ncangler.com*. Another good source for fishing information is *www.takemefishing.org*.

Local fisherman will need to obtain a basic hunting and fishing permit, along with any special permits for mountain trout. For more information on fishing regulations and permits, visit *www.ncwildlife.org/fs_index_03_fishing.htm* or call 919-707-0220.

Boating

Anyone over the age of 14 is allowed to operate a boat in North Carolina, though boaters 16 or under must have taken a boating safety course. (These courses can be found online at *www.ncwildlife.org/fs_index_05_boating.htm* or by calling 919-707-0031.)

In addition, boat owners are expected to register their watercraft with the wildlife commission. Registration lasts for a one or three year period, costing $15 or $40, respectively. Once registered, decals must be prominently displayed on your boat and your registration card must be available when the boat is on the water. For information on registering a boat or boating safety, call 800-NC-VESSEL. To register online, visit *www.ncwildlife.org/pg01_License/_Vessel/Menu.asp*. Or you may visit the commission office at 1751 Varsity Dr. on the N.C. State University Centennial campus.

For more on popular places for boating, see the "Sports and Recreation" chapter.

NOTES

THE GUIDE TO RALEIGH NORTH CAROLINA AREA REAL ESTATE

NOTES

THE GUIDE TO RALEIGH NORTH CAROLINA AREA REAL ESTATE

NOTES

THE GUIDE TO RALEIGH NORTH CAROLINA AREA REAL ESTATE

NOTES

We enjoyed writing this book for you, and we hope it was a big help! If you would like to talk to us about buying or selling a home, we would be honored to help you.

We work with local buyers and sellers every day, the initial consultation is always free, and there is no obligation.

Give us a call at
919-740-7000

or send an email to
mike@reganco.com

www.reganco.com

We're never too busy to help
you and your friends!

Call today for a free copy of our *Referral Directory*, a list of trusted vendors in the Raleigh area:

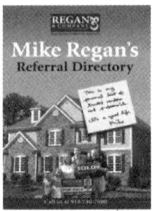